An American Gypsy

Around the World in 32,620 Days

D1714228

John Halbert

Endorsements

Come along for the ride on the life journey of a true American Gypsy. Be transported to an innocent time when children went swimming in a creek and when cheese had to be yellow and so shiny you could see your face reflected. Take a peek inside the underground command center of the Strategic Air Command at Offutt Air Force Base in Nebraska. Climb aboard the cockpit of a combat pilot who went on to become a journalist and public relations expert in the Air Force. This gypsy went from a life in a small town to travel on missions to all 50 states and 66 countries in six continents.

Thelma LeBrecht
Senior Correspondent, Associated Press Radio,
Washington D.C.

Tom Halbert has lived the American dream — and so much more. His multiple careers as journalist, editor, Air Forcer officer, and pilot, have given him access to the greatest show on earth, the human drama. Written with the honed skills of a professional reporter; an American Gypsy is a page turner — a non-fiction book with zip and sparkle of a first rate novel. As a fellow journalist who covered news of the Viet Nam war, I was fascinated by his account of serving as a briefing officer in Saigon and the "inside" view he gives of the challenge balancing the "truth" with the adherence to official government policy. More than 400 pages and none of them disappoints.

Mort Crim
Post-Newsweek Television, Retired
TV News Anchor in Chicago, Philadelphia & Detroit

You really evoke the sense of life in the Midwest in the 1940s. The story of leaving home with your shoes on but taking them off and hiding them in a small cave —only to be picked up and put on again on the way home from school that afternoon is verisimilitude that provides real feeling of time and place. Similarly, your mention of the business a small Midwestern town gives life to a place that many would assume has no/little life. Your discussion of flight training and numerous airplanes would seem boring on the face of it. But these details give a fulness and a kind of gravitas to your life. You have done a fine job here. From the catchy title to the end of your memoir was extremely entertaining because of your comments on history, culture and bureaucracy. Your PR and broadcasting experience enlivened the writing. You know your way around words.

Dave Harralson
Professor Utica College of Syracuse University, Retired

My wish for everyone is that we take time to hear the stories, ask questions, immerse ourselves in the presence of our seniors...not letting those precious nuggets of their lives to go to their graves before they are shared and passed down. But as older folks pass away I sense regret of missed opportunities to hear stories and gather every morsel of knowledge they had to share.

Craig Pleggenkuhle
Dubuque, Iowa
Reflections on Iowa's Greatest Resource

The two most important days in your life are the day you were born and the day you find out why

Mark Twain

When you are young your grandparents try to tell you their history and you don't care because it doesn't interest you at the time. Later on, you wish you had written down what they said

Understanding Compassion

The more that you read, the more things you will know. The more that you learn, the more places you'll go

Dr. Suess

Age appears to be best in four things; old wood best to burn, old wine to drink, old friends to trust, and old authors to read

Frances Bacon

Reading gives us somewhere to go
when we have to stay where we are

Kara Creates

OMG — This is so me
Nothing can replace holding a read book in your hands

Marcia Mackay
Community Leader - Indianapolis & Venice, Florida

Just to let you know, I have read your
book and enjoyed it very much,
providing me more understanding
of US culture and history

Ragnar Aoalsteinsson
Mosefellsbar, Iceland

You'll love this one!

Kenny DeCamp
Promoter, Public Relations Guru, Sarasota, Florida

Table of Contents

Prologue

Having reached an age that none of my forebears did and, as of 2021, being a father, grandfather, great-grandfather and great-great-grandfather, and having been urged to actually sit down and write the memories of my life – I have now consented to chronicle my life. I hope that my extended family will enjoy learning part of why and who they are today based on my factual remembrances and, at times, humorous life history.

I recognize that my descendants own their own future and that my decisions and those in my family trees who preceded me certainly impact and provide insight to the generations who follow.

This is a story of an adoptee born in a Sioux Falls, South Dakota, Lutheran home for unwed mothers who joined a down-to-earth Iowan family, had the luck to have a mother who guided me into gaining a college education, and a myriad of twists and turns that transformed me into an American Gypsy, taking me to all 50 states in the union and 63 countries on six continents in Asia, Africa, Europe, North America, South America and Australia. The continent I missed was Antarctica. We did have frequent C-130 missions from Sewart AFB in Tennessee across the Pacific to Christ Church, New Zealand, to Antarctica – one of the missions I never got to fly.

Here is a breakout by continent where I did fly.
- *Asia: Israel, Japan, Saudi Arabia, South Korea, South Viet Nam, Turkey*
- *Africa: Egypt, Libya, Morocco*
- *Australia: Perth, Western Australia, Sydney, New South Wales*
- *Europe: Andorra, Austria, Czech Republic, Denmark, England, France, Germany, Greece, Hungary, Italy, Liechtenstein, Poland, Slovakia, Soviet Union, Spain, Switzerland, Norway*
- *North America: Canada (Labrador, Manitoba, Newfoundland, New Brunswick, Nova Scotia, Ontario), Greenland, Mexico, Panama*
- *South America: Bolivia, Brazil, Colombia, Peru*

Islands included:
- *Atlantic Ocean Islands: Fuerteventura, Iceland, Jersey, Lanzarote in the Grand Canaries, Terceira in the Azores, Madeira*
- *Pacific Ocean Islands: Guam, Midway Island, Philippines (Corregidor, Luzon and Mactan), Hawaii, Oahu, Wake Island*
- *Mediterranean Islands: Cyprus, Sicily*
- *Caribbean Islands: Barbados, Cuba, Dominican Republic, Isla de Vieques, Puerto Rico*

This has been a major adventure for a farm town kid raised in Iowa who became a journalist, combat pilot in the U.S. Air Force, public relations and broadcast pioneer, community leader and a husband and father.

My goal in writing this memoir is to provide a record for my family and future members of my extended family tree that shows everyone can succeed, no matter what your heritage. My subtitle notes the time from when I was born until I finished writing this book — a total of 32,620 days.

I didn't learn until I was 14 that I was adopted. It was a shock and caused me to ponder for years, "Who am I?" But I did know that I was special and loved because I was chosen.

The other major factor on my life was that my father was an alcoholic. My mother and the family tried for years to change that factor, but when I was entering my senior year in high school, my parents divorced. That led my mother to move to Des Moines and become a librarian at Drake University. Her being a university employee meant I could get a degree tuition-free. It was a life changer and opened doors I never would have considered if we had remained in Red Oak. It was life full of opportunity, excitement and happiness.

I thank the patience of my extended family that has reached to the great-great-grandfather level, the loving encouragement and support of my life partner Gayle Maxey, and the gentle nudging from Irwin Starr, Jim Duffy, Burt Sherwood and Al Herskovitz of the Media Roundtable to get me off my butt and into stacking paragraphs about my life.

*And a special note of appreciation to Thelma LeBrecht, re-
tired Senior Washington Correspondent of Associated Press
Radio; Virginia Czaja, retired nurse in Washington D.C.,
who moved with her husband to nearby Port Charlotte and
began a second career using the pseudonym of Virginia Crane,
author of 19 romance novels; Kay Wight, former VP of CBS
News, and Burt Sherwood, a veteran of 50 years in broadcasting – both on-the-air and management. (We had unknow-
ingly crossed paths before when he played college football for
Bradley University and I was working as a sports reporter for
the Des Moines Register in the early 1950s.) All four helped
me immeasurably with spelling, grammar, format and clarity
corrections. One thing they all agreed on was when they broke
up laughing as they discovered a spellcheck error that turned
the Martin Luther King, Jr., assassination into 'assignation.'*

*In addition, initial reader feedback has been wonderful, espe-
cially by Venice residents David Sayer of Publishers Clearing
House fame who pointed out I have given President Franklin
D. Roosevelt an extra year of life and Brian Dietz who found
a fist full of typos missed by the professionals.*

*At the end, Gayle Maxey won an endurance medal for patient-
ly providing me corrections, clarity, and asking meaningful
questions time after time with each draft version as they were
created.*

Adoption & The Great Depression

My life journey began as Gerald Wayne Haas, born March 8, 1932, during the Great Depression to a young unwed mother in a Lutheran Home in Sioux Falls, South Dakota. Later in life, I learned that my birth mother was Alice Marie Haas of Rapid City, South Dakota. Alice Marie's father was a school teacher. Her mother was a daughter of a prominent rancher and a South Dakota State senator. I can only imagine what my birth mother went through – becoming pregnant at 16 years old, being forced to leave her home in Rapid City to give birth by herself clear across the state, giving her son up for adoption, and spending another year in exile with an older sister in Pierre, before being allowed to return home to Rapid City. I also learned that my birth father was John Thompson Hoar, a gold miner at the Homestake Mine at Lead, South Dakota. He was purportedly a friend of one of Alice Marie's brothers.

Sometime in the summer of 1932, I was adopted by Mary Pilkington Halbert and Russel Dillon Halbert residing in Sioux City, Iowa. I use the term 'birth parents' for those that created me and 'parents' for those who raised me as their son. My father had been a Swift & Company salesman living in Yankton, South Dakota, in 1923, before his transfer to Cherokee, Iowa, and then to Sioux City. I don't know if their Yankton time may have been how they knew about the Sioux Falls Home for Unwed Mothers' adoption opportunities, but I suspect it may have been a factor.

I fully understand and accept how my birth mother must have been torn with her options in the 1930s. Each Mother's Day, I still contemplate how this selfless young woman chose to give me life while surely enduring the heartache and pressure of being pregnant out of wedlock. I think of her struggle to carry a child for nine months, spend hours giving birth, and then handing over her first and only child for someone else to raise. It demonstrates love, concern, and deserves admiration.

During that era, sex outside of marriage was taboo, and being pregnant was extremely socially and morally unacceptable. Even in my youth, communities viewed unwed mothers as 'damaged,' and they were forced to carry the burden of shaming their families. My birth mother's prominent family did not disown Alice Marie. Still, she was secreted away across the state to hide her condition, give birth and then immediately give up her baby. She remained separated from her parents, suffering in silence for another year at her sister's home in Pierre, before returning to Rapid City.

I never had direct contact with my birth mother. My Iowa parents never told me about my adoption. I discovered my adoption documents inadvertently in our basement when I was 14. Because of concerns of crushing my mother with this information, I kept the secret to myself.

It wasn't until about a year before my birth mother's death that I made contact by mail with Alice Marie. I waited until she became a widow, as I did not want to do anything that might create a problem for her marriage. She did not reply to me directly. Instead, a neighbor friend responded to my letter confirming my already learned facts, including my research into the Haas family history.

I made two genealogy trips to Northern California while on trips to Sacramento after her death. There, I had lunch with four of Alice Marie's best friends. They provided me with information about her active civic interests and even some personal belongings Alice Marie had given them.

Children of the Great Depression

In 2010, Russell Friedman published his essay on *Children of the Great Recession*. His book resonated deeply with me and triggered the self-realization of a time that greatly affected my life and who I became. I found out the 'why' for many things that were not apparent before. These are things that Friedman, other researchers, and my own sensing identified about my generation that I found notable and deeply personal. These are the things I recognized as being part of what shaped Gerald Wayne Haas into becoming Tommy Halbert.

Those of us born in the 1930s is a special age group. We are a part of the smallest number of children born in the United States since the early 1900s. The 'Roaring '20s' came to abrupt end on October 24, 1929, as nervous investors sold stock en masse.

We are a generation who remember climbing out of a depression. The Depression began under newly-elected President

Herbert Hoover in 1929, three years before I was born, and continued to 1940 when I was seven. This economic disaster eventually resulted in more than 5,000 banks failing. There was a 25 percent unemployment rate with hundreds of thousands homeless and living in shantytowns. The Dow reached a Depression low of 41.22 in July 1932.

In the Midwest, farmers rebelled. A group called the Farmer's Holiday Association was formed, encouraging farmers to 'Stay at Home – Buy Nothing – Sell Nothing.' Their popular slogan was:

> "Let's call a Farmer's Holiday
> A Holiday let's hold
> We'll eat our wheat and ham and eggs
> And let them eat their Gold."

On the bright side, some good things did happen in the depression years before I was born:

> In 1929 the first color television was demonstrated by Bell Labs, and the Museum of Modern Art opened in New York City.

> In 1930, Mickey Mouse made his first appearance as a comic strip, Hostess Twinkies were invented, Scotch Tape was introduced, and the Chrysler Building was completed in New York.

> In 1931, *The Star-Spangled Banner* became the national anthem, and the Empire State Building was completed in New York.

In 1932, as I began my life, the Summer Olympics were held in Los Angeles, the Winter Olympics were held at Lake Placid, and Amelia Earhart became the first female pilot to fly non-stop across the Atlantic.

In 1933, I continued to advance toward being a pre-schooler. Franklin D. Roosevelt became President and began his famous radio fireside chats. The 21st Amendment to the Constitution went into effect, repealing prohibition and the World's Fair opened in Chicago.

In May 1934, Bonnie Parker and Clyde Barrow were killed by police. In July, John Dillinger, Public Enemy No. 1, was killed in a shoot-out in Chicago with the FBI. Also, in 1934, the Civilian Conservation Corps was organized with the first camp at South Dakota's Wind Cave National Park. A new law required all gold and gold certificates to be surrendered to the U.S. Department of Treasury.

In 1935, the Works Progress Administration began putting 8.5 million Americans to work across the nation, building such structures at the Hoover Dam and LaGuardia Airport. Alcoholics Anonymous was founded in Akron, Ohio. On the negative side, 1935 was the beginning of the devastating Dust Bowl that stretched from the Dakotas to Oklahoma and the worst hurricane to ever strike the U.S. resulting in 423 deaths.

In 1936, only 10 percent of rural areas in America had electricity. The Rural Electrification Act (REA) and the Tennessee Valley Authority (TVA) were other President Roosevelt initiatives to get Americans back to work. This long-term program raised the number of farm homes in America to have electricity to 90 percent by 1959. Other 1936 milestones included the worst heatwave ever causing thousands of deaths, Jessie Owens' gold medal in the 100-meter dash at the Olympics in Berlin, publication of *Gone with Wind*, *Life Magazine* becoming a weekly publication, and FDR being reelected for a second term.

As I began my formal school years in 1937, the drought and heatwave expanded well beyond the Midwest, the Hindenburg Zeppelin burst into flames after striking a mooring mast at Lakehurst, New Jersey. The Golden Gate Bridge opened for traffic, while Amelia Earhart and her navigator Fred Noonan disappeared after takeoff from New Guinea. Walt Disney's *Snow White and The Seven Dwarfs* became the first feature-length animated cartoon movie, and Detective Comics introduced Batman.

In 1938, the March of Dimes was established by President Roosevelt, Superman was introduced by Action Comics, and a new men's pant was introduced by Haggar who named them 'Slacks.' Also, President Roosevelt made it clear the U.S. would remain neutral after Nazi Germany occupied Czechoslovakia, and the Nazi Occupation of Austria began on March 1, 1938.

The year 1939 heralded the end of the Great Depression. The Nazi invasion of Poland began. The 1939 World's Fair opened in New York, and an Albert Einstein letter to President Roosevelt led to the development of the Atomic Bomb.

Following the Depression came the winds of war and the impact of World War II that shaped our daily lives for years. We were the last generation to remember ration books for everything from gas to sugar, to shoes to stoves. We saved newspapers, tin foil, all kinds of metal and poured fat into tin cans (a key ingredient for making bombs) for the war effort. We remember milk, blocks of ice (refrigerators had not been invented yet) and bakery goods being delivered to our front doors. We remember gold stars in windows of grieving neighbors whose sons died in the War. We saw our veterans return from Europe and the Pacific to build little houses and cause an explosion in our economy. The GI Bill gave vets a door to advanced education, and the number of colleges grew. We were the last generation who spent their childhood without television.

We viewed the world from the window of radio, magazines, and comic books. We grew up with the Pledge of Allegiance, Kate Smith singing *God Bless America*, Norman Rockwell's patriotic *Post* magazine covers, Rosie the Riveter, and Tokyo Rose. We laughed with Jack Benny, Fred Allen, and Fibber McGee's closet. Saturday afternoons were spent in a movie house with newsreels and cartoons sandwiched between watching Roy Rogers and Gene Autry westerns. Reading involved comic books and Big Little Books.

We played outside until the streetlights came on. There was no Little League. In Red Oak, there was one community park with a teeter-totter and metal slide. The news was for adults and obtained by radio at 10 p.m. and from respected daily newspapers and national weekly magazines. We had little understanding of the world. Our 'world' was mostly limited to our experiences within a 50-mile radius. Telephones were new, and party lines were common for those who had a telephone. Most hung on a kitchen wall and did not have a dial – you asked 'operator' to connect you by using the name of the person you were calling. Technology involved using typewriters driven by pounding fingers, throwing a carriage and changing ink ribbons. Television, the Internet, and Google were not envisioned, even in the futuristic world of *Buck Rogers* (the movie serial of the 1940s).

We came of age in the 1950s. We were the last generation to experience an interlude when there were no threats to our homeland. Polio was the most dreaded disease. The Korean War interrupted our age of overflowing plenty and opportunity and a time of feeling secure with our future. We began to instruct school children to duck under desks as part of air-raid training. Russia created the Iron Curtain. Eisenhower sent the first 'advisors' to Viet Nam, and Castro took over Cuba. Terrorism, global warming, and perpetual economic insecurity were not part of our world yet. It was an era of times that got better, not worse. And today, as we enter the 2020s, we are left wondering if we will be the last generation that will experience a wonderful era.

Sioux City Years (1932–1938)

Sometime after my birth, I was adopted by Mary Martha Pilkington Halbert and Russel Dillon Halbert, then residing in Sioux City, Iowa. My father (who spelled his first name with just one L) was employed during the Depression years as a salesman for Swift & Company with a territory of South Dakota. The family home was at 3805 Fourth Avenue – near Morningside University – in 1928. This is where my memories began.

My memories of Sioux City are minimal. But I do remember things like living in the basement of our home in brutally hot summers during the Dust Bowl, which was before exhaust fans or air conditioning. The upstairs of the home was shaded by drapes and darkening window shades during the day, and then opened in the evenings when cooling breezes provided relief. Based on family photos, it was normal to place me outside in winter months in a baby carriage for 'fresh air and sunshine.' My guardian at that time and after I began walking was our family Doberman, plus my mother's watchful eyes. I have memories of having Raggedy Ann and Black Sambo dolls, a tricycle and red wagon, and my protective Doberman preventing me from sledding down a steep hill by forcing my Flexible Flyer sled into the curb.

Young Tommy in Sioux City

I have vivid memories of family outings to the Sergeant Floyd Monument atop a bluff above the Missouri River, where you could see far into Nebraska and South Dakota. We watched thunderstorms move toward the east, seeing downpours in both states, with the bluffs blocking the storms from crossing into Iowa. Floyd was a member of the Louis and Clark Expedition who died at Sioux City as Lewis and Clark 'discovered' the West.

In 1936, I attended kindergarten in Morningside, although I can't recall whether it was associated with Morningside University or a Methodist Church. I have no memory of any teacher or classmates. At this time, I was hospitalized for the first time to have my tonsils removed.

Other memories centered around being at the Sioux City home of my Dad's cousin Vera Glee Fielding listening to radio – especially the *Kate Smith Hour*. Kate's rendition of *God Bless America* left me with deep patriotic feelings that I still have today. It was also the beginning of having popcorn every Sunday evening. This tradition lasted in the family as long as I lived at home with my parents. Glee was the daughter of Hester Dillon Iddings – my paternal grandfather's sister.

My Dad would frequently take me to the Sioux City Swift & Company complex to see the stockyards and racks and racks of beef aging in coolers. It was a treat to get out of the summer heat and be in the coolers at an age before air conditioning. It also was a time when I witnessed the impacts of the Great Depression (1928–1939). I recall long lines of men in soup lines; farmers blocking roads as they dumped milk from metal containers because product income was too low; strikes at the Swift plant where pickets blocked access and broke windows as protests grew violent.

Sioux City Stockyards were central to life in the Midwest for a better part of a century (1870–1960). It was home to the big three meatpackers, Swift, Cudahy, and Armour, making it one of the nation's most important meat packing centers. Meatpacking both built and shaped the Midwest. By 1910, Sioux City was the second-largest city in Iowa. By 1920, Sioux City had crept into the 100 largest cities in the nation. And by 1930, when my parents arrived in Sioux City, the population had doubled from 1910. Sioux City was remarkable for its ethnic diversity, with 38 percent of the population either foreign-born or of foreign parentage. It was noteworthy that even then, income within the industry allowed fathers to earn enough that moms could stay at home and be full-time homemakers.

The worst of the Depression began to abate in 1934 as President Franklin Roosevelt's New Deal WPA (Work's Project Administration) and CCC (Civilian Conservation Corps) began. But workers in the private sector had yet to benefit from the improving economy. Indeed the strikes at the Swift plant in Sioux City became so contentious in 1938 that the Iowa National Guard was deployed to resolve the Swift & Company strikes. At this time, my parents either elected or were forced to leave Sioux City and return to the family in Red Oak, Iowa – the county seat of Montgomery County.

Early Red Oak Years (1938–1942)

Red Oak was established on the mainline of Burlington Railroad, which connected Chicago and Omaha, Nebraska. The village was set in the rolling, fertile hills of Southwest Iowa, nestled along the banks of the Nishnabotna River, about 50 miles east of Omaha. Red Oak started out as Red Oak Junction in the 1850s during the surveying for the railroad. This was when both the Halbert and Pilkington families came as pioneers to Montgomery County. Iowa had just become a state in December 1846, with settlers primarily homesteading in the eastern portion of the state. Pioneers William Joseph and Sarah Morgan Halbert of rural Hancock County, Illinois, settled as farmers near Elliott, Iowa. In contrast, James Henry and Martha Mahetable Butterfield Pilkington of Bedford, Pennsylvania, settled in the community of Red Oak Junction shortly after the Civil War. Both families migrated by covered wagon.

This is where my paternal grandfather John Marion Halbert (son of William Joseph and Sarah Amelia Morgan) married Mary Ethel Dillon. Marion was a veteran of the Spanish American War, city assessor for the city of Red Oak, twice elected as Clerk of Court for Montgomery County, and was secretary of the board of the Independent School District of Red Oak. In the 1920s, he was associated with Wilson Concrete for eight years as a structural foreman in charge of building many of the county bridges, including the Coolbaugh Street Bridge across the Nishnabotna River. He also was engaged in building a huge bridge in Los Angeles, California.

My maternal grandparents were Harry and Maude Jeffers Pilkington, who lived directly across from the Montgomery County Court House at 103 Reed Street. It was a home normally filled with family. My mother had two sisters and a brother. My Dad, like me, was an only child. Harry told stories of his youth hanging around the blacksmith's shop where two notable things happened. He lost a finger in a shop accident, and he was asked by Frank James (of Jesse and Frank James notoriety) to hold his horse while dickering for services. Harry had lost his hearing before I came to Red Oak. For Harry, this was a wonderful advantage. When all the cousins got noisy, all Harry had to do was remove his hearing aids and enjoy peaceful quiet. When I got to know Harry, he pretty much would be in a lounge chair in the dining room with his plug of Horseshoe tobacco and his spittoon.

Maude was the matriarch, beloved by all the grandchildren. It was this serendipitous event that made moving to Red Oak so smooth. It provided instant playmates, all within walking distance in this town of about 5,000 citizens. My mother's oldest sister was Kathryn, who married Marion Thomas. They had two daughters, Marilyn and Susan. Her younger sister was Maurine, who married uncle Fred Replogle. They had one daughter, Jean. The youngest sibling was her brother Jim, who married Bernadine Atteberry. They had two sons, Jim and Ross. A second cousin, Roger Westerlund, was a part of the group. His father was Roy Westerlund, who married uncle Fred Replogle's sister.

Through the electronic editions of the *Red Oak Express* and *Red Oak Sun*, I later learned that I had visited Red

Oak many times before we moved there. Thus, while my memories of my cousins began with that move, my older cousins had met me several times when my parents periodically made visits 'home.' My first recorded visit was on December 23, 1932.

There were no such connections on the Halbert side of family. It wasn't till 2000, when I attended a 50-year class reunion, that I stumbled into the possible reason while doing genealogy research at the Red Oak library. By dumb luck, I found a *Red Oak Express* society article announcing that Mary Pilkington and Russell Halbert had eloped and were married in Omaha, Nebraska. As a kid, I was aware that my mother and my Dad's mother did not get along. Now I had just found out the reason why.

Both my mother and father had graduated from Red Oak High School just after the end of World War I. My grandfather, Marion Halbert, had used his political contacts to obtain an appointment for my father to attend the U.S. Naval Academy in Annapolis, Maryland, following his freshman year at the University of Wisconsin in Madison, Wisconsin. Once my parents were married, my father lost his eligibility to attend Annapolis. For me it was an 'aha' moment that explained the long, cold relationship between my grandmother Halbert and my mother.

History & Places that Shaped Me

Montgomery County was established on January 15, 1851. The first election occurred in 1853 when 18 ballots were cast for the first county judge. The first county courthouse was located in Frankfort. This early community was located north of Stanton and south of Elliott. The simple wood 20 by 40-foot county courthouse was moved by oxen to Red Oak in the winter of 1865 following an election decided by six votes.

When the Russel and Mary Halbert family arrived back home in1938, Red Oak was a small, quiet Midwest community that was a great place to raise kids. It was a town filled with hard-working people who both farmed and worked in town to make ends meet. The town square was active, covered with shade from beautiful elm trees, and with a unique river stone fountain in the center. It was also the home of weekly Red Oak High School band concerts on Wednesday evenings in the summertime. Besides the music, it was a special time to go to the ice cream shop and get a double-dip cone for a nickel. Red Oak was a place where I could walk anywhere or ride my bike anywhere. It was far from major population centers – it took an hour or more to drive to Omaha to shop. Iowa highways in the 1940s and 1950s were termed 'concrete cow paths' due to the constant curves and a two-lane narrowness with curbs on both sides that kept speeds to 50mph or lower. Highways went through the center of all communities along the way.

The elm trees not only provided beauty in the Red Oak town square. They also created a Currier and Ives postcard view of the community with wide green canopies providing a very welcome shade in the heat of Iowa summers. Red Oak prospered due to rich soil and the advent of the Burlington Railroad and the north and south branches to the mainline rail service. Red Oak's business section expanded around the Square, while the town expanded on the western flats, and many fine residences were constructed on the hills to the east. More than 30 of these splendid turn of the century (1900) homes on historic Heritage Hill remain today.

Famous residents of Red Oak have been rare. Probably best known was Johnny Carson of *Tonight Show* fame. When Johnny was born, his father, Homer Lloyd Carson, was a manager at Iowa Power and Light in nearby Corning. But Johnny also lived with his parents in nearby Clarinda and Red Oak, before moving to Norfolk, Nebraska.

Others of note include Clyde Cessna, founder Cessna Aircraft; Joni Ernst, current US Senator; Kenneth Evans, Iowa Lieutenant Governor; Kurt Griffey, guitarist for Creedence Clearwater Revisited; Actor Raymond Hatton, who appeared in 50 Silent & Talkies Hollywood films; Elvin Hutchison, Detroit Lions running back; Dick Kenworthy, Chicago White Sox third baseman; L. Welch Pogue, former CEO Civil Aeronautics Board, and Con Starkel, Washington Senators pitcher.

The county population peak occurred in 1900, as urbanization and the decline of family farms began. Although the family farm was still king in the Red Oak economy in the 1940s, several changes were transforming the way of life for the region that began with the Burlington Railroad access. Other than farming, the following major businesses were economic drivers in early Red Oak. Some still exist today. Many of those businesses that influenced my growing years and those of my grandparents and parents included:

Steinbrecher Brewery – 1870

Probably the first industry to be established in Red Oak, Steinbrecher Brewery was created to transform 2,000 to 3,000 bushels of barley into beer. It was located just south of the Burlington viaduct on what became Highway 48.

Red Oak Pottery – 1874

The Red Oak Pottery, operated by W. H. Close, processed 9,000 gallons of clay per month which was found one mile south of the works. He ran his pottery kiln on corn cobs, suspected to be the only place in the world to do so. During the 1880 season, he produced 1,500,000 bricks used to construct an expanding Red Oak. Like the pottery, they were fueled by burning corn cobs. The pottery also produced lard jars, milk crocks and flower pots.

Red Oak Greenhouses – Established 1879

The Red Oak Greenhouse complex grew into a major wholesale and retail grower of plants year-round for large and small retailers, garden centers, florists, and landscapers across the Midwest. The original location was south of Highway 48 on Reed Street near Replogle Mill. The mill and the greenhouse backed up to a series of large bayous east of the North Branch railroad. The original location still exists today, but has expanded to a large farm location with massive greenhouse buildings. It has become a national supplier of garden plants for Home Depot, Lowe's, and others. Even in the 1940s, the multiple heated greenhouses were a mecca to roam in the winter months full of grey skies, snow, and bitter cold.

Greenhouse Interior
One of a Dozen Buildings

Red Oak Courthouse – Constructed 1890

The landmark for Red Oak was (and still is) the 1890 red brick and red Missouri sandstone Montgomery County courthouse with a clock tower that extended to a height of 91 feet. The building was 72 feet wide and 60 feet tall. This was a magnet for young Tommy Halbert and friends in the late 1940s. Each Thursday, we could get the keys to the tower from the county sheriff's office to climb the 40-foot rickety metal stairs inside the tower to reach a landing that housed the clock mechanism. It was operated by stone-filled boxes acting as weights. The weights had to be cranked up once a week to keep the clock functioning. The weights for the minute hands were easy to crank, the heavier hour hand box much tougher.

Montgomery County Courthouse

It was not a desire to get involved in helping the sheriff that motivated us to community service. The hidden reason was rather that we could easily raise the platform cover atop the stair to gain access to the bell and get a fantastic 360-degree view of the town, the Nishnabotna valley, and Red Oak's hills. Frequently we would sneak a hammer to the bell tower and delight in being by the bell as the noon hour was struck. The hammer was critical, as it allowed us to make sure the bell pealed 13 times at noon. We also used the opportunity to capture squabs from pigeon nests in the tower. We sold these, allowing us to splurge on 'home style' ice cream at the Green Parrot Café on the Square.

Dan Gunn Buckskin Gloves – 1886

The glove factory employed 10–25 people, and its products were sold by five traveling salesmen all over the country. Their specialty was genuine buckskin gloves – one of a few factories that used real deerskin.

Replogle Flour Mill – Founded 1888

The huge flour mill was located at the west end of Coolbaugh Street, next to the North Branch railroad tracks and the bayous between tracks and Highway 48. It was very close to the Coolbaugh Street Bridge across the Nishnabotna River. All kinds of flour were produced here from grinding 300,000 bushels of grain annually. As I grew up in Red Oak, the mill was owned by decedents of the Replogle family. My uncle Fred Replogle managed it, the grandson of the mill founder Jacob M. Replogle, the pioneer miller in Red Oak.

What I enjoyed most was being able to sample freshly produced wheat germ. The plant was always busy, noisy, and dusty. It was also the place where the men of the Pilkington clan would gather Sunday with their pet rat terrier dogs to hunt rats behind the mill, along the bayou. The mill ceased operation in the late 1940s.

In the 1990s, when I made genealogy trips for my Haas family roots in Kork, Baden, Germany, I visited the French wine region along the Rhein just north of Strasbourg. I found the village where the Replogle descendants had emigrated from in the 1800s.

I gathered church records and photographed the town for second-cousin Roger Westerlund, whose mother married Fred Replogle's sister. I found the name Replogle comes from the baskets grape pickers used during harvest – *Reblogle: Reb was the word for grape, and Logle is a basket.*

Kerrihard Foundry – Founded About 1890

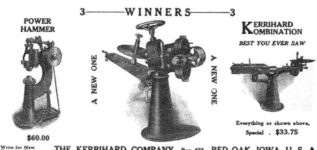

The Kerrihard Foundry produced many steel items, including its famous Power Hammer and the combined Emery Grinder saw table and disc used by blacksmiths. In 1938, as the blacksmith profession declined, the company began creating Ko-Z-Aire furnaces for home use. After WWII, the company changed its name to Ko-Z-Aire Manufacturing Company, until the company was sold to Anchor Post Products in Baltimore, Maryland, in 1948. The Ko-Z-Air furnace provided a hopper that shovels full of ping pong ball sized coal could load. A screw drive would then feed coal automatically into the furnace. The chore of putting coal manually in the furnace twice a day was reduced to once a week, making it very popular in Red Oak homes.

However, it didn't solve the problem of having to remove 'clinkers' and ash by hand.

Chicago, Burlington & Quincy Railroad Depot – Constructed 1903

Red Oak Train Station

The Burlington Railroad first extended west to Red Oak Junction and Emerson in 1869. The City of Red Oak was renamed in 1901, the year my parents were born. The Burlington was the newest and fastest transportation to open the west in the 1800s. Pioneers who came by foot or covered wagon didn't even have a defined road until the famous dirt trail called the 'Blue Grass Road' became the first cross-country road in 1911. It roughly followed today's Highway 34, the first paved highway to reach Red Oak in 1929. Having gravel country roads began in 1950.

The depot was the transportation center for salesmen, a la 'The Music Man.'

Grandfather Harry Pilkington, Uncle Marion Thomas and my Dad all used the Burlington while employed with meatpacking giant Swift & Company. That lasted until the 1940s, when the auto and concrete highways became the norm. The addition of the North and South branches was critical for farmers to sell crops between Shenandoah and Griswold. The largest crowd at the depot I can remember from the 1940s was when President Franklin Roosevelt made a whistle-stop campaign speech at the station.

This was the railroad station from where 16-year-old Chicago Cub fan Tommy traveled overnight to Chicago to attend a Boston Braves–Chicago Cubs doubleheader at Wrigley Field. I saved enough funds from working at the Red Oak Wholesale Fruit grocery store. It was my first trip to a major city, but I was able to take a taxi from the train station to Wrigley, and back to the train station after the game to go home. At Wrigley, I was petrified as I had never been anywhere with 40,000 people before. I never left my seat until the final out of game two. But I got to see my hero Andy Pafko, the Cubs' home run hitting third baseman, and that was what really mattered. The overnight train got me back to Red Oak the next morning.

Passenger service ended in 1971. And today, the historic depot is a WWII Memorial museum featuring Company M of the Iowa National Guard. The Third Battalion, 34th Infantry Division took nearly 90 percent of all Red Oak men of eligible age. The Division saw 600 days of combat, more than any other military unit. In the early days of WWII, *Life* magazine reported that Red Oak lost more sons per capita than any community in the U.S. The most tragic day was March 6, 1943, when more than 100 telegrams arrived in Red Oak announcing those missing in action. Also featured is WWI Company M, which fought battles of Belleau Woods, the Argonne Forest, Saint-Mihiel, and Soissons. Uncle Marion Thomas served with this unit of 250, with 160 casualties and 52 killed in action. My grandfather Marion Halbert was a member of Company M and a veteran of the Spanish American War in the late 1800s.

Red Oak Canning Company – 1902

The Red Oak Canning Company was organized in 1902 near the Nishnabotna river on West Coolbaugh St. The primary products were peas and corn. In 1933, it was sold to the Otoe company of Scottsbluff, Nebraska. Otoe became a national brand.

Thomas D. Murphy Calendar Company – 1905

The Thomas D. Murphy Calendar Company was created in Red Oak. Thomas D. Murphy was recognized as the first person that successfully developed advertising art calendars. He is the individual who is most responsible for the creation, development, and expansion of the art calendar industry. The original location was on the Square in downtown Red Oak. The factory building followed beginning in 1905 south of town near the Burlington Railroad. It was expanded in 1907 and then again in 1920. The power plant part of the historic designation was part of the 1920 expansion. It was listed on the National Register of Historic Places in 2008.

My grandmother Maude Jeffers Pilkington was an employee in her 20s in the downtown location. My mother, Mary Pilkington, was the featured calendar girl for a WWI bond drive poster as a teenager.

Chautauqua Park – Constructed 1907

Chautauqua Park is a historic pavilion located in Red Oak. The first Chautauqua in Iowa was established at Clear Lake, Iowa, in 1876. By the 1920s, there were as many as 500 Chautauqua assemblies in the state. Most of the structures used for the organization's functions in Iowa were tents. Red Oak became the exception when this pavilion was built in 1908. The circular structure was built for about $5,200, and it had a seating capacity between 3,500 and 5,000. Speakers on the inaugural program included orator and politician William Jennings Bryan, social reformer Jane Adams, Wisconsin Governor Robert M. La Follette, and evangelist Gypsy Smith. Children's programs were held on weekday mornings.

It continued to host annual Chautauqua programs until 1929. Chautauqua Park in Red Oak was listed on the National Register of Important Places in 1972. It was a very special program and space for my grandparents and their children.

The original Chautauqua age began in Red Oak from June 29 to July 6, 1905, at the county fairgrounds in a 3,000-person tent. It featured electricity for the tents, dining hall, and campgrounds. Season tickets were $1.50 and $2.00. Overnight sleeping was 25-cents per day. Tents and camping space were $2.50 to $6.00 per season. Discount round trip railroad tickets were available up to 150 miles from Red Oak on the Burlington line.

But for the kids of Red Oak, it was more important as the location of playground swings and slides plus the lighted softball field, and the original water standpipe that could be seen for miles. The park was on U.S. Highway 34 where the road climbed the steepest hill on the highway between the prairies of Nebraska and Chicago.

Carnegie Library – Constructed 1909

Red Oak's Carnegie Library

Andrew Carnegie accepted the city's application for a grant to build the Red Oak Public Library for $12,500 on November 27, 1906. The Chicago architectural firm of Patton & Miller designed the Tudor Revival structure, and the formal dedication was held on October 8, 1909. The two-story building features a side-gable plan and rustic brick-and-half-timbered style. The corners are buttresses that rise from the base in a concave curve and disappear into the walls before they emerge above the eaves as parapets. A two-story addition was built onto the rear of the building in 1924 to house a new book stack, and another two-story addition was built on the south side to house reading rooms. Both additions complement the structure's original design. The building was individually listed on the National Register of Historic Places in 1983. In 2016, it was included as a contributing property in the Red Oak Downtown Historic District.

As a genealogy note, my uncle Marion Thomas and the Thomas family donated a model replica of the British Navy Ship. Marion's father, Dr. Louis Thomas, was a teenage crew member before his immigration to the U.S. Dr. Thomas built the replica after he immigrated to Iowa. The replica was housed in the glass case on the library's second floor.

Red Oak Country Club – Established 1923

Red Oak Country Club

My parents had a family club membership while living in Red Oak – both my mother and father were golfers. It was the first golf course I ever played and worked at as a caddy. When I was young, we had frequent family outings enjoying a great hide and seek wooded area for kids and an exclusive family restaurant. When I was a caddy, I passed out and ended up hospitalized with typhoid fever. After about three days, I woke up in the hospital and was released after about a week. Diagnosis: caused by a cut in my foot in Red Oak Creek, where I had been swimming on a hot summer day in 1947.

Today, the club pitches that the amenities are nice, but the real star of the show at Red Oak Country Club is the course design. Red Oak boasts an 18-hole, par 72, championship golf course that is easily one of the most challenging and picturesque in all of Western Iowa. The course spans 6,176 yards for a rating of 70.5 and a slope of 124 from the championship tees. The course is carved among gorgeous natural scenery. Players will encounter water hazards, sand traps, doglegs and blind shots to the greens, as well as uphill and downhill lies and many mature trees. Today the Red Oak Country Club features a driving range, swimming pool, and a lounge area with televisions, a full-service restaurant, golf lessons, a junior golf program and club-sponsored parties throughout the year.

Wilson Concrete Company – Established 1925

Wilson Concrete began as a small family manufacturing company, which produced concrete culverts and various products for roadwork in Montgomery County. The company had six to eight employees, one of which was my grandfather Marion Halbert.

Wilson Concrete Truck Fleet

Following WWII, the business expanded into areas such as Council Bluffs and Omaha, Nebraska, with structural precast and architectural products. Concrete products were in high demand for the post-war reconstruction.

Wilson Concrete began serving contractors and architects in four Midwestern states. The company produced all sizes of concrete pipe and building components for roads, bridges, railroads, parking structures, hospitals and ballpark stadiums. Wilson Concrete eventually had manufacturing plants in four Midwestern states, offices in Red Oak and Omaha, and 700 employees.

Fund-raising completed in April 2007. The groundbreaking ceremony for Red Oak's Wilson Oakview Performing Arts Center was in September. However, construction struggled with mud throughout that fall and winter, so building work continued throughout 2008. The doors were officially opened on February 10, 2009.

Halbert Hybrid Corn Processing Plant: 1936–1946

Halbert Seed Company established one of the first hybrid seed corn plants under the Pfister Seed Corn banner by my grandfather, who had become a pioneer in the hybrid corn industry. Pfister became a top brand after being founded in El Paso, Illinois, in the 1930s. Other major competitors included DeKalb and Pioneer.

Before hybrid seed corn, Iowa farmers were producing 35–40 bushels of corn per acre. Hybrid corn resulted in yields exceeding 100 bushels per acre.

The large Halbert Seed Corn plant was located on Bridge Street, one block south of the intersection of old US Highway 34 and Iowa Highway 48, near the banks of the Nishnabotna River and the bayous to the south of the plant. The plant encompassed a collection of single-story long bins, a building for shucking and removing corn kernels from the cobs, an office complex and the huge multistory processing plant that contained the dryers and separators for bagging next year's seed crop.

There was also a 'downtown' office at 415 Coolbaugh Street, directly across from the Grand Theater and next door to a Swedish Bakery. The two offices shared the same phone number – 479. That was before dial phones existed. So, you would pick up the phone and tell the operator to connect you to four-seven-nine.

In addition, my grandfather also leased a section of land (640 acres) known as 'Harris Pasture,' one mile east and one mile south of the Coolbaugh Street Bridge. One acre was used to raise bluegrass. All other acreage was for growing seed corn. No homes were on this property, but there was one shed for a tractor, plows, and harrows.

The shed also housed one horse that was fed daily out of my Dad's car. I got to ride the horse frequently. The biggest hazard was I would be at the far reaches of the farm when my Dad would arrive in his car. Pavlov's dog rule prevailed. It would be the only time the horse would run. The car equaled food. There was no stopping him. I would hang on, but the corn leaves would cut my arms and face as the horse ran the shortest line to get to the car. I soon had an expanded vocabulary.

One of the impacts was that Halbert Hybrid Seed Corn became the highest paying employer for teenagers each summer. Iowa was famous as that state 'where the tall corn grows.' For nearly two to four weeks in late summer 'detasselers' were hired to walk through cornfields for up to 10 hours per day removing corn tassels.

The pay was about $2 per hour at a time when the average pay for teenagers was 50 cents per hour. It was a rural rite of passage in the Corn Belt. Normally four rows were detasseled, with two rows in between retaining tassels for cross-pollination. The harvested detasseled rows became the source of next year's seed corn. By the 1960s, 'gene' technology eliminated the need for manual detasseling.

The tassel of a corn plant

My father and his mother sold the company in 1946. It was purchased by Confections Inc. of Chicago, who had just created wildly popular Snacks Popcorn. The product at the plant changed to processing popcorn seed in place of field corn seed. Uncle Fred Replogle, former manager of the Replogle Mill in Red Oak, became the new manager (Fred was married to my mother's sister Maurine). The seed corn plant was destroyed by fire in the late 1940s.

Civilian Conservation Corps Company 2723 Red Oak, Iowa: 1935–1942

The Red Oak CCC camp was located just south of Burlington train station and the Highway 48 underpass. The Civilian Conservation Corps was another of President Roosevelt's New Deal programs, initiated on March 31, 1933, during the Great Depression. Its purpose was to conserve natural resources and salvage the lives of unemployed young men between the ages of 18 and 25. Participants had to buy their own uniforms and were paid $30 a month.

CCC workers building hillside terraces

In Montgomery County, many of the efforts were directed toward building levees and soil and water conservation projects. Before the CCC era, farmers would burn fields following each harvest to have the land ready for planting the following spring. Fields were plowed in as they lay, resulting in loss of soil as melting snow or rain washed down the hillsides. The camp partnered with the Montgomery County Soil Conservation Association to conduct soil demonstrations around the county. By 1939–1940 terracing of farms started, and remaining corn stalks or stubble were plowed under in place of burning to add nutrients back to the soil. By May 1940, the Montgomery County Soil and Water Conservation District became a reality, becoming the first countywide soil and water district in Iowa. The Red Oak Civilian Conservation Corps was closed in 1942. World War II efforts began to shape a whole new world for all of us, leaving the impacts of the Depression years behind.

Legion Park WPA Swimming Pool – Constructed 1937

www.delcampe.net

41

Red Oak was noted for having the largest public swimming pool in Southwest Iowa, created as a water reservoir by the Works Progress Administration (WPA). It was a benefit following President Roosevelt's work program of 1936 to employ millions of job seekers during the Depression Era to construct public buildings, roads, and other projects.

It is where I learned to swim. The pool featured high and low diving boards, two large rafts, and a long slide. Access was by individual ticket or annual pass. Cousin Jim Pilkington was a lifeguard during his high school years. Lighting allowed open hours from 10 a.m. to 10 p.m. daily. (We also swam in the bayous along Highway 48, where an IGA grocery store stands today. We created pools by damming Red Oak Creek. The bends of the Nishnabotna River provided high banks and overhanging trees to tie ropes for 'Tarzan' swings. Also, the falls of Walnut Creek to the west of town supplied our first water slides.)

Unfortunately, the colossal swimming pool no longer exists. Age and repair costs caused the pool to be replaced by a new, smaller pool – no longer the really special pool Red Oak was noted for throughout the Midwest.

Legion Park also housed a large indoor skating rink, the lighted Red Oak High School football field and semi-pro baseball field, plus the county fairgrounds with additional space for traveling carnivals and the Ringling Circus. I played third base on this baseball field. Here, I became noted for three things: I found out that sometimes the ball can find the bat, I could make spectacular catches of routine fly balls, and I was responsible for the winning run many times when I dropped the ball. I actually got paid $5 per game.

National Carbon Company – Constructed 1948

National Carbon was a pioneer in dry cell batteries used in flashlights under the name of Eveready Batteries. The plant was located in a field across the street from the Halbert Hybrid Seed Corn facility on Highway 48 and the corner of old U.S. Highway 34. The Red Oak plant produced batteries for use in portable radios, hearing aids, and other uses under contract to the U.S. Army Signal Corps, the U.S. Air Force, Navy, and Weather Bureau.

Tommy's Red Oak

Red Oak became my 'hometown' for life. This is where I was molded and shaped – where I became who I turned out to be. Here I had roots where I had none before. It is where I lived the longest, except for my time in Germany. I began my education here, got my first jobs, made lifelong friends, and learned life lessons. Here I got my anchor before I became an American gypsy wandering all over the world.

It is also where my father's alcoholism would become the positive roots that caused my horizons to leap so far beyond rural Red Oak. For this reason, my mother left Red Oak in 1949 for Des Moines to take a job as a librarian at Drake University. That event allowed me to gain a free college degree as the son of a Drake employee. And it was the Korean War that paused my plans to be a journalist and nudged me into becoming an Air Force pilot.

Note: World War II and the Korean War also impacted many of my relatives. In World War II, Uncle Jim Pilkington was in the Air Force serving combat duty in the China, Burma and India Theater as a sergeant. Marilyn Thomas, the oldest cousin, was an employee at the Glenn Martin Bomber Plant at Ft. Crook just south of Omaha. Cousin Jean Replogle became a Navy Ensign as a nurse based in Chicago. The Korean Conflict ensnared cousin Jim Pilkington who became a Marine Lieutenant based at Quantico just south of Washington D.C. Cousin Ross Pilkington became an Air Force Sergeant based at Charleston AFB in South Carolina. Second cousin Roger Westerlund served as a doctor in the Public Health

Service, supporting American Indian tribes in the American Southwest.

My early years in Red Oak were centered on elementary school, family get-togethers, visits to the family seed corn plant, bike riding, and Sunday dinner at the Johnson House restaurant. I played hide-and-seek with other kids at the golf course, chased lightning bugs, and built hollyhock dolls for my mother. I played with the neighborhood children. We played in caves, built tree houses, constructed dams in Red Oak Creek, and explored Indian Gulley, going barefoot as much as possible.

Our first home was 1021 Corning Street, just a couple of blocks from my Halbert grandparents' home on Heritage Hill and Webster Elementary School. Webster was where I attended first to fourth grades.

Just up the street was the home of widow Hester Iddings, my grandfather Halbert's sister. Her husband Frank had a large farm about three miles north of town on both sides of a country road and the Nishnabotna River at the back of the property. Part of the land included a large, wooded area full of hickory trees where we had frequent picnic outings. It also abutted a pioneer cemetery on the west side of this grove.

Aunt Hester's home was one of the Red Oak classical heritage homes. It was unique for me because she had an incinerator built into a hilly bank on a side street. In those days, any yard or house waste that you could destroy by fire – you did. When I was in first grade, the incinerator was no longer used. It provided an ideal hiding space that I used to go to school barefoot during the spring and fall. So on the way past her house to first grade at Webster School, I would take off my shoes and socks, and place them in the unused incinerator. After school, I would retrieve my shoes and go home. I don't believe my mother ever knew.

My first-grade teacher was Miss Lampson and was the first teacher I can remember. It's also where I gained my initial tools for reading and writing. Best of all was that the desks were arranged perfectly for dipping pigtails into inkwells.

My second and third-grade teacher was Miss Schmidt. This was much tougher and the fun parts of kindergarten and first grade were gone. But the elementary school had the benefit of recess. The fire escape on the side of the school was our jungle gym. During the winter, the back of the school became a great hill for snow sledding. Miss Schmidt was probably my first employer. When I was in sixth grade, she paid me to shovel her sidewalk after snowstorms during the winter months. And I learned as a result that working could lead to the acquisition of spritz cookies at the Swedish bakery or even gain entrance to the Grand or Iowana movie theaters.

Nearby was 1020 Boundary Street – one of the majestic Heritage Hill houses. The home and attached carriage house were well maintained, but no one lived there. Roger Westerlund, my newly-discovered second cousin, and I found a basement window that was not locked. From time to time, we would explore the home. The attached carriage house had a second floor for storage. The treasure trove we found was hundreds of old magazines, plat books and Montgomery

County business journals. One of the ads that appeared in those journals was for 'Halbert's Hair Restorer' available at Charles B. Halbert's drug store in Elliott, Iowa. He was a brother of my grandfather Halbert, one of the many aunts and uncles I never knew I had. The 'Hair Restorer' caught my interest, as my Dad, my grandfather, and all the male Halberts on the family photos were all bald.

It is also a time when Roger and I ended up before the Mayor of Red Oak for destroying Bert Schafer's back porch with claw hammers. Bert's house was also empty and not being maintained for livability. Looking back, I guess Roger and I thought we were just involved in a community improvement project. Mayor Reilly was also the family doctor for both of us and knew us well. We got off with a stern warning – but did notice a twinkle in Mayor Reilly's eyes.

A couple of years later, we moved to 910 Miller Avenue, about three blocks away but still close to my grandfather Halbert's home and just two blocks from Roger Westerlund. The home was on a large area of property at, what then was, the end of Red Oak to the East. We had upstairs bedrooms with stairs down to the living room and stairs down to the kitchen. The basement was for the furnace, washroom and storage. The back lawn was terraced and included a large outdoor goldfish pond. To the east were pastures and tall trees for climbing and building tree houses.

It was normal in Midwest communities to have both named streets and alleys between streets. I recall that the alleys were for pickup and delivery access to houses between streets. Pickups were garbage, yard waste, clinkers

from furnaces, and old items no longer wanted. There
was no street pickup. The amount of garbage created was
very small as compared with today. Anything metal, paper products, and other items determined to be useful
to the war effort were collected in an early form of recy-
cling. Flour was sold in large cloth sacks that had floral
and other designs. These became clothing as nearly every
housewife had a sewing machine and made many clothing items for the family. In addition, most housewives
did their own baking of bread, cakes, cookies, and pies.
Refrigerators were brand new, and freezers did not exist.
The family bought groceries several times a week. Seldom
was it more than two bags. Most everything was seasonal
and fresh.

Our family went on summer vacations to Lake Okoboji in
northern Iowa. The cabin was owned by the Replogle family. In articles from the *Red Oak Express* and *Red Oak Sun*,
I learned that my parents vacationed at Lake Okoboji beginning in 1930. My first trip there as a Halbert was with
my parents in1933. After that, we frequently visited while
residing in Sioux City and later in Red Oak.

The lake resort was famous for being on the only gla-
cier-dug lake in Iowa. It also boasted the massive Arnold's
Park Entertainment Complex and the excursion Mississippi River Steamer-style paddle boat nearby. The area
was interconnected with five lakes: West Okoboji, East
Okoboji, Upper Gar, Lower Gar, and Spirit Lake. At the
cabin, we had access to the dock where a Chris Craft pow-
erboat and canoes were available. The dock also provided
a place to dive into the cold waters of the crystal clear

lake. The highlight was Arnold's Park with a house of mirrors, a haunted house, and long wooden slides where you sat on carpets to whiz to the bottom.

Cross county trips were rare. Going to Omaha, Council Bluffs, and Des Moines by car were fairly common. However, in 1941 we did make a driving vacation to the Colorado Rockies and Yellowstone National Park. I learned that, once you got west of Lincoln, Nebraska, you were in a desert full of cattle and devoid of anything green. The biggest natural products seemed to be livestock and sugar beets carried to market in trucks. The boring scenery finally gave way as we approached the magnificent Rockies in Colorado and followed them to Grand Teton National Park and Yellowstone in Wyoming. The return trip was through the Bad Lands of South Dakota, Mount Rushmore, Rapid City, and Sioux Falls – places where I had no idea I had family history connections.

Tommy at Yellowstone National Park

These were golden years for the family. The seed corn business was thriving, and life was easy. I had my first bike, and I had a whole world in town and the countryside to explore. But it was also the time when childhood sicknesses were rampant, including measles, mumps, and chickenpox. I had them all on Miller Avenue. Dr. Riley would show up at the house, prescribe medicines, and then carefully tack a sign at the front door announcing there was an infectious disease in the home and the house was quarantined.

Early one spring evening on April 26, 1941, as the sun was setting, I was riding my bike at the seed corn plant with instructions not to leave the complex. The plant was set alongside a seldom-used dead-end dirt road. Busy Highway 48 was one block east, and the dirt road ended at the Nishnabotna River to the west. There were no homes or businesses along this road. Traffic was rare. So I was confident when I turned onto this road that nothing could happen. Shorty Sands, a cemetery employee, was just as confident as he turned from Hwy 48 on to the road, and we collided. The handlebar of the bike pinned me down. It took about two weeks for me to recover from knee injuries. It also ended of my bike adventures in the time remaining before my mother and I moved to Omaha, Nebraska. It was also when I instilled my interest (possibly passion) for the outdoors, including hiking state parks, fishing in rivers too thick to drink and too thin to plow, and hunting in the stubble of fall corn and soybean fields for pheasant.

In September 2000, I returned to Red Oak for the 50th Anniversary of my High School class graduation. I actually graduated from Roosevelt High School in Des Moines. I was a member of the Red Oak class of 1950 from grade school through my junior year of high school. My Red Oak classmates always considered me a member of the class of '50 in Red Oak.

While on this trip, I spent time doing additional genealogy research at the Red Oak library and the Red Oak Historical Society building. I presented two items to the Historical Society including a weathered barn wood framed Halbert Hybrid Seed Corn sack from 1940 and the Halbert family history I had compiled as of 2000. The donations were noted in a 2-column news story in the *Red Oak Express* headlined "Halbert donates extensive family history documents" on October 31, 2000.

Deaths of Grandparents and Franklin D. Roosevelt 1939–1946

The first family death I experienced was my paternal grandfather John Marion Halbert. He died on April 5, 1939, at the age of 62, about two years after we moved from Sioux City to Red Oak. Then, on July 5, 1945, 'Papoo' died at the age of 74. He was my maternal grandfather, Harry Walker Pilkington. My maternal grandmother, Maude Jeffers Pilkington, died a year later, on July 20, 1946, at the age of 70.

And while not a relative by any stretch of the imagination came the death of President Delano Roosevelt on April 12, 1945 in the middle of World War II. When I was born, Iowan Herbert Hoover was president, but Roosevelt was the only president I had ever known in my early years.

Even today, I'm convinced if Roosevelt hadn't died, he'd still be president. I did see him once when he was making a whistle-stop tour. He was greeted by about everybody in Montgomery County during his 15-minute campaign speech on a balcony of the last train car before continuing on to Omaha.

Roadside Weeds for the War Effort Now Known as Cannabis

Beginning in 1942 and throughout World War II, rural ditches between the fences and roads were used to grow cannabis. The cannabis replaced hemp used for making rope, cloth, and cordage necessary for the war. Cannabis was a 'Victory Crop' that every farm family was familiar with. There were no synthetic fibers in those years. The world's hemp supply mainly came from the Philippines, which was occupied by Japan. The roadside weed provided source material for 40 fiber-processing plants in the Midwest to produce cordage for the U.S. Navy.

We had cannabis growing all around rural Iowa but had no idea it was anything but a weed. My young buddies and I spent our time experimenting smoking 'corn silk.'

World War II Years in Omaha: 1943–1944

World War II resulted in family upheaval as my Dad volunteered for a civilian position with the U.S. Navy Seabees. His assignment took him to Adak Island in the Aleutian Chain, part of Alaska. My mother elected to move to Omaha, Nebraska, to run a rooming house where my oldest cousin Marilyn Thomas resided. Marilyn was employed at the Glenn L. Martin Aircraft factory at Ft. Crook, which later became Offutt AFB. (This was the factory where 536 B-29 Superfortress bombers were built – including the famous *Enola Gay* and *Bockscar* that dropped the first nuclear weapons on Japan.) All of those in the rooming house were working at the factory.

The house was on the west side of Hanscom Park in midtown Omaha. It was the oldest park in Omaha with an upscale residential neighborhood. Two of those who had previously lived in the area included the Henry Fonda family of Hollywood fame and the birthplace of former President Gerald Ford. The huge park included two lakes, a cascade, extensive flowerbeds, 2.5 miles of macadamized roadway, fountains, and a magnificent growth of trees.

Two blocks west was Field Club Elementary School, where I attended fifth grade. Across the street to the west was Field Club golf course founded in 1898, and beyond that was pastureland. We lived on 32nd Street, where the streetcars ran day and night. Field Club School and the golf course were on 34th street. It was the end of Omaha to the west, which today extends well beyond 120th street.

Omaha, at that time, was the home of several regional breweries, including Metz, Storz, and Krug. In the late 1940s old Ft. Crook and the Glenn Martin Bomber plant became the home of the Strategic Air Command (SAC) at what became known as Offutt AFB.

My previous knowledge of Omaha was limited to occasional family trips for shopping, visiting the stockyards, the Joslyn Art Museum, Burlington/Union Pacific railroad stations, and dinners at King Fong. This was known as Omaha's oldest restaurant serving excellent Chinese food in a unique setting since the early 1920s.

King Fong Marquee

That knowledge helped me become a fast learner when we moved to Hanscom Park. I was also immediately able to walk downtown by following the streetcar tracks or joining forces with classmate buddies I had just met at school.

The one deep shock I had while in Omaha happened after I had met a neighbor kid who was of Japanese heritage. We became close friends, as we were both new to the school. We saw each other daily at school or in the park. Then one day he was no longer around. He and his family had been rounded up by federal authorities. They were sent to a concentration camp in California for the duration of the war. It left a deep scar – knowing I had just lost a new friend and could do absolutely nothing about it.

I spent lots of time helping my mother with chores and collecting all the things wanted for the war effort like printed materials, cooking grease, aluminum and other metal. We used any money we earned to buy saving stamps to paste in booklets and eventually trade in for war bonds. We put on a circus at the nearby Heaton house that even drew Abbott & Costello, two famous Hollywood comedians, to the event. They were in Omaha for live appearances at the Orpheum Theater.

Besides the interruption of life and losing contact with my friends in Red Oak, sleeping became a problem. Not from pressure of the interruption – but from the constant clatter of the streetcars across the street at night. I would later find out that the reverse would happen when we moved back to Red Oak and the country silence at night would be deafening. The other constant in Omaha was the odor from the stockyards anytime the wind blew from the southeast. It was called the smell of money!

Return to Hometown
Red Oak: 1944–1948

Returning to your hometown is special. You are back where you are known and where everything you want is where it's supposed to be, including the sounds of trucks changing gears to climb the U.S. Highway 34 hill on the north side of town and Burlington freight trains whistle all night on the south side of town.

Dad returned to Red Oak from his Seabee tour of duty in the Aleutian Islands in 1945 and joined his mother in running Halbert Hybrid Seed Corn again. But things had changed. Strange things began to happen. It took a while, but I realized that my father had become an alcoholic. The family was no longer engaged in the community. We now lived in a small rental home at 704 Maple Street while the corn plant was being sold. After my Dad became a traveling salesman again, we moved to another rental home at 509 Nuckols Street in the south part of town.

He was being treated for alcoholism in clinics in Council Bluffs (the Iowa city on the Missouri river across from Omaha, Nebraska). My mother worked for Bertha Faunce at her clothing store, but times were tough. Mom made frequent visits to the clinic in Council Bluffs. Sometimes, I went with her, although I had to wait outside the clinic. It was a parklike setting. I remember seeing and feeding pure black squirrels for the first time. Those in trees of Red Oak were exclusively red squirrels. The trip took more than an hour to drive there and another hour to return on two-lane concrete cow paths. Eventually, my mother filed for divorce in 1948, and we moved to Des Moines.

My life centered on school and part-time work at the Faunce Ladies' Ready-to-wear store washing windows and vacuuming floors. I also sacked groceries at Safeway and the Red Oak Wholesale Fruit Company, delivered the *Des Moines Register* and weekly national magazines like *Saturday Evening Post* and *Colliers*, coached little league baseball, and matured.

I entered sixth grade at Lincoln School on return from Omaha. I have very few memories from that class year, except for the Coke truck showing up during recess at times and handing out free Cokes for anyone who could spell Coca Cola. Then came Junior High that was my parents' high school building. Lincoln School was located atop a high hill, so steep that Model-T Fords had to climb the hill in reverse gear. Best memories here were learning to square dance and sing in a chorus during music classes. I was on top of my game with geography as I had become a stamp collector and knew a lot about countries of the world.

It was also when Lake Okoboji became the location where I attended a boy's summer camp at Camp Foster. We would be put aboard a bus in Red Oak for the annual two-week camp. Heading north, we would stop along the way and pick up others along the route. As happens at this age, the kids you bond with at school or two-week camp vacations become friends for life. Besides swimming and canoeing, we learned crafts, had fireside hotdogs and marshmallow roasts, followed by the telling of ghost stories. Big items were making square and round bracelets and lanyards out of plastic strips thinner than a shoelace. This talent was used as I entered Junior High School to sell bracelets to classmates. I earned enough to buy homestyle ice cream at the Green Parrot, and tickets to movies at the Grand and Iowana theaters.

Chores were assigned by the cabin where you bunked. They included prep of canoes, setting chow hall tables, washing dishes, and cleaning the camp. Classes were held for learning crafts and the camp area's flora and fauna. During evening campfire sessions, I gained an interest in Robert W. Service poetry, and actually memorized and recited a few of them, including:

The Bread Knife Ballad Refrain

Please mother don't kill father with the bread knife
Remember it was a gift when you were wed
But if you must kill father with the bread knife,
Please use another for the bread.

The other two were the 15 stanzas of the *Cremation of Sam McGee* and the 10 stanzas of *Dangerous Dan McGrew*.

This was when 'old timers' (ones who were not at camp for the first time) learned to be especially careful with salads. Jack-in-the-pulpit plants grew profusely in the woods. As the plant matured, it would produce its famous flower, and then morph into a miniature stalk of seeds. It looked much like a miniature green ear of corn. Those seeds, when eaten, would set your mouth afire – feeling like you had needles sticking you everywhere in your mouth. Drinking water made it worse. So being boys, this was the ultimate prank to pull on 'newbies.' And the reason that 'vets' usually skipped salad. This was usually accomplished when your cabin was responsible for setting up chow hall tables.

Boyhood in Red Oak

We had lots of outings to the Red Oak Golf Course. Both of my parents were active golfers. It was the center of social life for Red Oak. It provided opportunities for the adults to dance, socialize and dine. But for us kids, it was all about hide-and-seek, red light green light, and catching fireflies during summer evenings. These were the years I made money by shoveling snow, mowing grass, picking and selling bittersweet gooseberries, hickory nuts and walnuts. Roger and I ran a fur trapline, I sold ringneck snakes captured along the Burlington railroad tracks, nightcrawlers from yards all over the hills of Red Oak, and squabs taken from nests in buildings and barns. I even raised baby chickens in the backyard. Another way I made money was by flattening pennies. I would go to the Burlington train tracks, put pennies on the rails, wait until the train came by, and then recover the flattened pennies I could sell for a nickel.

One time while in a barn between town and the golf course to get squabs, I fell from the barn's rafters. By sheer luck, I hit a beam and was flipped in the direction of a manure pile. That was a good thing. Had I not hit the beam, I would have fallen 25 feet to the concrete floor below.

I learned to drive at the age of 13. Iowa had no driver's licenses at the time. The accepted requirement to drive was just to be able to see over the hood from the driver's seat. The road rules were 'reasonable and proper' with no specific speed or age limits. Restrictions were your own depending on the car's capabilities, the driver's skill, and the layout of the road. It was considered fast when you could go 50 mph on the narrow, hilly, and curvy highways. We really enjoyed it when a friend took us on a joy ride in his family car with a rumble seat. This was a seat facing forward that was hidden out of sight in what is now the trunk of a car. This joy was greatest on the thrill hills – rural dirt roads that you could launch the car off the ground when topping an ungraded hill at high speed.

My parents never gave me 'the talk.' My sex education was from 'big boys' behind the barn. It was augmented when I visited my Aunt Maurine's home as her husband Fred subscribed to *Esquire* and *National Geographic* magazines. The Vargas Girls of *Esquire* and the topless natives in *National Geographic* were of keen interest. My cousin Jean had Vargas Girl posters in her bedroom when she still lived at home.

The two shoeshine shops downtown sold paperback books, and this is where I discovered *God's Little Acre* and eroticism. The Red Oak library provided access to the erotic writings of Guy de Maupassant. Roger and I would sometimes skip school and go to the matinees at the Grand Theater (one of two movie houses in Red Oak). They had Swedish films where female nudity was standard. Friends would share 8-page comic books 'borrowed' from their parents' bedrooms that featured explicit drawings. That was basically my sex education as I grew up.

… Except for an unexpected event during the summer before I entered Junior High School. That summer, my mother arranged for my father to obtain treatments at an alcohol clinic in Hot Springs, Arkansas. My mother arranged for me to stay with one of her golfing partners, whose husband was on a business trip to Colorado. This first weekend was the annual Red Oak Country Club golf tournament. The champion was Bill Victor, a charismatic traveling salesman who resided in an apartment in my grandparents' home at 103 Reed Street. Following the tournament was the tournament banquet where the awards were presented, with celebrations in the bar area following.

I had gone to bed about 10 p.m. Shortly after midnight, I was awakened by strange noises from the living room. I quietly got up and sat high on the stairs where I would not be seen, but could see what was going on in the dimly lit living room. My mother's golf partner had returned home with Bill Victor and another male golfer I did not know. All were naked. I was frozen in place, viewing actual sex for the first time. My mother's friend was providing oral pleasure to the male I did not know, while Bill was providing enjoyment to her doggie style. Due to fear of being discovered, I quietly returned to my room. It was a powerful event that left me with a strong lifelong knowledge that women are actually more sexually capable than men.

I assumed that, after the tournament banquet and then celebrating until the bar closed, she came home totally forgetting that I was in the house. Even so, it became my "Here's to you, Mrs. Robinson" moment.

I did have a 'family life' course as a junior at Red Oak High taught by the girl's athletic coach. That course did not last long, as she responded to a question asking if the size of a woman's breast had any correlation to breast sensitivity. Parent uproar caused her to be fired the next day, and it was back to the behind-the-barn classroom.

One of the highlights in my freshman and sophomore years at Red Oak High School was the boys and girls summer camp at Simpson College in Indianola, Iowa. The college facilities and nearby Lake Ahquabi State Park offered our first coed opportunity other than school. We had classes and activities galore, and bus transportation to Lake Ahquabi offered a relaxing escape from the summer heat. Swimming, sunbathing, boating, and fishing were popular activities on the pristine man-made lake. With rental boats available, we could enjoy the water from a canoe, paddleboat or kayak. It was also great to wander along shady trails. For both years I had a duck call and slide whistle 'garage band' group that provided entertainment at the school theater stage. We were big on *Woody Woodpecker*.

Lake Ahquabi State Park – Indianola, Iowa

Our adult camp leader was Reverend Glenn Lamb, a young Methodist preacher. Later, he was the pastor of Grace Methodist Church in Des Moines, right across the street from my Theta Chi fraternity house. Another coincidence was that one young lady who attended both years ended up as a student nurse at the Des Moines Methodist Hospital. She became the wife of my fraternity pledge son, Lon Jensen, after both graduated from Drake University.

Methodist Churches in Iowa always had Wednesday evening set aside for potluck dinners. Each family brought a dish to share. It was this tradition that sprung how we identified particular churches. The Catholics were known for the rosary they wore and those of Hebrew faith by the Star of David. Methodists were known for their casserole dish.

My freshman class at Red Oak High School totaled 77 students. I was with this class through my junior year. I was not a great student – struggling with math, getting by in English and Spanish and doing fine in Family Living class. But looking back, the most important class I took was typing. This was my game changer. Without that skill, I don't believe I would have done so well in journalism in college and beyond.

I never dated during my high school time in Red Oak. But I did participate in sock hops at various homes, learned to dance, and actually got to hold a girl for the first time. It was a period in my life where I was a chick maggot. *Yep, maggot is not a typo.* In the community, during 1944–1946 I sang (actually, I was filling a robe) in the Methodist Church choir and acted as an usher for Sunday services. I became a Boy Scout and joined DeMolay – the Masonic group for high school boys.

Time of Discovery

At this time, in the basement of our home on 509 Nuckols Street, I came across my South Dakota adoption papers. I was stunned. But, I never mentioned this discovery to my parents. I knew it would crush my mother, who did everything in her power to make me feel loved and wanted as I was growing up. It did, of course, weigh heavily on me. The questions of who am I? What are my roots? Why was I put up for adoption? Do I have any Sioux Indian heritage? Those thoughts and more ran through my mind.

I never took any action to find answers to those questions until after I was on my own working for the *Cedar Falls Daily Record*. I contacted the unwed mothers' home in Sioux Falls and received a letter providing my birth mother's name, some basic information, and the name of my birth father. It wasn't until my mother died in 1975 that I began detailed research to learn who I was and my background. This was a time when my birth mother was still alive.

I made no effort to contact her for years after, as I did not want to do anything that might disrupt her marriage. I determined that my birth mother did not have any other offspring during her marriage.

Broadcasting and Media Impacts
That Sparked my Journalism Interest

Subconsciously, my interests in the media began to grow in my early high school years. It was still the early days of radio, and television was not even on the horizon. We had two radio stations in nearby Shenandoah, termed the 'Friendly Farmer Stations.' Shenandoah was the mail-order seed and nursery capital of America. Ten active nursery companies were operating in the fertile valleys of Southwest Iowa, with Henry Field and Earl May companies leading the way. Both got the broadcasting bug by appearing on weekly shows on WOAW in Omaha to promote their businesses.

Fed up with the long drive to Omaha, Field constructed his own radio station in Shenandoah. On February 24, 1924, it went on air with Field as the main announcer. The newly established KFNF reached an audience throughout Iowa and adjoining states. Earl May countered and, by September 1, 1925, began his competing station KMA — 'The Corn Belt Station in the Heart of the Nation.' Both stations provided a mix of talks on agriculture, poultry, old-time religion, and folksy, homespun philosophy. Both stations had no advertising revenue.

Each station created buildings for audiences. May's investment now totaled $90,000 for his station, another $100,000 for his auditorium, with monthly operating costs of $1,000. Everything was supported by their booming catalog seed business. By 1930, attendance at the two stations reached nearly 440,000 people.

Fast forward in the late 1940s … both stations were still going strong. Young, teenage Tommy and his friends would hop on the South Branch train from Red Oak to Shenandoah to watch radio shows and grand piano or pipe organ concerts at the Mayfair Auditorium.

Our radio station of choice for network news, especially in the WWII years, and for entertainment was WOW in Omaha. Like KFNF and KMA, it too was created when there were no radio laws or regulations. The stations just 'turned on the juice' and began broadcasting.

Television came to Omaha and Southwest Iowa in 1949, but not in time for my mother and I to see any programming. We had moved to Des Moines, with the first TV station in the area going on air in Ames in 1952.

In Red Oak in the 1940s we had two weekly newspapers. The *Red Oak Sun* was established in 1884, and the *Red Oak Express* that was first published on March 28, 1868. Our daily newspaper options were the *Omaha World Herald* and the *Des Moines Register*, both papers with morning and afternoon editions plus stellar reputations.

College Years in
Des Moines: 1949–1955

My parents divorced on June 20, 1949, ending a marriage that began on January 13, 1921, when they eloped to Omaha for the ceremony. It was just after I had completed my junior year of high school. My mother obtained a job at Drake University in Des Moines as a librarian for the Cowles Library on campus. As a result, my mother and I left 509 Nuckols Street in Red Oak. We temporarily moved in with her sister at 2701 High Street in Des Moines – the home of Kathryn and Marion Thomas. Their youngest daughter, Susan, also resided in the home and was a student at Drake University. The biggest impact for me was moving in my final year of high school, away from all my friends and support base – to begin a new life where I knew almost no one.

It was a tough year for me but was cushioned by my experiences with DeMolay and my Methodist Youth Fellowship in Red Oak. That provided one common thread in making new friends. My new high school was Roosevelt High, where my class size went from 77 to 400. Beyond the new friends I forged with DeMolay and church, my new base was being formed by those assigned to my homeroom. The classroom facilities at Roosevelt were beyond what I had experienced in rural Red Oak.

Opportunities for 'the great outdoors' became limited living in the city. My transportation was curb liners (an electric bus) or walking. But I made trips to the Des Moines

Water Works Park, which had large ponds for bass fishing along the Raccoon River.

It was a mixed bag for me educationally. I was fortunate to have Mr. Frank Hildreth for English, and he was the spark that spurred my interest in English and the theater. He could bring writers and playwrights to life – in ways no other teacher had done for me before. The school also had an indoor swimming pool, providing a welcome expansion for physical training and extreme pleasure during the cold and grey Iowa winters. The uniform for this class was your Adam costume.

On the other hand, my physics teacher obviously knew his subject – but he was unable to translate what he was instructing into something I could understand. It was a tough transition year. And one that proved invaluable as I began as a freshman at Drake University.

A life-changing moment happened in the spring semester my freshman year. The Missouri River at Omaha faced record flooding. Many of us at Drake volunteered to help and drove to Omaha to fill sandbags to protect homes and businesses. We were in the Little Italy section of Omaha just south of the Union Pacific and Burlington train stations. The life-changing moment came as a result. It was the first time I had ever eaten in an Italian restaurant and the first time I ever had a salad with Italian dressing. It was more than a wow!

I grew up in an entire family structure that only used French dressing for salad – a taste I have never acquired. As a result,

I avoided salad. The Italian dressing became my favorite and opened the door to me eating salad from that day on.

I did not get involved with extra-curricular activities at Roosevelt. My spare time was spent as a soda jerk with Bright Drug store at the corner of 28th Street and Ingersoll Avenue. It was a small business district two blocks from my Aunt Kathryn's home. One long block south of Ingersoll was Grand Avenue – the main street in the center of Des Moines lined with huge mansions. And just one block away on Grand Avenue was the home of the Governor of Iowa. I first got to know him, as Gov. William Beardsley frequently came to the drug store to buy pulp westerns.

The best thing about attending Roosevelt High was that it prepared me extremely well to make the transition to Drake. I had adjusted to changing from a class of 77 to one of 400. So, the change to school attended by 6,000 students was not overwhelming. In fact, the Drake student body was composed of about 2,000 students from Des Moines, 2,000 from the state of Iowa, and 2,000 from Chicago and Illinois. As a result, I already knew a large percentage of my class.

I was not someone who knew why he was in college or had any specific goals or targets. Guidance counselor aptitude tests were not much help either. I did get all my requirements out of the way as a freshman and sophomore – but entering my junior year, I still had no idea at all why I was in college. I only knew my mother expected me to attend and excel.

The Korean War impact was always in the background. With help and guidance from my Uncle Marion Thomas, I joined the Iowa National Guard as a private while attending Drake. My first military serial number was 26780091. The Iowa Guard was not called to active duty during that war, but the Iowa Air Guard was. So I had the protection of remaining in college to temporarily avoid the draft. My guard duty was as an enlisted finance clerk in the Headquarters & Headquarters Detachment of the Iowa Guard in Des Moines. My uncle's brother, Jim Thomas, was the commanding officer. This was a political unit assigned directly under the Governor Bourke B. Hickenlooper, a governor I also knew from the Bright Drug store.

As a guardsman, I showed up for four hours training each Monday evening. I was twice deployed for three weeks each summer to Camp McCoy, Wisconsin – not far from the Wisconsin Dells. During my first deployment, I was tasked to be the driver for Governor Beardsley during his official visit. He arrived in a two-engine C-47 Gooney Bird at a grass strip at the Camp. When the aircraft stopped, I drove around between a wing and the fuselage to get close. I didn't notice a fire truck had pulled in behind me. I backed up with the Governor aboard to get away from the aircraft wing and crunch! … I hit the fire truck with a Governor in the car. The only impact was I never served as a driver again.

All in all, I served two years, seven months, and eight days in the Iowa National Guard. I earned one promotion when I became Private First Class on September 25, 1951. To my benefit, that military time counted through my military career in reaching pay scale increases and counted toward time served for retirement.

Two things happened at that time. The Korean War draft was in the background for all 20-year-olds, and Air Force Reserve Officer Training Corp options began at Drake. For a junior, I would have to take ROTC classes for four semesters in 1952–53 and 1953–54, including summer school between both years. To enter Officer training, I had to resign from the Iowa National Guard – and I did.

I had my first taste of being in the active-duty Air Force between my junior and senior year. I attended a four-week orientation training at Lowry AFB in Denver, Colorado. We were mixed together with several hundred ROTC students living in barracks at the base. We were restricted from leaving the base, except on Sunday as the 'workday' in the military was Monday through Saturday. Most everyone followed the rules, but one adventurous cadet managed to get through the fence and base guards to be picked up by a girlfriend waiting in a car.

One evening we got a 'schadenfreude' moment, to use the German word to explain 'that wonderful feeling you get from someone else's misfortune.' The barracks were set up for sleeping in a barn-like area, with rows of cots on both sides. After 'lights out' one night, we removed 'Romeo's' cot and closed up the arrangement so there would be no empty cot where his had been. When he returned that night, he spent considerable time looking for his bed, double-checking to see if he was in the right barracks. He even checked out other barracks nearby. But it took daylight before he could figure out his cot was gone, but his clothes locker was still intact.

Lowry AFB Barracks – 1953

The highlight of my training at Lowry was to be selected as one of a handful of cadets for a flight in a B-29 Superfortress, as Lowry was the training base for B-29 crews. This one was special, as we flew to Eglin AFB in north Florida to witness a 'Firepower' demonstration. I had seen the B-29 frequently when I was a fifth-grade student in Omaha during the War. It was the first truly long-range bomber. The range was 5,600 miles with a 20,000-pound bomb load.

World War II B-29 Superfortress Bomber

B-29s were built at the Martin Bomber plant on Ft. Crook (later Offutt AFB, where I was assigned in the late 1950s). During World War II, the Martin Bomber plant built more than 500 four-engine B-29s and another 1,500 twin en-gine B-26 Marauders. The B-29 was the first pressurized aircraft and used remote-controlled guns for defense.

Two of the B-29s produced at this plan were the *Enola Gay* and *Bockscar* that dropped the atomic bombs on Hiroshi-ma and Nagasaki in Japan, resulting in the end of World War II. My Florida flight marked the first time I ever sat in the pilot's seat and handled the controls.

At Drake, it was decision time. I had to declare a major. I went to the top rows of the Drake Fieldhouse, and looked down. The shortest line for signup was Journalism, so I became a journalist. I had taken broadcast courses during my freshman and sophomore years. There was no Drake radio station – just a classroom. Professor Jim Duncan was a one-man department. His classroom in Cole Hall business school had a glassed-in studio with speakers. The training centered on being a disk jockey or announcer, creating spots, and acting in soap operas. Now my direc-tion changed. Professor Bob Bliss was the head of the one-man Journalism department in New York Hall, a World War II temporary building that remained on campus for years. His curriculum was augmented by reporters and editors from the *Des Moines Register & Tribune*; Associ-ated Press, United Press and International News Service, *Better Homes & Gardens* and *Look* magazines. We were pounded with the mantra of 'accuracy, accuracy, accuracy and spell names right.'

The student publication was distributed twice each week. I was the managing editor of the *Drake Times Delphic* for the 1953–54 school year. As managing editor, I was responsible for tasking 20 reporters and being at the printers twice a week when the newspaper was printed (beginning Volume 72, Number 1). The trips to the printers were to insure the layout concept we did in advance would actually fit, and to make corrections on the spot if the Linotype operators had hit a wrong key while putting copy to lead. We also had to create headlines when needed because the ones we created in advance would not fit for the typeface we had selected. I learned to proof type that was set to go to press – when it was upside down and backwards. Here is where I got my love for the smell of printers ink. I was getting good at intelligently stacking paragraphs, editing copy, and taking notes during interviews. I remember Bob Bliss' charge to us after graduation with diplomas in hand was, "Now this is just the beginning of your education." A very accurate and telling statement that I found to be true, there is no finish line as there is so much to learn.

PEOPLE ARE NO DAMN GOOD

The *New Yorker* cartoon that identified my *Times Delphic* desk

Who's Who in American Colleges and Universities

In February 1954, I was selected for recognition and listing in *Who's Who in American Colleges and Universities*, honored as one of 34 from Drake University from our class of 1,200 graduates. The only other journalism graduate listed was Bill Wallace. He later became my mentor as I settled in Sarasota nearly 50 years later.

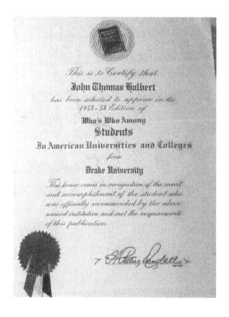

The Real World Of 1954

It wasn't all modern by 1954. Department stores and hotels in Des Moines had white-gloved elevator operators, and pneumatic tubes carried money and receipts to and from cashiers. However, it was a world of U.S. economic leadership. The nation produced 80 percent of the world's electrical goods, 40 percent of its electricity, 60 percent of its oil and 60 percent of its steel. America's five percent of the world's population had more wealth than the other 95 percent. By 1954, a total of 99.93 out of every 100 cars sold were U.S. brands. GM was a bigger economy than Belgium, and Los Angeles had more cars than Asia. It was the last time people were thrilled to own a toaster or waffle iron.

At the end of my freshman year of college, only 40 percent of Americans had seen television – and Des Moines was still a year away from getting TV service. As I began my senior year of college, Boston residents gained the reputation for having more TVs in their homes than bathtubs.

Things not invented yet by 1954 included ballpoint pens, credit cards, instant coffee, dishwashers, Matchbox toys, Mr. Potato Head, and garbage disposals. Words we no longer heard included 'iceboxes,' 'running boards,' and 'dime stores.' The only 'foreign' food was French toast. Loose meat Made Rite hamburgers were popular but never beat out Tenderloin sandwiches as the No. 1 choice. Bread had to be white, and spices were salt, pepper, and maple syrup. Cheese had to be yellow and shiny enough to see your reflection.

Smoking was marketed as 'healthful' for soothing jangled minds and sharpening dull minds. X-rays were so benign that shoe stores everywhere installed them to learn exact shoe sizes.

In 1954, additions to the world included Butterball turkey, M&M candy, Reddi-Whip in place of real whipped cream, and transistor radios. The price of an average new home reached $22,000, and annual incomes rose to $3,953. Gasoline was 29 cents a gallon, while an Oldsmobile 88 cost $2,362. Lettuce was 29 cents for two heads, bread was 17 cents, and first-class postage was three cents. The minimum wage was 75 cents per hour. The DOW average was 292.

We recognize now that our childhood was much better than our children's. We were pushed out the door by eight in the morning for unsupervised, unregulated, robust play and adventures. We only came home for lunch or occasions when we would be actively bleeding. On the other hand, our children grew up to be Olympic-class shoppers and being indoors at malls. Nothing has changed more for the worse than childhood.

Beginning of My Quest for Bylines 1953–1955

My first paying journalism job was as editor and columnist for the *Hawkeye Beverage Association Beer Distributor* magazine in early 1952. My column was titled 'Froth from the Spigot.' At the time, I was not old enough to purchase a beer.

I began working as a sports reporter for the *Des Moines Register* in May 1952, covering local sports and professional wrestling at KRNT Theater. Professional wrestling was reluctantly covered by the *Register*. The editorial policy was that I could write about the costumes and the audience reaction but never write that anyone won or lost. Professional wrestling, featuring 'stars' like crowd favorite Vern Gagne and drop-kick specialist Argentine Rocca, was an exhibition, not a sport.

At the time, the *Des Moines Register* was Iowa's largest and most influential statewide newspaper, with a circulation of 500,000. It was termed 'The Newspaper Iowa Depends Upon' being delivered to all four corners of the state by train and trucks. The Cowles family also founded and owed KRNT radio and KRNT-TV.

A hidden landmark in Des Moines was in the lobby of the *Des Moines Register*. In 1950, a 6-foot-diameter world globe featuring 114 square feet of geography was installed to honor the *Register's* 100th anniversary. It was a jewel I remember first viewing as a senior at Roosevelt High

School. I then was it daily as I became a sports reporter at the *Register* in 1952 at a salary of $50 a week.

Both publications were Cowles family properties. The *Register* globe underwent last-minute editing (as appropriate for any newspaper of record at the time). An hour before the globe was to leave New York in a heated railroad car, the Rand McNally cartographers scrambled to edit name of the capital of Indonesia to Jakarta. For years before, the capital had been known as 'Batavia.' The globe was motorized, allowing it to spin. The globe was moved to the State Historical Museum when the *Register* downsized from its multi-story building on Locust Street. A twin globe was built for the *Minneapolis Star Tribune*.

Register & *Tribune* World Globe

My next job began in May 1953 as a staff reporter for United Press, doing general reporting for the news and radio wires and covering the Iowa State House at $75 a week. I opened the office at 5 a.m. alone to generate both newswire and radio wire copy. It wasn't until 7 a.m. that the Bureau Chief, another staff reporter, and a union Teletype operator would begin their day. I did not have this support when I opened the office each day. I had to punch Teletype paper tape to run on the news wire split, while I also had to type live copy for the radio wire split. The next big part of the day began at 10 a.m. when I became a statehouse beat reporter. I got to know the secretaries in the various offices, where I got most tips of what was happening new in each major office, each day. There were no press offices or public relations staff at the time. At 2 p.m., I was through for the day. I liked the hours because I had time to play golf every afternoon.

One of my 'great' scoops came during a flood of the Raccoon and Des Moines rivers that merge near the Class A professional baseball park. As the river was rising, I attended a press conference by the Mayor of Des Moines. While in the office, I noticed a secretary had a handwritten telephone number on her desk. I copied the number and found it was an unlisted number that provided river levels. We now had an exclusive way of finding out the height of the floodwaters. We checked the levels frequently, and they continued to rise. Then it leveled off – for four hours straight. Using this information, I now had my first real 'scoop.' We declared the flood had crested. None of us had sense enough to look out the window and see that the water level was still climbing. The fact was the measuring device had become stuck.

Competition was tough as United Press had a staff of eight. In contrast, Associated Press had 22 staffers. They

also received carbon copies in advance of every story gen-
erated by all the reporters for the *Des Moines Register* (the
morning paper) and the *Tribune* (the afternoon paper).
Another competition was *International News Service* that
had a staff of two.

I graduated from Drake University in Des Moines in early
June of 1954 with a degree in journalism and a commission
as a Second Lieutenant in the Air Force. My new military
service serial number was now A02206767. It was at the
time of the Korean War. I was facing a four-year commit
ment to serve four years in the Air Force in payment for my
college deferment. The war was winding down, and the Air
Force rules were changing. I now had the option to serve
just two years, holding an Air Force Reserve commission
of Second Lieutenant but agreeing to enter as an enlisted
man. The only other option was to enter pilot training and
accept my commission as an officer and serve four years. I
became a pilot.

We then had to declare if we wanted 'immediate active
duty' or be delayed for later entry if desired. Not knowing how 'military thinking' worked, I asked for immediate active duty. My classmates who asked for a delay to
active duty all went before me. I did not enter active duty
until late January 1955. Lesson learned: Air Force Personnel people use reverse logic. For example, I learned if you
wanted to be assigned to a base in the southern U.S., make
sure you ask for a northern assignment. Other Air Force
rules that became apparent in later years were: If you were
assigned to a base you liked, it would be closed. The No.1
military rule of 'any change is progress' prevailed.

Sports Editor, Photographer, Police Reporter, Circulation Manager and Janitor of the *Cedar Falls* (Iowa) *Daily Record*

Shortly after graduating from Drake, I resigned from my job with United Press, expecting to enter the Air Force almost immediately. When it became apparent that this would not happen, I scrambled and applied to newspapers all over Iowa. Bill Anthony, the publisher of the *Cedar Falls Daily Record*, responded.

So, I packed my 1950 Frazer in August 1954 and moved to Cedar Falls. I joined a team of five other journalists and fell into the daily routine of putting together the daily community newspaper. The writing was what I was used to; my beat was covering anything having to do with the police department, high school and college sports, plus photography.

The photography was new. The *Des Moines Register* photographers had been on the leading edge using 35mm Leicas and relying on natural light (existing darkness as we called it). I was to use the classic 4x5 Speed Graphic. Modern cameras had roll film. Speed Graphic used film holders inserted manually into the back of the camera. Also necessary was a supply of flashbulbs. You would take a shot, pull a sheet of paper out of the way, and take another shot with a maximum of 8 shots. Luckily, I only had to shoot photos. Another employee processed them in his basement.

I was expected to cover home and away high school games in person, and all home Iowa State Teachers College games. Bill had no objections to my doubling as a stringer for both news and sports reports. This gave me additional income from both the *Des Moines Register* and United Press.

The toughest journalism day I ever had was in Cedar Falls. Six Iowa State Teacher College coeds were driving a convertible at night and had run under a parked semi-trailer. All of them were decapitated. Even in all of my military experience, there was never any experience that topped the impact of that disaster.

As time went by, I learned Bill had his first job with the *Ames Tribune*. The publisher of that daily provided Bill the opportunity and backing to eventually purchase the Cedar Falls paper. Bill had looked over my resume, conducted a short interview, and hired me knowing I would eventually leave for Air Force duty. It turned out to be an audition. Bill wanted to groom someone and offer his backing to buy that candidate a newspaper in Iowa. The paper turned out to be the *Marion Gazette* near Cedar Rapids, Iowa. It was an outstanding opportunity, one I would keep in the back of my mind to seriously consider when I completed my four-year active duty requirement with the Air Force.

Jumping forward four years, we last talked about his offer when I was assigned to Headquarters Strategic Air Command in Offutt AFB, Nebraska. Bill was with a bunch of Iowa community leaders brought to the headquarters for briefings on the command. I was the command briefer. I had just been selected for a regular officer appointment – no longer to be a reserve officer (which was considered to be 'Christmas help'). At this point, I was getting Captain's pay, flight pay, and a significant housing allowance. My 'Depression baby' era syndrome had kicked in. I told Bill I appreciated his offer, but I was pre-set for security above all other concerns. The other factor was I enjoyed flying and, at the same time, was using my journalism skills. I remember telling him that even as a Second Lieutenant, my bosses would listen to me. I had not had the kind of experience with the Des Moines Register *or* United Press. *He said he understood and that the door would remain open should I change my mind later in my life.*

The End of an Engagement and a 2-Year Romance

Two years before, I had become engaged to Marlys Holland of Thompson, Iowa, who was working in Des Moines as a Northwest Bell telephone operator. We had been dating after meeting in Bright Drug store, about a block from where she and her roommates lived. That two-year romance dissolved when the reality hit that she would be married to an Air Force Officer facing four years of active duty. Marlys decided it was not the life she wanted and instead moved to Minneapolis to attend the Moody Bible School. It was our last contact.

Air Force Primary Pilot Training
Spence Field, Moultrie, Georgia:
March 1955 – August 1955

In late January 25, 1955, I left my home at 966 21st Street in Des Moines in my new black, grey and white tricolor Buick Special. I was off to Lackland AFB in San Antonio, Texas, for two months of 'pre-flight' assignment. That home and entire hill were removed to construct an Interstate Highway.

The new car was made possible by a conviction I would become a student pilot. Then, I would earn a $222 a month salary and get $47.88 monthly for 'subsistence.' On beginning pilot training, my pay would increase by another $100 a month for flight pay. Our housing was free if we lived in Air Force barracks. Those who were married, and lived in 'economy' housing got an additional $90 a month tax-free as a housing allowance.

At this point, I became a veteran of the Korean War – by just six days. I was officially on active duty on January 25 with orders to report to Lackland on January 28, 1955, to begin training. Eligibility for this 'war time' credit ended on February 1, 1955. I got a campaign ribbon to wear on my dress uniform just freshly purchased at nearby Kellac Village, a shopping center between Kelly and Lackland AFBs.

At Lackland, we underwent final flight physicals and bought our initial uniforms using a one-time payment. We attended classes for officer training, accomplished all types of physical and team-building tests, and marched for the a class. Here is where we received our class This grouping became Class 56-J based on the projected completion of basic and intermediate flying training in March 1956.

In March 1955, those of us in pre-flight training at Lackland joined others who had gone through officer training schools and from Allied nations for initial flight training at several civilian contract schools throughout the United States. These included nine bases in Texas, Missouri, Mississippi, Florida, and Georgia. My class group joined together at Spence Field in Moultrie, in South Georgia, on March 7, 1955, one day before my 23rd birthday. Spence was operated by Hawthorne School of Aeronautics, headed by Bevo Howard. He was a world-renowned aerobatic pilot melded with military supervision provided by the 3302nd Pilot Training Squadron of the USAF Air Training Command. All instructors were civilians, and each instructor was assigned four students. Allied students were all from the Netherlands and were integrated throughout the training.

The routine was a half-day of flying and a half-day of ground school instruction. The classes were alternated weekly for six months (if you flew mornings the first week, you had classes first the next week). Class 56-J was the first to fly the Beechcraft T-34 and North American T-28, replacing the Piper PA-18 and North American T-6 trainers. Both the T-34 and T-28 were tricycle gear – while the PA-18 and T-6 were taildraggers.

At Spence, my flight training in the T-34 involved 24 hours and 58 minutes of dual flying time (flying with an instructor) and 15 hours and 2 minutes of solo flying time, while logging 95 landings. The T-28 experience involved 52 hours and 25 minutes of dual flying time with another 37 hours and 37 minutes of solo time. The T-28 time breakout also included an additional 25 hours flying on instruments while hooded and 3 hours and 5 minutes of weather flying time, and 110 landings in the T-28.

The flying training took place at Spence and three other auxiliary fields in Thomasville, Coolidge, and Tifton. Actual flying training typically entailed 40 flying hours in the smaller first-phase aircraft, and 90 hours in the complex second-phase aircraft. Ground school focused on aircraft engineering, principles of flight, weather, and navigation. Our graduation from primary flying training at Spence was on September 3, 1955.

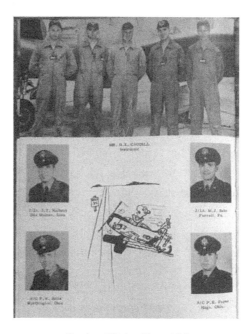

Gopher Flight Class 56-J

Historically, Spence was active as a training base from the 1951–1961 decade. More than one million flying hours were logged, with 2.5 million takeoffs and landings and 6,400 flight students completing the course. In addition to those in the USAF, military exchange students were from Belgium, Bolivia, Brazil, Columbia, Cuba, Denmark, Ecuador, France, Germany, Great Britain, Greece, Norway, Pakistan, Paraguay, Peru, Philippine Islands, Puerto Rico, Saudi Arabia, Spain, Thailand, Turkey, Venezuela, and Viet Nam.

Nearly all of the civilian instructor pilots at Spence moonlighted as crop dusters. In fact, one of the instructors had a very embarrassing experience with crop dusting. He was to dust a field south of town, and could not locate it while in the air. Seeing a car along the road, he throttled back and opened the side door of the aircraft to yell out where was so and so's farm. He hit the only tree around for miles. He was slow enough to just get caught in the tree, requiring fire department rescue and assistance to get the aircraft out of the tree.

South Georgia was a culture shock for this Iowan, who had limited experience beyond the Midwest. Moultrie was actually twice the population of my hometown in Red Oak. Likewise, it was a county seat. Spence Field was probably the largest industry. Like Red Oak, it was primarily a community that supported the farm industry centered on tobacco, lumber, turpentine, and pecans.

Segregation still existed in South Georgia. Blacks had separate entrances at movie theaters and bus stations, separate public water fountains and restrooms, with no integration of schools or housing. Black officers in training at Spence could not sit in theaters together in Moultrie with their White classmates. Our fellow students were from all over the United States, most from areas where we had no experience with segregation. Sometimes, as many as 30 of us would go to the Moultrie movie theater with Black classmates. All the White guys would buy tickets first, and one or two Black classmates bought them last. The Blacks were not allowed to buy tickets on the first floor, where we all had tickets. When that happened, we all marched back to the ticket office and demanded refunds since we could not all sit together.

It was not the only time the Yankees in Moultrie would piss off the natives. Saturday was the big market day. The tradition was for the natives to walk the business square clockwise. We noted that and purposely walked counter-clockwise to disturb the flow. At restaurants, we would order chocolate-covered grits. We were a pretty obnoxious group.

One of the strange facts of life in South Georgia (at least to an Iowan) was the stores were closed every Wednesday at noon so employees could go fishing. There were lots of bass ponds created on farms, the picturesque Ochlocknee river lined by live oaks draped by Spanish moss, Lake Talquin, Lake Iamonia, and Lake Jackson on the Georgia-Florida border, and the Gulf of Mexico south of Tallahassee.

While flight training took up nearly all our time as flight students, we had free weekends. The attraction was nearby Tallahassee, where Florida State University had just become a coed school. Historically, it had been a girl's only university. It still had a large majority of female students. Class 56-J at Spence was primarily composed of college grads. It was not unusual for many of us to head to Tallahassee for the weekend. We grabbed a six-pack of beer at the Georgia border on Spanish moss-covered live oak tree-lined Highway 301, picked up a coed on campus, and headed for Wakulla Springs State Park for swimming and exploration.

But it was in Belk's Clothing store in Moultrie where I met my wife-to-be. Four months after I left Spence Field, I returned during the Christmas break to marry Elaine Goff in rural Coolidge, Georgia. We started married life in Laredo, Texas. Elaine was a graduate of Moultrie High School. Georgia schools at the time ended after three years of high school, leaving the only opportunities to either go to college or begin full-time employment. Elaine became a bookkeeper at Belk's.

Following primary training, we were assigned to basic training at five active-duty bases in Texas. Those selected for multi-engine aircraft assignments were sent to Goodfellow AFB San Angelo or Reece AFB in Lubbock. Those selected for single-engine aircraft assignments were sent to Bryan AFB (today's home of Texas A&M University), Laredo AFB, or Webb AFB in Big Springs. I was sent to Laredo AFB on the U.S. Mexico border in South Texas.

Air Force Basic Jet Pilot Training
Laredo AFB, Texas
September 1955 – March 1956

I packed all my belongs in my 1955 Buick Special after graduation at Spence, and was on the road again to Laredo, Texas. It was still before the interstates, so my marathon drive began on U.S. Highways along the Gulf Coast to Texas, and then south to the emptiness of South Texas and Laredo. The Air Training Command base was outside the town, near the Rio Grande River and the Mexico border.

Here we started with 28 instructor pilots and 112 fledgling jet pilot students. This was our entry into flying jets with the entire six-month course involving the tricycle gear North American T-28 and the jet Lockheed T-33. We got outfitted with hardhat helmets and oxygen masks. When flying, we wore the same greenish cotton, multi-zippered flight suits we wore in basic training. But now, we were in a military environment, and our flight suits had unit patches sewed on.

We began ground school with classes on weather, instrument and cross country flying, the inner workings of jet engines. We were issued our aircraft 'bible,' the Dash-1, a heavy by weight and heavy by reading manual. The book detailed every part and system of the aircraft. (Every aircraft in the Air Force inventory has a Dash-1).

North American T-28 Trojan and
Lockheed T-33 Shooting Star

We were introduced to our instructors and eventually got our dollar ride. This was the introductory flight with an instructor to get the feeling of being in the jet, learning the procedure to taxi to the runway, take off, fly and land. The student was always in the front seat – the instructor sat in the rear seat with dual controls.

The primary lesson you learned was there is nothing out there on the ground around Laredo but cactus and mesquite. It may look benign – but if you have a serious problem – always bail out – do not try to crash land. The terrain is too rough. A secondary rule was if you ever get lost, always head south, and you would find the Rio Grande. This was known as the rule of FTR (follow the river). It will lead you back to the base or a community you can identify by its water tower. It's good to know, but it was weeks before we flew solo without our 'seeing-eye dog' in the back seat.

One of the biggest problems was learning to taxi. If you taxied too slow, the tricycle gear in the front would end up cocked 90-degrees. You could only go in circles when that happened (and it did). To get out of it, you hit the brakes and used a burst of power to make the aircraft's nose bounce. Or be forced to call for help (embarrassing!).

Other big observations: The nearest community in our flying areas was Cotulla, about 50 miles north. There were no signs of human existence between Laredo and Cotulla – especially at night. On a moonless night, all you had visibly below were oil-rig fires. These blended with the stars. You had no horizon to keep you on track if you were right side up or upside down. This was especially a problem when flying formation as a wingman.

But it was especially neat to know that in a T-33 that Cotulla was only eight minutes away, and San Antonio was only 15 minutes north. When you drove to San Antonio, you would bitch all the way that it would take an hour to drive to Cotulla – or two hours to get to San Antonio.

We began each day early with flying or classroom instruction beginning at 7 a.m. Our alarm clock was a clock radio set for the station in Nuevo Laredo, which began programming daily by playing Ravel's *Bolero*. We were inventive in the flight shacks. Some mornings when we were to fly, we faced being socked in by dense fog coming up the Rio Grande. We would have to wait it out and hope for clear skies. This is when we found out cockroaches are not just big in the Mexican songbook. Our flight shacks were loaded. This gave us time on mornings when we were weathered in to catch a group of roaches, tie yarn around their bodies, mark out short runs on the floor – and then bet on which cockroach could get from one end to the other first.

It wasn't long before we mastered a basic flying task before we began another. Instrument flying, cross country flying, instrument landings using ground-controlled voice approach guidance or radio beacons, flying formation, night flying, acrobatics, and emergency procedures.

Jet Pilot Trainee

At Laredo, the flight training at the beginning was in the T-28. I added another 26 hours and 5 minutes dual flying time and 13 hours and 55 minutes solo, and another 57 landings. Instrument flying time totaled 9 more hours while being hooded from seeing outside the cockpit, plus 1 hour and 30 minutes dual weather time and 2 hours and 30 minutes solo weather time.

The Lockheed T-33 jet training added up to 157 hours and 20 minutes of dual training with 93 hours and 55 minutes solo and 344 landings. Instrument flying time totaled 54 hours and 15 minutes hooded, 10 hours and 50 minutes weather dual and 10 hours and 40 minutes solo in weather. I also had 45 hours flying in a simulator to learn and be tested on emergency procedures.

Laredo offered other opportunities as Nuevo Laredo was just across the Rio Grande Bridge. We would go in batches across to shop for silver jewelry, enjoy Mariachi music, have dinner at the Cadillac Bar, buy cheap booze and go to bullfights. The biggest time of year in Nuevo Laredo at the time was Washington's Birthday in February. Their rationale for this was, "February is a great time of year. Christmas is too cold, Cinco de Mayo is too hot – February is perfect for a fiesta."

There also was a large lake with rental boats on private land just east of the base runway. Not many people fished there, but I found it an outstanding lake for bass, catching many between 2–4 pounds. The Officer's club kitchen gladly made a catch of the day meal for us.

We also experienced Blue Norther's – cold fronts that came all the way from Canada to South Texas. It got down to freezing. Laredo homes did not have heating systems. It was not an issue on base, but for the inhabitants of Laredo, it was serious. Emergency shelters were opened each time this occurred.

During the Christmas break, I left Laredo for Coolidge, Georgia, to marry Elaine Goff at the small country church that her parents and family attended. After the wedding reception, we headed toward Laredo – spending our honeymoon nights in Marianna, Florida, and the French Quarter of New Orleans. I had found our first apartment in Laredo before I left – so we had a home to come to on our return.

Newlyweds at first home in Laredo, Texas

Our start in Laredo was made easier for Elaine, as she knew many of my classmates from our time at Spence and Moultrie. The apartment was furnished. The most important addition we made was a blonde cabinet Grundig Hi-Fi stereo consul – which followed us to Lincoln and Omaha, Nebraska, in later years.

Our class graduated, and we became full-fledged U.S. Air Force jet fighter pilots on March 7, 1956. A total of 131 new jet pilots had just entered the roles of combat pilots in the U.S. Air Force. But it was an unusual time in 1956 as the Air Force was trimming down and making drastic adjustments following the end of the Korean War. All the fighter combat training bases were closed.

The options for our class were to become air traffic controllers or go to multi-engine assignment in the Strategic Air Command. I chose SAC and Lincoln AFB, Nebraska. Lincoln was just 50 miles from my hometown – and I was still considering the offer from Bill Anthony to start a small town daily newspaper in Iowa.

Strategic Air Command
KC-97 Pilot & PIO
Lincoln AFB, Nebraska
March 1956 – July 1958

Elaine and I packed our belongings in the 1955 Buick Special after graduation. We were setting off on the drive through Texas, Oklahoma, and Kansas to reach Lincoln. We rented a small apartment in south Lincoln, not far from the famous salt mines of that city.

Lincoln AFB was a Strategic Air Command base under the 818th Air Division housing 90 Boeing B-47 swept-wing, six-jet engine bombers, and 40 Boeing KC-97 air-refueling tankers powered by four propeller-driven reciprocating engines. The KC-97 was created from the World War II B-29 Superfortress. The base had been active during the Korean War, was dormant for a short time, and was brought back to life by SAC in 1956. The base was in the countryside, a few miles west of the city of Lincoln.

I was assigned as a co-pilot in the 307th Air Refueling Squadron flying the KC-97 on the crew commanded by Major John Gallagher with 2nd Lieutenant Bernard Randolph as Navigator. The crew also included a flight engineer, a load-master, and an air refueling boom operator. Our mission was to refuel B-47 bombers in the air as they proceeded on combat missions. My first flight as a KC-97 crew member was on April 2, 1956.

KC-97 StratoTanker

Because of its slow cruising speed and low cruising altitude, the KC-97 had difficulty being an efficient refueler to high-speed, swept-wing jet aircraft. To refuel a faster jet aircraft, we performed a maneuver called 'tobogganing.' The refueling would begin at 20,000 feet, and then the tanker and jet bomber flew 'downhill' together, picking up speed to allow the jet to not stall out.

Lincoln AFB was huge. It was a self-contained, self-sufficient city in its own right. Population-wise, Lincoln AFB was the fifth largest city in Nebraska. After finding a duplex apartment and signing in for duty at the base, Elaine and

I created our first real home. SAC in those days was a six-day-a-week job – the only day off was Sunday.

Lincoln AFB Flight Line Open House Display

My first challenge was to complete the initial KC-97 aircraft aircrew familiarization course conducted by the 408th Field Training Detachment Lincoln in March 1956. Every aircraft in the Air Force has a basic bible or manual called the Dash-1.

This very thick book details everything about a specific aircraft. Many of us would study it at night, especially if we were having trouble sleeping. Twice a year, pilots would have 'stand-board' exams, including in-flight checks, evaluation of handling emergency procedures in a simulator, and written exams.

Examiners were not always straightforward. They delighted in throwing you curve balls such as, "What do you do with a wing fire?" The correct answer was, "Surround the building, lock the doors, and don't let the wieners out." Another favorite was, "How many ASH Receivers are in the aircraft?" For this one, you need to know Dash-1 terminology as ASH Receivers was the military jargon for ashtrays.

While I did begin flying with the 307th Air Refueling Squadron on April 3, 1956, I was on hold, as I needed to go to the formal C-97 school for classroom and simulator training. That required driving to West Palm Beach, Florida. The class was from May 15 to July 15. This became my first assignment to Florida. Elaine and I settled in a motel in Palm Beach, enjoying the Florida life with beaches and tourist bennies. Elaine had lots of time at the motel pool while I was in classrooms during the day and flying the simulator at all hours of the night.

I returned to Lincoln just in time to make my first SAC deployment. Flying across the Atlantic on July 18, 1956 – just three days after completing training at West Palm Beach. At the time, bombers and tankers were deployed worldwide in support of SAC's role of providing the nuclear deterrent for the free world. That boiled down to a routine of six months at a home base and six months overseas. The 307th was assigned to operate out of RAF Greenham Common at Newbury, England – about an hour west by train from London.

Elaine elected to return to her hometown of Moultrie, Georgia, to be with family until I would return to Lincoln in mid-October.

Lt. Halbert and his Aerospace Vehicle
RAF Greenham Common

During this deployment, a lasting friendship for me was begun with the navigator on our crew, Bernard Randolph, and his wife Lucille, both from New Orleans. About six months later, Randy switched from being a navigator on the KC-97 to becoming a navigator on the B-47. But we still kept in touch. I even flew with his crew on a B-47 flight to England in my role as a public information officer. After I went to SAC Headquarters, Randy would fly with me on T-33 flights on weekends, going to Maine for lobsters or the Mexican border on booze runs. We were later together in Viet Nam when we were majors.

Randy was a guy who loved to read. He was a fast learner, and even as a Lieutenant in B-47, he rapidly became a lead navigator and gained a spot promotion to Captain well ahead of our pack. When we were together in the Pentagon, he was selected by the Secretary of the Air Force to be a Lt. General. I remember being at an Air Force Association event in Arlington, Virginia, where I saw Lucille across the room and said hello. Her response was, "Tom, can you believe this?" referring to his promotion to 3-star general. Randy later got his fourth star and final assignment as Commander of the Air Force Systems Command. When he got that promotion, I was in Germany. Still, the editor of *Aviation Week* magazine found me, as he knew about our long history together. He wanted background on Randy as a Lieutenant. He asked if Randy faced any discrimination issues while he was at Lincoln. I told him, "Yes." He asked, "Was that because he was Black?" I replied, "No, because he was a navigator."

Lt. Randolph & Lt. Halbert Await
Pub Opening Time

The increasing Soviet threat caused a major change for the deterrent force. The concept of being deployed declined from 1957. A rapid response alert force at each base evolved. Like firemen, you would stand alert in a base facility and be ready anytime, day or night, to take off on a combat mission within 15 minutes. Now you would be at your home base spending one week on alert and having two weeks for flying training missions. While on alert you would spend hours in ground school, but you would have time to shop in the base exchange, go to base theaters for movies, or go to the officer's club. However, when the klaxon alarm would sound, you had to be able to take off in 15 minutes.

SAC was famous for no-notice Operation Training Inspections (or OTIs). The first one I was involved in ended up in failure. The Air Division commander and several others were fired, including those in the entire base public information office. Brig. General Perry M. Hoisington III replaced the Division commander. His nickname was Mach 2. One of the first things he did was seek assistance in rebuilding his public affairs office. One of the senior officers at Headquarters SAC public affairs was Ward Koons. I had worked with Ward for two years when I was studying journalism. He was the editor/owner of a weekly newspaper in Stuart, Iowa. Ward was also a Drake grad. So he knew me, and he knew that I was based in Lincoln.

Bottom line: In March 1957, I became the Assistant Chief of Information for the 818th Air Division, joining Maj. John Ruehle who was brought in from a B-47 pilot assignment at Lockbourne AFB in Ohio. (At the time to become a base Public Affairs officer, you had to be rated as a senior pilot and be able to drink three martinis without falling on your ass). We matched up well and built a group who became recognized as the best public affairs office in SAC.

Going from being a line pilot tasked to fly at squadron level to being assigned to work at wing headquarters level opened you to slurs from your squadron buddies. The two most common terms were 'Seagull' and 'LSD.' Seagull implied that when you became a 'wing wienie,' all you did was squawk, shit, and never fly. Also, your aerospace vehicle was no longer an airplane, but an LSD or a large steel desk.

We faced a major problem at Lincoln AFB. From the start of 1955, there was a rash of B-47 accidents that happened on Fridays when bombers crashed following takeoff at nearby Ceresco, Nebraska. The National Safety Board and SAC Inspector General organization did not find a reason until late 1957. Lincoln shared airspace with the commercial airport in Omaha and Offutt AFB, Nebraska, south of Omaha. That required at times for Lincoln departing aircraft to stay low until getting past an air traffic air lane. Only B-47s were having this issue. All other aircraft had no problems.

The cause was finally determined to be a problem caused by the swept wing of the B-47. After takeoff, the B-47 pilots kept flying at high speed to get under the air lane, expecting to climb rapidly once they got by. The high speed at low level was causing aileron reversal. Pilots would turn left to depart the controlled area, but the airplane would turn to the right. The pilot would correct even more to the left, and the aircraft would turn even tighter in the opposite direction. This caused the aircraft to crash out of control. Problem solved, but not until after a significant loss of aircraft and crews.

One Saturday morning, I was filling in for Major Ruehle at a General Hoisington staff meeting. The famous cigar-smoking commander of SAC was Curtis LeMay. He just happened to visit Lincoln that morning. He came around the conference table to shake hands with the staff, all Colonels and Lt. Colonels, and me. He was taken aback to see a Lieutenant at the table – looked at me and said, "What do you do, son?" I said I was a public information officer – Sir. He continued his stare and asked, "Have you ever been fired?" I proudly said, "No Sir!" He paused and then said, "You aren't worth a damn, are you?" End of conversation. I never met him again. But what he said rang true. All of us in public affairs knew that we were in a profession where your contract was renewed daily.

General Hoisington was one of only two commanders I worked for who was really public relations savvy. He took a keen interest in what we were doing. Even when Major Ruehle was unavailable, he would call me and ask for public relations advice. That was pretty heady. I never had an editor ever ask me anything. General Hoisington gave us an open check to rebuild the office. The manning authorization was for three officers (Major John Ruehle, Lt. Humphreys Hodge, and myself), a senior non-commissioned officer (MSgt. Manley Floyd), a base newspaper editor (SSgt. Ken Allen), two enlisted staff members, and two historians. We shortly had an office with four officers, an NCO, editor, ten enlisted members, and two historians, plus the opportunity for additional augmentation if needed. We also set up the office in an unused mess hall that gave us tons of space.

North American B-25 Bomber

I was no longer a crew dog on KC-97s but had to maintain flying proficiency to keep getting flight pay. So I started flying with base flight. The primary aircraft was the WWII B-25 bomber, with leather helmets, throat mikes, and parachutes as your bucket seat cushion. One wag called the B-25 the 'mother-in-law' as it was dumpy, dependable, and loud. The B-25 was the work horse in World War II, flying combat missions to Sicily, Tunisia and Sardinia. They disrupted Rommel's supply chain usually without fighter protection, as the range of the B-25 were too great.

Occasionally I flew the C-47 Dakota (another World War II vintage aircraft). Most of the flying was around the flagpole, but occasionally we would fly to Washington, D.C. We were also on call for emergency support missions when civil authorities needed eyes-in-the-sky assistance. The C-47 was the first aircraft I ever flew that was slower than a car. On extremely windy nights in the Midwest, cars on the highway below were going faster than we were because of fighting headwinds. Our base flight C-47 was serial number 43-49507. It had 20,831 flying hours and was the last operational C-47 in Air Force Service. Today, it lives on at the Air Force Museum at Wright-Patterson AFB in Dayton, Ohio.

The Legacy of Lincoln AFB Base Flight C-47 43-49507

Including my orientation flight in the B-29 at Lowry AFB, I had now added two more World War II aircraft in the flying log book.

Fishing opportunities at Lincoln were rare. I grew up where there were lots of trees, cornfields, rivers, and creeks. Lincoln turned out to be the end of the world for those elements. West of Lincoln, you find a vast, humid desert, all the way to the Rockies. At Ogallala is McConaughy Reservoir, the largest lake in Nebraska. It turned out to be a lot of water but no fish.

Setting Up a New Office

MSgt. Manly Floyd was a genius in scrounging things. (In the Air Force, you are a scrounge if you are Staff Sergeant and above, for lower ranks, you're a thief.) His first acquisition was a multi-lithe machine for our exclusive use to be able to produce instant news releases. The normal process was centralized, and it could take days to get something printed.

I found out each safety office had 16mm motion picture cameras to document accidents. They had no idea how to use them. I arranged for them to provide us the cameras. We would respond to any requirement they had, and we could use them to produce black and white footage of base activities. I also arranged for the TV stations to provide us film. We would shoot and hand-deliver raw films and news releases to the Lincoln station and use commercial bus services to get the products to the Omaha stations.

We arranged for the major papers and broadcast stations to have beat reporters to cover base activities and also arranged for them to fly on refueling missions and deployments overseas. The public information office was charged with four responsibilities: internal (or employee) information, public information, community relations, and major unit histories.

Public Information:

Our obvious prime resources were the *Lincoln Tribune* and the *Omaha World Herald* (area community weekly papers) and the electronic media (including three television stations in Lincoln and Omaha, and Associated Press, United Press and International News Service).

Internal Information:

The major vehicle for communication internally was the base newspaper, which was published weekly. The contract printer was in South Omaha, which meant the editor would drive to Omaha each Thursday to supervise layout and make any instant changes that might arise.

The other vehicle was the monthly commander's call program. We would assist unit commanders in providing topics, slide briefings, and select films for their individualized programs. Wing commanders would make monthly presentations in the base theater. But General Hoisington preferred to reach out to the officers, NCOs, and enlisted wives' clubs to ensure spouses were in the loop.

Community Relations:

Every base had programs to reach out into the community. This could be chaplains from the base with ministers in the community, or base commanders and supporting staff with mayors and supporting staff. But General Hoisington put this type of program on steroids.

His underlying concern was low retention rates, especially when his base was compared with those in the south. His first active program was creating a squadron adoption program. He got civic organizations to adopt a squadron, and it took off like a wildfire. A Rotary Club would adopt a maintenance squadron inviting airmen to their events. The squadron would host picnics or tours for Rotarians and their families. On an individual basis, families would invite airmen into their homes for a holiday. He got each community organization to donate furniture, TVs and pool tables for dormitory dayrooms. Over time, a very active 'getting to know you' verve grew on base and in Lincoln.

History Office:

The public affairs office also had two historians – one for the 98th Bomb Wing and one for the 307th Bomb Wing. They were charged with compiling a semi-annual history of their units. It was the single most important program that gave legitimacy to the broader reach now encompassed with government public affairs. By 1990, that 'cover' was deemed no longer necessary, and the history mission was no longer part of the public affairs mission.

History was a major factor in the early days of public information. It also provided insight as to why the military and other government organizations did not and still do not have public relations offices. Congress in the first decade of the 1900s had passed a law that prohibited the use of government funds for the 'hiring of Pinkerton guards and public relations.' That law still exists today. (Cite: 5-3107

Employment of publicity experts; restrictions.) In government, all public relations offices have been labeled information service, public information, or public affairs offices.

The Age of PowerPoint

It was the beginning of the dominance of PowerPoint as a primary means of communication, whether presentations at staff meetings, for visiting news media, or civic leaders – everything was done with PowerPoint. Have projector – just dim the lights, and it's showtime.

Roper/Gallup Air Force Attitude and Opinion Research Seminar New York City: April 22–24, 1957

The New York Air Force Office of Public Information created an opinion research seminar at a Manhattan hotel presented by the opinion poll giants Elmo Roper and George Gallup organizations. I was one of 14 public information officers in the command selected to attend when the command had 21 bases worldwide, with 164 public information officers assigned. It was my first time in New York City – quite a change for a country kid from Red Oak. The course was great and provided a background that would be helpful in years to come in either creating polls or reviewing results from polls.

It also provided me my first contact with this key Air Force public information office in New York. So, when I was transferred to HQ SAC the next year, I already knew the key players in that office and where the office was located. The Air Force team in New York comprised a core who had been in their jobs for the past 10 years or more, as the value of having a Rolodex of contacts and continuity was critical. Another valuable asset in the world's media capital was the Air Force Reserve squadron manned by those working full-time in media organizations in the New York area. It is where I first met Len Gumley. Len was a WWII glider pilot, involved deeply with the major networks, and later retired in Sarasota. Len was the key to getting me involved with the prestigious Flyboys, the Media Round Table, and Broadcast Pioneers in Sarasota nearly 50 years later.

Charlie Starkweather/Carlin Ann Fugate Murder Spree December 1957 – January 1958

One of the most unusual and frightening days of my life and those of my young wife were during the time of the Starkweather/Fugate murder spree in Lincoln. The first death in this spree was in December, which didn't get much attention. But beginning on January 21, 1958, 19-year-old Charlie Starkweather and his 14-year-old girlfriend Carlin Ann Fugate grabbed national headlines by killing 11 people before they were captured on January 28, 1958.

If was a very frightening time in Lincoln, Nebraska, and the whole Midwest. I had been on a night training mission flying as co-pilot on a KC-97. After landing and completing the maintenance debriefing, we left the base to drive to our homes. We reached Lincoln shortly after daylight and returned to a city with no vehicle traffic. It became obvious something was really wrong.

At most every home you passed driving on residential streets, you saw a resident on the porch armed with rifles and shotguns. It was a real puzzle. When I got home, I heard news reports on the radio about the first four killings. The pair evaded the police effectively, killing seven more people before being apprehended a week later.

Robbers' Cave – Lincoln, Nebraska

In many communities, you might have memories of remarkable outdoor places that you enjoyed. In Lincoln, it was Robbers' Cave. It was a naturally eroded limestone cave that had two levels. It offered natural air conditioning in the summer and had electricity and lighting. We would rent the cave occasionally for booze, burgers, music, and exploration. Local legends, all unsubstantiated, included the cave was used by Pawnee Indians for spiritual practices, it had been a stop on the Civil War underground railroad for assisting slaves to get to freedom in Canada, or it was a Jesse James gang hideout. For our group, it was for party, party, party.

Bowling Lake – Lincoln AFB, Nebraska

The most impressive effort of all was the creation of Bowling Lake. This was created on a base where there was nothing in the past but prairie grass. Here again, the underlying concern was low retention rates. General Hoisington was convinced Lincoln AFB needed a lake for water skiing and recreation, which would provide a reason for more airmen to reenlist. The base did have Salt Creek flowing from one end to the other – but no bayou or ponds had ever been there. Hoisington put his base engineer in charge of the lake building project.

Sources of surplus heavy earth moving equipment were located and were shipped to the base. Squadrons 'volunteered' to provide manpower to operate the equipment to gain 'wartime disaster training' skills. Slowly, a huge circular area was dug out. A temporary dam was created nearby on Salt Creek. Surplus pumps were acquired, and a lake, large enough for water skiing, was formed. The island left in the middle provided space for Bowling Lodge that was funded by squadron adoption organizations. All this took more than a year to complete.

Bowling Lake – Lincoln AFB, Nebraska

In the winter of 1957, Major Ruehle and I went to outdoor shows from Chicago to Denver. We recruited more than 100 vendors to participate in the commemoration of Bowling Lake the following summer. Major Ruehle also arranged for the Wisconsin-based Tommy Bartlett Water Ski Show to be an event highlight. Also participating would be performances of three premier air shows flown by the U.S. Air Force Thunderbirds, the Navy Blue Angels and the Colorado Air National Guard Minutemen.

The Aqua Air Show was held on Thursday, Friday, and Saturday, June 19–21, 1958. More than 166,000 people attended the three-day event. Guests attending the dedication ceremony included the Governor of Nebraska, the Mayor of Lincoln, and Hollywood actor Andy Devine, who contributed the funds to build a mock lighthouse at the lake. Fireworks provided a spectacular ending to the show every night. Entry to the base was restricted to one gate and an entry/parking fee was charged. The funds raised were used for the construction of Bowling Lodge on the Island Lake.

It was a spectacular celebration of airpower and the 'elbow grease' of countless 'volunteer' officers and airmen who created the base lake. It also was the impetus for several congressional investigations questioning the use of government funds and 'forced labor' to build the lake. But it was all smoke in D.C. – the investigations came and went without any real action.

The lake became the property of the Lincoln Airport Authority after the base closed in 1966 and is now a fishing and recreation spot. After 2000, the lake was dredged, and lingering signs of the days of Lincoln AFB were removed, including the Andy Devine lighthouse and keystones denoting the contributions of the 307th and 98th Bomb Wings in building the lake.

Following this event the base information office under Major Ruehle was selected as the best in the command and received an award from SAC Commander General Tom Power at SAC Headquarters. It also marked the end of my time at Lincoln AFB. I was transferred to SAC Headquarters and became one of four Lieutenants assigned to headquarters.

Career Decision Time

In a mentor role, General Hoisington wrote to his boss, who was the three-star commander of Eighth Air Force at Westover AFB in Massachusetts, nominating me to become a regular officer. It was a two-page letter requesting special consideration from his boss to select me from the ranks of reserve officers to become a member of the elite group of regular officers.

This endorsement resulted in my being selected on January 25, 1958, to officially become a regular officer and was provided with the appropriate certificate signed by President Eisenhower. I also got a new serial number (my third) and became 56808A.

General Hoisington was a great mentor and was wonderful to work for. He accepted me at staff meetings (no one under the rank of Lt. Colonel was on the staff). He would call frequently, and if Major Ruehle was not available, he would ask me for public affairs advice. It was heady stuff for a young Lieutenant. Undoubtedly, it was why I continued my Air Force career. He also helped me fill out my Personnel Dream sheet. One item was to identify your career goal. He said there is only one goal to note: to be Chief of Staff of the Air Force. It is advice I have followed throughout my Air Force career and since. General Hoisington would also move on from Lincoln. In 1961 he was assigned to the Pentagon, becoming Director of Legislative Liaison for the Air Force. He retired as a Major General. (*His sister was also in the military and became the first female General Officer in the U.S. Army.*)

Beginning a Family

Really major family events happened at Lincoln. The first was when we lived at 830 South 45th Street. Elaine gave birth to our first child and oldest daughter. Debra Elaine Halbert arrived at 4:25 p.m. on January 2, 1957, in St. Elizabeth's hospital. Debi was delivered by Dr. John Epps and entered the world at nine pounds. We were ecstatically happy with our first daughter. Although, in the back of my mind, I was hoping that she would arrive in December to give us a welcome tax deduction. No such luck. We even tried driving on bumpy rural roads, but Debi stuck to her own schedule.

Our second daughter, Tomajean Halbert, was born at 7:19 p.m. on May 1, 1958 – also in St. Elizabeth Hospital in Lincoln, assisted by Dr. Epps. At this time, we were living at 1228 Pawnee Street in Lincoln. With the second daughter I was convinced I would not have a son. So, I pressured Elaine to name our new daughter Tomajean. I reasoned she could either choose to be called Tomi or Jean. She did neither. She settled on TJ.

Elaine had taken up golf for the first time. What made it somewhat unusual is the courses in Lincoln had 'sand greens.' Once you got on the 'green,' you had to pick up your ball and move it to a putting path to the hole. But it got her started on a sport she would enjoy for years.

Our life was interspersed with happy hours and dinners at the Officer's Club on base, outings to Omaha and my mother's favorite Nebraska site, the Morton Lodge in Nebraska City, and my hometown of Red Oak, Iowa.

Most outstanding was the restaurant in Emerald, Nebraska, just west of the city of Lincoln and just south of Lincoln AFB. Calling it a small town would be an exaggeration. Emerald had a restaurant, one store, and two churches. However, Emerald's restaurant was famous for steak dinners, so huge that they hung over large plates.

Our wonderful 1955 Buick Special became a down payment for a Ford station wagon that could handle the transportation requirements of two adults and two young daughters. The move to Omaha had expanded to the needs of the four of us.

Headquarters Strategic Air Command Offutt AFB, Nebraska, July 1958 – October 1961

I had now been in the Air Force for nearly five years. At that time, it took seven years to become a Captain. It was rare for a Lieutenant to be in a major command headquarters. The commander was now General Thomas Power. The head of public affairs was Col. Don Foster. Armed with Power's words, "The only war I'm fighting is a war of information," Foster successfully expanded the SAC Information Services from 30 positions to 65 positions. He actually had a third of all SAC public affairs in the command at the headquarters. I arrived for duty on August 27, 1958.

This was an office of 'stars,' staffed with outstanding professionals at the working level. The bosses were Col. Don Foster as Director and Col. Charles VanVliet as his deputy. As part of the Media Division I was responsible to Division Chief Major John Oswald. My Branch Chief was Capt. Don Roberts (later replaced by Capt. Jack Olsen). Books and Magazine Chief was Major Ed Derryberry.

Ed spent most of his time promoting himself. He was noted for being loud and always answering his phone by saying, "Ed Derryberry – ten letters, one word." His goal was to be based in Hawaii. He almost got his wish when Col. Reade Tilley, former director of SAC Information was the Director of Information at Pacific Air Forces headquartered at Hickam Field in Honolulu. Reade did not have a space for him at the Headquarters, but got him assigned to the base PIO job, saying he would be moved to the headquarters when the next opening occurred. Ed said thanks, but no thanks. That pissed off Colonel Tilley and Ed was reassigned to Da Nang AB, Viet Nam.

The quiet one in the office was Capt. Russ Turner who was given the job of decorating the halls of the bleak three-story headquarters building by Gen. Curtis LeMay. Russ was an artist at heart and slowly began filling hallways with works of art depicting the Strategic Air Command. When General LeMay became head of the U.S. Air Force, he moved Russ to the Pentagon to begin hanging art in the hallways throughout the fourth floor of the building.

Russ realized that the shelf life of broadcasts was measured in hours, newspapers by days, and magazines by months. But art has a shelf life of years. Russ created a program to offer artists the opportunity to travel with the Air Force to locations around the world to witness military facilities and exercises to record these events in the form of paintings. Artists were selected from the Societies of Illustrators in New York, Los Angeles, and San Francisco.

Today there are nearly 9,000 works in the Air Force Art Program documenting Air Force personnel, equipment, locations, and activities. These are displayed throughout the Pentagon, State Department, Congressional offices, the White House, and museums – even on trailers equipped at mobile art galleries that travel to cities throughout the U.S.

The Air Force accorded artists all courtesies and privileges as a GS-15, the highest civil service rank equivalent to the rank of a Colonel. This meant artists had travel status on Air Force aircraft, housing on bases and reimbursement expenses at the standard per diem rates. The artists' income and opportunities were suspended during the assignment and creation of the work. Additionally, all work is donated to the Air Force without any tax deductions.

Chuck Burlingame was the first Chief Master Sergeant in the Air Force and handled manpower and assignments. Following retirement, Chuck became the head of public relations for Toyota of America in California. *On a tragic note: Chuck's son was the pilot of the American Airlines passenger jet that crashed into the Pentagon during the 9/11 attacks in Washington, New York City, and Pennsylvania.*

Chief Master Sergeant William Lummus was our staff photographer. He was the one who taught me to always carry a tree limb when photographing on flight lines. Flight lines are barren except for concrete and aircraft. A tree limb provides framing for the photo and adds greatly to having attractive photos.

The other three lieutenants who arrived about the same time were Lou Cantelou, Steve Emerine, and Jim Hendricks. Lou ended up as an Assistant Director of Public Affairs in the Pentagon, Steve became an elected official in Tucson, Arizona, and Jim became a writer/editor at the prestigious *Aviation Week* magazine. Two young Captains, Jerry Dalton and Dave Schillerstrom, became part of the new 'young Turks' that joined the office during this buildup. Both became legends in Air Force Public Affairs history. Jerry retired after being the first information officer to become the Director of Public Affairs for the Air Force, who was not a pilot. Dave ended up as Jerry's deputy in the Pentagon.

One highlight of this assignment happened in 1959. I was privileged meet Senator and now Presidential candidate John F. Kennedy and Jacqueline Kennedy as they visited SAC Headquarters, including the famous underground command center.

One unique program that we all were working on was the test of deploying the Minuteman missile throughout the United States on trains. Captain Dalton, as chief of plans, was the primary public information action officer for this test. It was a Cold War initiative to deploy trains as launch vehicles of the missiles using periodic movement for security from targeting by the Soviet missile force. The trains were operational with five of 10 cars for living and working quarters for the launch crews. It included a control section where two launch officers would sit at duplicate panels – separated by bullet-proof glass.

On January 27, 1961, the test train left Chicago for a two-week test of switching facilities with launching cars weighing 127 tons, each equipped with four extra wheels to bear the weight of the 30-ton missile. It traveled through the Midwest and West. Jerry was a member of the test crew. The program was derailed a year later due to costs and lack of Congressional support.

On the north side of the base, across the long runway, was the Base Commander's office. That was where Lt. Herb

Babb was assistant base information office. He also became one of the young Turks and frequently joined us at Friday night happy hours at the club. Like me, Herb was also a pilot who had to complete monthly day and night flying requirements. And at the base shop periodically was Maj. Nick Lamberto. Nick was one of the stellar reporters at the *Des Moines Register* that I worked alongside in the late 1950s. They knew each other well. But they had a surprise meeting near the Des Moines Airport. Herb was flying as co-pilot of a B-25 when the aircraft crashed. Nick was the *Des Moines Register* reporter at the crash scene to report on the event. Nick was dumbfounded that Herb got from Omaha to the crash scene in Des Moines so soon after the accident. Herb had to explain he was one of the pilots.

I was just getting settled into the new job as the deputy in the Broadcast branch of the office. I was also settling in the first home I ever bought in a subdivision in southwest Omaha. It was two houses off M Street, the main highway used by hundreds of truck drivers daily to the stockyards with cattle and hogs.

I was able to qualify for a VA loan and approval from the builder solely because one of the key members of the builders' team was my cousin Jean's husband. With the help of discount furniture stores, we were able to outfit the three-bedroom, single-bath home. As a new housing project, our yard was just beginning to show growth. One of the best ideas I ever had involved that yard. Weeks later, I staged a weed-pulling party. I offered beer or drinks for every five weeds picked. It went fast at first, but then it got harder to find weeds. It was the most weed-free yard I ever had. The location was great, atop a high hill in easy driving distance to Offutt AFB, the restaurants of south Omaha, the new shopping center on 42nd Street, and Aksarben. Aksarben was famous in the Midwest for its horse racing track and in the Omaha region for its civic involvement. One of first things I learned in the new job was that all officers at SAC were 'required' to become Aksarben. This was a civic organization, and its name was a coined word that was Nebraska spelled backwards.

Elaine was pregnant again. This time, she would give birth to John Michael Halbert, born in the Offutt AFB Hospital on April 11, 1959. We now had a son and two daughters. It was now seven months we were in Omaha. We figured he was conceived when we were still drinking Lincoln water, just as had happened with his two sisters. We found out later that was not the reason at all.

My mother was also living in Omaha at this time. She was employed by the University of Nebraska in Omaha in the medical library, sharing an apartment with Elizabeth Kentopp, head of the Nebraska Medical Center College of Nursing. This provided Elaine a little help with our young brood, as grandmothers are prone to do. I don't know what caused my mother to leave Drake, but it was just after her second divorce from my father. I suspect she learned about the job opportunity with the College of Nursing and took it, giving her increased income and job advancement.

When I got orders to Newfoundland in 1962, Mom and Liz moved into our home on South 52nd Street. This gave them cheap rent and allowed Elaine and me to continue to build equity. They lived in the house more than six years until we moved from Massachusetts to Nashville. It turned out well for both of us, and we would need the equity from the Omaha house to purchase our new home in Nashville.

Headquarters SAC at Offutt AFB

Offutt gained international prominence when it became the host base for Headquarters, Strategic Air Command. Air Force Secretary Stuart Symington chose Offutt as the head-quarters of the Air Force's crucial long-range atomic strike force because the base was centrally located on the North American continent. This was well beyond the existing range of potentially hostile bombers or missiles at the time.

Our office was just inside the front door on the first floor, across the hall from the SAC Elite Guard office. Parking was in a huge lot behind the building. The photo shows the building and its Minuteman missile display from the

Officer's Club parking lot below the hill. The headquarters was moved from the old Martin bomber complex to Building 500 in 1957, just before I was assigned.

In SAC, everything had a backup. The famous 3-story underground SAC command center – 45 feet beneath Building 500 – was backed up by KC-135 jets outfitted at airborne command posts flying 24 hours a day. In the SAC underground was the first-ever-built Univac computer. It was huge and was housed in special air-conditioned rooms. Since there was no other computer as a backup, the solution was a red, metal, wall-mounted 'in case of emergency' notated box. Inside a breakable glass window was a Chinese abacus. Also housed in the underground was the Air Force Global Weather Central, the Joint War Targeting Center, and the control center for the total SAC alert force of bombers, tankers and intercontinental missiles.

The SAC underground command center war room

The XB-70 Valkyrie
Mach 3 Strategic Bomber

The highly classified XB-70 North American Aviation nuclear armed, deep-penetration, strategic bomber prototype became public knowledge in the late 1950s. The 6-engine, Mach 3 jet bomber was to fly at 70,000 feet, using altitude and speed to avoid interception. The bomber's official name was the Valkyrie. It never got funded by Congress. The prototype was initially only seen in the factory by those with special clearance. The nickname that those who were allowed to view it became the 'Savior.' That is because when anyone who viewed it would slowly exclaim, "Gee-sus Key-rye-'st."

PR Technological
Breakthrough of 1958

While the Univac Computer was a major breakthrough for SAC war planning, another breakthrough advance was happening all over the world. It was the invention of the Rolodex and it became the must-have item on desks in the PR and business world. On a Rolodex, you could store individuals' contact information on notched cards that could be snapped in or out of a rotating spindle. It fast became the most important item on your desk, giving you instant alphabetical access to key contacts. This resulted in a new form of competition – who had the most listings on their Rolodex. Your listings grew and grew and allowed space for including personal information beyond just phone and address data. Your Rolodex became personal and traveled with you throughout your career from job assignment to job assignment.

A Very Skinny Rolodex

My primary job at SAC involved generating and marketing story ideas with national and regional broadcast networks through personal contact – primarily in New York City and Los Angeles. As result more, than 150 broadcast productions were aired featuring the command. Another aspect of my job was to escort news media down the tunnels to the command center. I was deputy of the broadcasting branch of the SAC Office of Information. So, I assisted producers and actors from Hollywood, newspaper editors, columnists, reporters from major daily papers, and film teams and broadcasters from worldwide locations.

Those I remember best, included broadcasters Walter Cronkite of CBS, Roy Neal of NBC, Chuck Connors (former Chicago Cubs 3rd baseman turned actor for the *Rifleman* TV series), Hollywood columnist Hedda Hopper, actress Joan Crawford, actor Jimmy Stewart, and Hollywood Producers Bernie Lay and Norman Foster. I met many regional and local news people, including WHAM-TV of Rochester, New York, who showed up with a team of 12 to document the underground command center. The networks usually had a team of two or three persons.

The actor that I remember best was Johnny Crawford, who played the son of the Rifleman on TV because he asked great questions and was totally interested. I was least impressed with Hedda Hopper and Joan Crawford, who had no interest in what they saw. Hedda used the term 'slitch' during their conversation about a prominent Hollywood actress. It was a new word to me and I asked naively what it meant. Hedda replied, "That's a combination of slut and bitch." I also keenly remember a producer and motion photographer team from *Weekly Reader* who had expanded outreach from a grade school print news format to a weekly motion picture format.

Lt. Halbert and Hedda Hopper in the
SAC Underground Command Center

Persons of prominence were common due to the nuclear mission of Strategic Air Command. Probably most prominent was on August 9, 1959, when Presidential Candidate John F. Kennedy toured the headquarters and was briefed in the underground command center. My responsibility was assisting the press corps during the visit.

But I had one more advantage that I brought to the office. I was required to fly a minimum of eight hours monthly to ensure I qualified for flight pay. And the base flight aircraft available included the two-seat T-33 trainer. I used that opportunity to fly visitors to the headquarters where no combat aircraft were present. This included Lincoln AFB so they could experience firsthand B-47 Bomber/KC-97 tanker alert teams and underground Atlas missile sites. I could fly to bases near New York City and Los Angeles to provide story ideas to film and electronic media producers.

I had 'door openers' in both media centers. Each had an Office of Information that represented the Air Force Office of Information in Washington, D.C. Each had an officer manned by longtime specialists who worked daily with those in the industry. They would review the proposals we created and set up appointments with those they believed might be interested.

Part of my duties included being a technical advisor for production support decisions of films and network TV shows including the first Playhouse 90 TV production based on Pat Frank's *Forbidden Area* book. The storyline involved an aircraft that was in flight when the pilots were notified of a bomb on board. It was set to explode as the jet descended below 4,000 feet in an approach for landing. Spoiler alert: the aircraft diverts to Denver that is above 5,000 feet.

As technical advisor, other movie productions that I was involved in included *Strategic Air Command* with Jimmy Stewart and June Allyson, *Bombers B-52* with Natalie Wood and Karl Malden, and *A Gathering of Eagles* with Rod Taylor. Part of the involvement was a review of the scripts before agreeing to production support. Minor successes included the TV series *Steve Canyon*. The series got bought and started to air. But after a few episodes, the company ran into script problems. Scripts required Air Force approval. The production company finally resorted to going to the Air Force film library at Wright-Patterson AFB in Ohio and purchased footage of Air Force aircraft accidents, a disaster for both the production company and the Air Force. That experience resulted in a growing strong reluctance by the industry against making military TV shows. They did not have to get any approvals to make westerns – and so they did.

A sidebar: SAC crews all were assigned radio call signs that were considered classified at the confidential level. If the scriptwriter inadvertently created a call sign that was classified by SAC, it had to be changed. The best source for creating call signs was to use the sports pages to get unique ones, primarily using the names of racehorses in the daily results columns.

I also became the 'motor pool' for legendary Col. Barney Oldfield. He was Director of Public Affairs at the North American Air Defense Command (NORAD) Headquarters, jointly manned by US and Canadian forces. I often would pick him up in a T-33 at Peterson Field in Colorado Springs and fly him in the back seat to where he needed to go. Barney was a leader in Air Force public relations. He also had years of experience as a publicist and press agent for stars such as Errol Flynn, Ronald Reagan and Elizabeth Taylor.

During World War II, he was a press aide to Allied commander Gen. Dwight D. Eisenhower. He also liked that I was a Midwest product since he was born in Tecumseh, Nebraska, and graduated from the University of Nebraska. His first job was as a reporter for the *Lincoln Journal*. Barney was a major factor in my acceptance in the motion picture and media world.

He was also a founding member of the Radio and Television News Directors Foundation. The foundation's Barney Oldfield Distinguished Service Award was created in his honor. It is presented annually to an individual who, through their own efforts, has contributed to the growth and success of RTNDA.

Probably the best success was the in-house creation of SAC Radio News. We took a corner of the office and made a small studio. We had no professional equipment, except for an Ampex tape recorder. At the time I got to SAC, a young airman named James (Buzz) Sims joined the broadcast section. He had worked for a radio station at his hometown in North Carolina and for me at Lincoln AFB. At the time, NBC radio had a hot news show, called *Monitor*. Our product featured short audio reports with wild sound in the background. Buzz was our voice and the two of us created SAC Radio News in the NBC *Monitor* format.

We concentrated on interviews on current subjects the command was involved in. We recorded wild sound for backgrounds on flight lines, maintenance hangars, alert facilities – anywhere – and added the sounds at a controlled level to the interviews. The product was eventually provided to 250 radio stations nationwide and frequently aired by NBC *Monitor*.

In October 1959, I became a member of the Radio and Television News Director Association as a result of creating the SAC Radio News Service.

Buzz was at the end of his Air Force tour of duty and returned to North Carolina where he reached another claim to fame. He was the guy featured in Haines underwear ads on a Lambretta motor scooter for print and TV advertisements.

Based on a tip, I flew my T-33 jet to Vandenberg AFB in California to meet Airman Mort Crim. Mort was in the information office at Vandenberg, SAC's missile training and launch base on the West Coast. As a result, Col. Don Foster, the director of information for SAC, got dispensation from SAC Commander General Tom Power to curtail Mort's assignment at Vandenberg and bring him to SAC Headquarters.

Mort was from Chicago. His home shared backyards with Don McNeil of the 1940–50s radio show *Don McNeil's Breakfast Club.* That apparently sparked his interest in broadcasting. He could raise the bar with ease to produce products for SAC Radio Service and work with broadcasters from everywhere who visited the headquarters frequently. We teamed up well, leading to another long-term passion Mort acquired.

Mort and Tom at 2016 Broadcasters Club Luncheon in Sarasota

Mort was impressed with my being able to fly while on the job. He joined the SAC Aero Club at Offutt and quickly went from student pilot to getting his pilot license. He has been flying ever since. It is also the reason he chose to 'retire' in Jacksonville, Florida. It was as far south as he could get from Detroit on a non-stop flight piloting his single-engine aircraft. In Jacksonville, Mort earned his highest 'rank,' becoming Commodore of the Queen's Harbor Yacht Club. In 1989, Mort gave a commencement address at Anderson University in Indiana. One of the students was impressed and wrote Mort her thoughts on his speech. That resulted in Mort flying back to Indiana for their first date that led to his marriage with Renee.

Once he completed his Air Force duty, Mort gained his undergraduate and master's degrees at Medill School of Journalism at Northwestern University. (Mort was a classmate of Mike Eisgrau, who became a close friend of Gayle and myself through the Media Roundtable and Broadcasters Club of Florida in Sarasota). Mort's television journey began as news anchor for WBBM-TV in Chicago, WHAS-TV, Louisville, Kentucky, KYW-TV in Philadelphia, and WDIV-TV Detroit. His longest stint, 19 years, was Detroit where he retired in 1997.

He also frequently filled in on radio for Paul Harvey, including creating his own "And now you know the rest of the story" narratives. Mort used many of these reports to create several books. My favorite is *How to be that Wonderful Person Your Dog Thinks You Are*. Mort remained active as a syndicated commentator and keynote speaker, addressing conventions and conferences across the country. He gained further fame when actor Will Ferrell credited Mort in *Rolling Stone* as being the inspiration for the Ron Burgundy character in the 2004 hit Hollywood movie *Anchorman*.

Boston University Introduction to Public Relations June, 1960

My personal quest to obtain a master's degree got a significant boost in June 1960, when I obtained 10 hours of credit toward that goal. Lt. Lou Cantelou and I were sent to an Air Force Short Course in Public Relations and Communications at Boston University School of Public Relations and Communications. The course centered on the history of public relations, an in-depth review of legal aspects, what professional public relations are today, and forecasts into the future. For me, the eye-opening experience was the difference between the 'cookbook public relations' learned in college and the awaking of the depth of professional PR.

I already had a good understanding from college and on the job. What was new here and eye-opening was answering the question, why? This provided the foundation for my growth from a publicist to a professional PR practitioner. The professors and course set me in a new direction. I understood that my primary job would be as an advisor, expected to provide critical advice that would be factored into management decisions.

The Air Force had given me three legs up on being a pro. The first was a special three-day course in public opinion polling with Roper and Gallup, and now a newly-found understanding of what my job really entailed at Boston University. The third leg was being accepted as a regular officer.

First Overseas Assignment – Barely
Ernest Harmon AB, Newfoundland, Canada
October 1961 – September 1964

By 1961 I got caught in the Air Force Personnel system and tapped for an overseas assignment. I had a choice of Newfoundland or Spain. I chose Spain – still not understanding how personnel people think. So I ended up going to Ernest Harmon AB at Stephenville on the west coast of the Canadian Province of Newfoundland. Newfoundland was originally the oldest commonwealth in the British Empire. Its residents had just voted to become a province of Canada a short time before. (That was a classic textbook election – and the voters chose Canada by just one vote). The alternative was to petition to become a state in the United States. But now Newfoundland was considered overseas – but we drove to this Canadian island province where the entire population of Newfoundland was around 470,000. That was equivalent to the size of the city of Denver.

Note: The reference to AB in place of AFB is used by the military to designate whether the base is in the United States or its territories, or whether in a foreign country where we share facilities but do not own them.

This time, the move involved five of us and we now had a 1961 Rambler station wagon. We made the trip in two parts: first was to take Elaine and the kids to Moultrie, Georgia, where they would live until I could find housing at Harmon. After getting them settled, the second was for Elaine to drive me to the SAC base at Savannah, Georgia, where I caught a flight to Harmon. The KC-97 unit

139

at Savannah was charged with standing alert at Harmon, making a convenient, seamless connection.

I checked in at Harmon, living in the bachelor officer's dorm, and settled into my new office. I also began hunting for a house in Stephenville. I quickly lucked out by getting a three-bedroom home with a kitchen, bath, living, and dining room. However, there was one odd factor. It was the first house I had ever seen with a floor furnace. The only register was in the living room, which meant the heat had to circulate to heat the other rooms. During the winter, it was not too efficient. You could be comfortable in the living room but would need to bundle up in other rooms. It was not unusual for the inside walls of our bedrooms to be covered in frost.

But it was a home where we could all be together, and I flew back on leave to Savannah, where I was picked up and driven to Moultrie. We packed all our belongings and headed north to Newfoundland in a Rambler station wagon. It took us several days. Eventually, we crossed the Gulf of St. Lawrence on the Blue Nose Ferry that took us from Sydney, Nova Scotia, to Port Au Basque, Newfoundland. We then drove the unpaved TransCanada Highway to Stephenville.

Debra Elaine   Tomajean   John Michael

We lived in Stephenville a few months and finally got base housing, a really wonderful duplex with three bedrooms, living and dining rooms, kitchen, basement, and a garage. The house had a real furnace! Harmon AB was a self-sustaining town with a shopping center (the base exchange), commissary, gas station with a cost of 15 cents per gallon for regular, a golf course, bowling alley, lakes for fishing, and a radio and TV station. The nearest large town was Corner Brook, 50 miles north.

The population of Stephenville grew from about 1,000 in 1941 when the base was surveyed. It exploded to 7,000 when the construction of the base was finished on June 23, 1941. A sleepy French-speaking fishing village had now become an English-speaking community as Harmon Field morphed into the largest U.S. Army airfield outside of the United States during WWII.

For Elaine, it was a great location. We had a live-in maid to help with the kids. She could play golf nine months per year, be involved with the officer's wives club, and for a time hosted a daily TV show.

The nine-hole golf course was located alongside St. George's Bay Beach Road. What made it really unique was the fox that lived in the woods on Hole #2. Between the tee and the green was a raised maintenance road. You would normally use a driver to where the ball carried over the road but landed out of sight because of the raised road. But no problem. You knew the ball would be in the fairway as you dragged your golf cart onward. Then would come the surprise. For some reason, the fox loved golf balls. She would run out hidden by a raised road, grab a ball, and take it into the woods. But the golfer would have no idea what happened.

It was not until a ground crew member stumbled across a huge pile of golf balls in the woods that Harmon golfers learned what happened. Colonel Goyt, as senior commander at the base, declared that the fox was protected and that this issue at Hole #2 should just be considered a hazard.

Another time Elaine and I encountered the fox was on Hole #8. It was fairly flat except for a small creek that was right at the approach to the hole. Here the fox would lie in wait, and when you made your pitch shot to the green, she would run up on the green and grab the ball. The fox would wait for you at the green, and then the dance would begin. You move toward the fox – the fox backed up. You move away from the fox – the fox would move toward you. Eventually, the fox would apparently think, "That's enough fun for now," and drop the ball to disappear down the creek bed.

We were also involved with the local community that centered on the Catholic Church and Corner Brook, a harbor town hosting the huge Bowater's Paper Company. We had many friends in Corner Brook, the second-largest city on the island, where we attended dances, learned to curl, and played golf. They, in turn, loved visiting Harmon for the slot machines and golfing. Our closest friends were Rocky and his wife 'George' Schulstad. Rocky was an anchor for the CBC TV station in Corner Brook and an avid outdoorsman. He is the one who taught me the art of tying fishing flies.

We had several unique golf experiences at Corner Brook. The first was in a friendly golf tournament. The players behind us were all doctors from the Harmon Base Hospital. Hole #2 had a long fairway ending in a steep drop to a green below. When we got to where we could see the green, we also saw there was a horse on the green. We waited, and he left exiting stage right. We had just finished putting and were headed to the Hole #3 tee box. The green and tee box were separated by a thick, wooded area. We heard a ball hit a tree and drop to the ground. By earshot, we had a good idea of where the ball would be and went to the spot to mark where the ball was lying. There was the ball, and next to it, a fresh pile of horse manure. I couldn't resist. I picked up the ball and placed it on the manure.

Then I thought the ball actually came down with force, so I used a putter to tap it in a bit more firmly. The doctor shows up, we direct him toward the ball, and he discovers where the ball is lying. He goes through the golfer routine of looking at the ball, the tree branches, and the green. He addressed the ball, backing up a bit; backing up another bit, and then says, "What a shitty shot." He swings, and the ball comes out of the woods onto the green.

Two other times we had experiences you would never think you'd have. The first was on Hole #3. We were delayed 30 minutes from getting close to the green, as a bear and her cubs were relaxing there. The other time was on Hole #9, where a moose had walked across the green the night before and left large footprint holes. It was impossible to find any angle where you could even use sand green rules and move the ball circular to find a path to putt.

I learned the sport of 'curling' at Corner Brook. Curling involved manually sliding a 40-pound polished granite stone down a sheet of ice controlled at the start by an embedded handle. The only other piece of equipment was a straw broom. No special clothing, except for having pair of foot rubbers (although you only wore one to allow one foot to slide on the ice). The best thing about this sport is that rinks always have a bar. The first time you do this, be prepared for pains the morning after. If you have never lifted 40 pounds backwards before in your life, the next day your shoulder shouts, "What have you done?"

I learned enough to become a member of the Harmon AB competition curling team for three years. Like bowling, it involved a team of four – male, female or combination. The positions on the team are by rank. Skip is the leader. Mate is the No. 2 player. Second is the team member who follows 'Lead.' Lead is the team member that goes last. I made 'Mate.' So for the uninitiated, the game involves sliding the rock down the rink, using a twist of the handle when setting the rock free to curl it to the right or the left at the right speed to get it into the 'house.' You get points based on the color scheme of the circular house.

But it gets more complicated. Before sending the stone toward the 'house,' you learn that each end has four concentric, colored circles marked on the ice. Each team has eight stones, so each player throws two per 'end.' A game consisted of eight to 10 ends. Skip or Mate would mark a spot in the house with a broom where they wanted your stone to land. Two players, not releasing the rock, move ahead of it, following commands from the skip to sweep or not in front of the moving rock. The theory was that the sweeping creates a vacuum in front of the rock making it go faster, and/or the sweeping heats the ice, making the rock slide farther. My thought was all the sweeping did was get the straw out of the way left from previous sweepers' brooms.

Elaine also made another friend in Stephenville. She was the daughter of a storeowner who enjoyed bridge. She became Elaine's frequent bridge partner at the Officer's Club. Many of the officers' wives viewed Newfoundlanders to be 'below their station' but eventually accepted the guest – reluctantly. They never knew that her father had been an elected member of the Canadian Parliament. Her husband was the CEO of Pan American Airlines. (Pan Am was a major worldwide airline at the time.) When she wasn't visiting family in Newfoundland, she would be residing with the wealthy at her homes in Miami, Hawaii and Spain.

The weather was a pleasant surprise. We came to call Newfoundland the Miami of the North. The Gulf Stream was just offshore, resulting in relatively mild winters. The lows in winter normally reached 20 degrees Fahrenheit. Night flying provided us viewing of the spectacular Northern Lights that played on the horizon. Snow didn't begin until mid-December and would be over by March. It did snow frequently, but you could use a broom instead of a shovel to remove it. Summers were super, with some days reaching 70 degrees. Those would be days our wing commander declared a down day for golf – wanting everyone to take advantage of any day when the temperature got that warm.

In 1963, we had an Arctic hurricane while living on base. Snow piled up over the first floor of our house. We were without electricity for three days. The furnace failed. We kept warm by bundling up and staying in one room heated by candles. We all slept on one bed, snuggling together for warmth. During the day we got warm by shoveling snow from around our door, garage, and driveway. The base handled it extremely well. Because of the base mission, the runways and base had to be kept open by a civil engineer team composed of civilian employees. In winter, their full-time was to remove snow. In summer, their job was grass cutting. (Except for England, I had never seen grass grow so green and fast, aided by constant drizzle and long summer days.)

The mission at Ernest Harmon AB was to maintain a tanker alert force to provide air-to-air refueling support to SAC jet bombers en route to targets. The KC-97 was still essential to this task. The base was also a primary air-refueling stop for transatlantic military flights and supported three Air Defense radar sites. Our night flights gave us hours to enjoy the beauty of Canada's Northern Lights.

I was on the staff of Col. Gordon F. Goyt, the senior commander at the base. Colonel Goyt was unusual for two idiosyncrasies. He was bald and always wore his hat in the office. His Air Force vehicle was flamboyant. In addition to the normal commander license plate, it was festooned with two American flags – on each side of the front of his car. He had a reputation for creating golf courses around the U.S. and had been the 8th Air Force Inspector General before this assignment. His inspection of Harmon a few months before resulted in the firing of the then commander after an operational readiness inspection. His boss at 8th Air Force at Westover AFB in Massachusetts then named him commander at Harmon.

Another mark from Colonel Goyt's time at Harmon was when his wife determined renovations for the Officer's Club. Most notable was the use of heavy maroon drapes throughout the building. Many thought the change made the club look like a French house of horizontal pleasure.

My job was Director of Information for Ernest Harmon AB. I had a deputy, a non-commissioned officer, an editor for the base newspaper, two enlisted writers, and a wing historian in my primary office. I was also responsible for the programming and operation of our base radio station (licensed by the government of Newfoundland as VOHF before Newfoundland became a province of Canada). I had the same duties with CFSN-TV which was licensed by the Canadian Government. It served both the Stephenville area and the base. We had a CBC representative to monitor our operation of the stations. We coordinated all station programming decisions through our local CBC manager.

He reported to William Calgay, as manager of all CBC broadcast outlets in Newfoundland and Labrador based at St. John's, the province's capital.

The radio and TV stations had a staff of seven Air Force enlisted men. They were housed in an unheated Quonset hut protected from winter cold by being covered with earth and heated inside by the lights in the TV studio. The radio antenna was a long wire on a base dormitory. The TV had a normal tower and reached the coastal communities along St. George's Bay. The radio reached only the base and perhaps five miles around the bay on a good day.

The biggest benefit to this arrangement was that we had live CBC-TV feeds by microwave, giving us high-quality black and white programing. Our other programming primarily was provided in kinescopes by the Armed Forces Radio and Television Service in Los Angeles, shipped by huge containers by mail. We would have a three-week supply of programming to cover in case weather caused shipping delays. Kinescopes were copies of live broadcasts filmed from a TV screen. The kinescopes really came across as very poor quality, especially compared to the live microwave service from CBC.

Radio was on 18 hours from 6 a.m. to midnight daily. Each morning VOHF signed on playing national anthems. Actually: four national anthems (*God Save the Queen* for the United Kingdom; *Oh Canada* for Canada; the *Newfoundland Anthem* from days gone by, and the *Star-Spangled Banner*). Altogether, it took 12 minutes before scheduled broadcasting could begin.

Our American radio news was provided by the short wave service from Armed Forces Radio in Los Angeles. The frequency we could receive was not reliable as the signal was aimed for bases in North Africa. Our workaround was two-fold. The early morning newscast was at 7 a.m. Newfoundland time (90 minutes ahead of Eastern time zone). WPAT out of Patterson, New Jersey, saved our day. Their signal was crystal clear at night. We would record a late-night newscast, delete all the commercials, and lead with that newscast each day. This was augmented by our own team using the Associated Press Radio Wire for copy. That, too, was a workaround as we obtained a printer setup by our communications squadron on base for on-the-minute written United Press and Associated Press news copy.

VOHF (Voice of Harmon Field) was originally licensed by the Broadcast Corporation of Newfoundland, sometime between the construction of the base in 1941 and the time the BCN was absorbed into the Canadian Broadcasting Corporation in 1949. This was when Newfoundland was no longer the oldest commonwealth in the British Empire and became a province of Canada. VOHF had three sister Armed Forces Radio Service stations licensed by the BCN, including VOUS at Pepperell AB, VOAR at Argentia U.S. Navy base, and VOGB at Goose Bay AB in Labrador.

When I arrive, the television service at Harmon AB was transmitted from 3 p.m. to midnight daily. That soon changed. The Canadian government created strict content rules. Fifty percent of all TV in Canada had to be Canadian content, have Canada as a subject, originated in Canada, or have a Canadian-born actor in the program. Canadian

Content rules caused us scheduling problems, making it tough for us to air the U.S. programming that we wanted to provide our military audience and their families.

We did have a bonus available to us. For example, all U.S. network programming we had third-showing rights access to, were Disney and documentary programs filmed in Canada. Many U.S. entertainment programming had a Canadian actor or actress like Lorne Green on *Bonanza*, Gisele MacKenzie on *Your Hit Parade* plus many musical shows also had Canadian talent. But we still had a hard time meeting the requirement.

My first solution was to go on air with TV at 8 a.m. We put a live camera on a goldfish bowl and had music from the AFRTS radio disc package played underneath. That gave us seven hours of Canadian content, before we began regular programming at 3 p.m. (We actually built a large audience for the goldfish as we mixed sound from the latest transcription records we had just received or from our library. Our listeners liked that as they could record the music at home in an uninterrupted format.) Goldfish worked for several months, but eventually, the CBC in Ottawa found out and we had to find another solution. CBC was sympathetic to our unusual joint service and volunteered to pay for any programming locally produced.

On the positive side, CBC gave us funding for creating local studio productions. We were given $125 per half hour for live studio programming origination. That made CFSN-TV the highest paying industry on the West Coast of Newfoundland. My first efforts here were to arrange for the traveling musical groups that visited the military offi-cer and NCO clubs to play live in our 2-camera Quonset hut studio. We created talk shows on any subject we could come up with. The pay was the same. That is how Elaine became a TV talk host until we could find someone inter-ested to get away from the perception of nepotism.

It was one of the musical groups that added to my humor repertory with this four-line poem which continues to be on target 60 years later:

> The bee is such a busy soul
> He has no time for birth control
> So that is why in times like these
> There are so many sons of bees.

I discovered a company making portable dictation ma-chines for our local news services, taking a cue from what I had already done at HQ SAC. The Mohawk Midgetape was a handheld, battery-operated recorder any of my team could use anywhere on the ground or aboard an aircraft for in-flight 'actualities.'

Step 2: For TV news, I found a company in Milwaukee that made the Milsco 16mm film processor. Again, based on how we built SAC radio service on one Ampex recorder, I began to find ways to create both audio and film news for VOHF and CFSN-TV. We had no budget, and funding was always tight. My solution was to go to the NCO club on base and ask them to buy the processor for us from their profits from slot machines. The NCO Club in return would get airtime credit by a 'tag' announcing, "News film coverage provided by the Harmon AB NCO Club." It worked, and we got the necessary funds.

Step 3: Get the wing safety office to give us their authorized 16mm camera, using the same logic I had used at Lincoln AFB. We agreed to cover their documentation requirements for continued access to the camera. They had no one that knew how to use the camera – it was a win/win agreement.

Step 4: Designate one of my young military broadcasters to get a quick course in using the motion film processor. That requirement was done when Airman Ron Sott went to Milwaukee to pick up the processor. Ron was our one-man local news department for both VOHF and CFSN-TV. It also became a major benefit to his professional career when he left the Air Force. Ron got a job shooting news films for Ralph Renick's TV station in Miami. He was recognized as the Radio & Television News Directors Association news photographer of the year in the late 1960s.

That pretty much did the trick. We aired our mix of U.S. shows we felt were essential despite being of kinescope quality, especially if they qualified for Canadian Content. Lots of U.S. programs qualified. Disney and Wild Life productions and many others provided additional Canadian content when airing U.S. programming. I also added a lot of Canadian Film Board travel movies to the mix. But I still think the goldfish was the best solution.

Every year we had a major open house that would attract several thousand visitors. CBC assisted and ensured that we had live TV coverage of open house events and aircraft flyovers. It was the only remote coverage we had each year.

At the time, Air Force bands existed at all levels – in Washington D.C., various command headquarters, and some bases. All were assigned to the public information offices. So I was also responsible for scheduling the Air Force Band at Harmon AB, particularly for their public appearances locally and throughout the province.

I still was required to fly to get monthly flight pay. I checked out flying the de Havilland Beaver, a single-engine aircraft used throughout Canada for servicing remote locations. During the winter months the aircraft was on wheels, but with 'ice out,' we flew it as a floatplane. It was the most fun flying I ever did, especially landing on lakes to take VIPs to moose hunting areas or fishing lakes. Altogether I amassed 99 water landings in the Beaver. This was another aircraft I flew that, in high-wind conditions, was passed by traffic on the roads.

The de Havilland Beaver

During the Cuban Missile Crisis, I was flying locally. I noticed a large container ship with no origin or country markings in St. George's Bay. I had wild thoughts – perhaps it might have missiles onboard to attack the base! I reported that to authorities on base by radio. I was told to keep an eye on it while it was being checked out. About 20 minutes later it was determined by Canadian maritime authorities the boat was a Great Lakes ore boat that had been bought by an English company and it was in St. George's Bay for safe harbor as a hurricane was forecast in the Atlantic. So much for saving the world!

The Cuban Missile Crisis in October 1962 did have a personal impact on me, though. This time it was the Air Force Personnel people again. The crisis resulted in all pilots in staff jobs being immediately assigned to combat units. Because I had been a KC-97 pilot before, I was now being transferred to the KC-97 Air Refueling Squadron based at Harmon. I had a short refresher and became a KC-97 pilot for the second time. My assignment at Harmon ended in August 1964 when I was transferred to Westover AFB in Chicopee, Massachusetts.

Regarding our family, we had two major events. Debi, our oldest daughter, began first grade at the Department of Defense School in 1962. Elaine gave birth to our youngest son, Curtis Charles Halbert, on January 28, 1961. This was how we found out that it was not the water in Lincoln that caused kids.

A storied local Stephenville old-time fishing guide, Charles White (pronounced 'Wheet' in the Newfoundland dialect), provided me and our local Hudson's Bay store manager Ken Saunders the techniques of fly fishing in an open field. We both became semi-proficient on casting for both wet and dry flies. When our instructor was confident we had the basics, he took us to nearby Harry's River, famous for Atlantic salmon fishing. However, the reality on the river differed greatly from our training in an open field. We quickly learned about bushes and trees behind us that we hooked more often than we got a fly on the water.

Ken was of Ukrainian heritage who grew up in Manitoba Province in western Canada. He and his wife were among the community leaders in Stephenville and we became great friends. As we were leaving Harmon AB for Westover AFB, he gave us a special gift that I still have today. It has graced the entry of every home I have lived in since. The gift was a very large and heavy walrus bone – actually the penis bone of a walrus. It even has an identification certificate that explained a walrus needs the bone to maintain the capability of reproduction in cold water.

Salmon fishing requires wading. You must have felt material glued to the bottom of your chest-high wader boots. The moss on the rocks and strong current made it tough to maintain balance as you cross the river to fish from 'beaches' of river rock. You had to cross the river frequently as you trekked from 'pool to pool' because the bending river had high banks across from the beaches. Our guide would sometimes be with us, giving us corrections and advice. But more often, he would be on the high bank where he could see salmon in each pool. With his guidance and 'suggestions' we would try to cast where he said the fish were.

Atlantic salmon are in Newfoundland rivers for one purpose only: to lay eggs or spray eggs with sperm in a nest created by the female. And it has to be at a spot in the river where they themselves were born. No human knows why. But the salmon do. Thus, they do not feed while they make this trek from ocean to 'their' river. Your job is to pass a fly in front of them sufficient times to irritate them, and they bite in retaliation. Atlantic salmon are uniquely different from the Pacific varieties. Their flesh is white, not pink or red. And more important, after they spawn, they return to the ocean to return another year.

But once you get one hooked, it becomes a battle of tactics. It takes roughly 10 minutes a pound to land a salmon. Your tackle is not built for just reeling in a big fish in a strong current, and you're standing on slippery rocks. Your job is to get the salmon to swim upstream and wear them until they become docile and are floating on their sides. Then, you ease them into a net or slowly beach them on the pebbled river bank. They remain calm until you touch them. Often, when you are not prepared, they have just enough strength to flip into the river without even waving goodbye.

My first fish on Harry's River was a three-pound sea trout. I was hooked and spent much of my free time when climate and free time allowed my fishing for salmon. My many hours on alert were spent in the newly constructed underground alert facility or 'mole hole' tying hundreds of salmon flies. It cost me about eight cents to create a fly. I sold them for 25 cents each. It was the only time in my life where a simple homemade product paid for all my fishing equipment, waders and gas.

Tom's first Atlantic Salmon – Harry's River, Newfoundland

Salmon fishing is never a sure thing. The first year I had only the sea trout and lots of 'grilse' or baby salmon that had not yet gone to sea. The second year, I caught four real salmon, and the third year I ended up catching 22. Our base locker plant that was operated by the military commissary allowed us to put footlockers in their freezers to store moose meat and fish. My last year, I knew I would be transferring to Westover AB – so I had them all safely frozen to take them there when I would return as a KC-97 crew member to stand alert. Spoiler Alert #2: I hadn't told Elaine of my plan. So as we were packing our household goods, she gave all the salmon to our maid! Seeing a grown man cry is not a pleasant sight.

In March 1963, I participated in Arctic Survival Training, where we were on our own in the frozen, barren marsh-land out of sight of the base for five days. On about day four, I was cutting a parachute cord to make a snare and the knife cut through the tendon of my left index finger. I ended up in surgery in the base hospital and then eventually home to recover. It was daughter Debi who became my biggest helper, as with only one hand, I could not do zippers. She saved me time after time from helplessness and embarrassment.

In late May 1964, I was pulled from the mole-hole alert facility and learned that my father had died in Des Moines. He was just 62. In a whirlwind of events I was put on a T-39 executive jet and flown non-stop to Des Moines Airport. My uncle Marion Thomas met me, gave information about my Dad's death, and informed me about the preliminary funeral arrangements. From there, we drove to Red Oak for services and burial. My trip back was not as rapid as I caught military flights at Offutt AFB back to Newfoundland.

A year later, when it came close to the time for the move to Westover AFB, we took advantage of NATO discounts to purchase a Chevrolet Impala. If you were overseas in a NATO country, you could factory order cars at 25 percent or more off a dealer's price. This car was special as it was built to order on a convertible frame and had an extra radiator installed. We had the travel trailer bug and quickly purchased a Holiday Rambler near the base that would hold a family of six. This time, the trip was smoother, heading out on the now paved TransCanada highway to Port Au Basque. We boarded the Blue Nose ferry to Nova Scotia and finally to Westover in Western Massachusetts.

Westover AFB, Chicopee, Massachusetts
Final Assignment in SAC: 1964–1965

We checked into Westover in June 1964 and moved into base housing. The homes were all single-storied, almost joined together in pairs, separated by a covered sidewalk, and with entries facing each other. We had yards with flowerbeds along the side of the building. Since it was spring, one of the first duties I had after we got semi-settled was to plant the flowerbed.

But I did take time to take my three oldest kids (Debi, Tomi, and Mike) fishing on a nearby pond. They were skilled in using fly rods and popping bugs, and among all of us, we caught more than 50 bluegills. (State law required killing any panfish caught in Massachusetts as they were overpopulating ponds.) When we got home, I knew from my grade school history classes that the Pilgrims were taught by the Indians to put down a fish for fertilizer when planting corn. So we put the bluegills through a grinder, and as I dug up the flowerbed – put the fish mixture down, covered it with soil, and topped it all with young plants. Nowhere in history books do they mention cats. For the entire summer, our flower bed was the hit for the cats in the neighborhood who would dig up the plants thinking there must be a fish someplace.

The kids were free from school until September. We made good use of this opportunity when I was home – not flying locally or standing alert at Harmon, where our squadron rotated every third week. There was so much history all around us. We traveled to Boston, Plymouth Rock, and historical sites to the Berkshires on the New York state border. Debra entered second grade and Tomajean started first grade. Mike entered first grade a year later as Debi and Tomi advanced one grade. These schools were local school district schools, but were physically located on the base.

Our nearest lake of size was Lake Webster on the Massachusetts-Connecticut border. It was popular for water skiing with a surface area of 1,442 acres. It was better known by a much longer name having 45 letters comprising fourteen syllables: Lake Chargoggagoggmanchauggagoggchaubunagungamaugg. The name attracts many tourists. It is well known simply because it is the longest name of any place in United States.

Our fishing was for shad in the Connecticut River or bluegills in our local pond. Debi, Tomi, Mike, and I used fly rods and roll casting to get the floating line out from shore. We knew if the line stopped moving, it was because of a fish. The fish would then be hooked with a flick of the wrist. Shad fishing was unique that way. And even after the lesson about cats, we continued popping bug fishing in our nearby pond.

Culinary wise we were where we could easily get fresh lobster. Our favorite location was the Yankee Peddler in nearby Holyoke. Occasionally Elaine and I would go to Boston for historical and gourmet outings. Favorite locals were the Union Oyster House and Durgin Park, still one of Boston's oldest continuously running establishments.

Again I was a KC-97 aircraft commander and became the head of a new crew at Westover. I had just been designated on October 8, 1965, as a Senior pilot. This signified I had reached a combination of seven years of flying experience with more than 2,000 hours of flying time.

We did local flying (taking off and landing at the same airfield) to refuel B-47s on air refueling tracks across New England and into Canada. As had been the case since my assignment at Lincoln AFB, the KC-97 had to descend to be fast enough for the B-47 to maintain flight. For an off-load, you figured you would have to go from 20,000 feet to 10,000 feet while refueling in 30-minutes or so.

Every third week, several crews would fly to Harmon AB in Newfoundland to stand alert there. It was a morning briefing in the alert facility at Harmon in September 1965 when we learned that the Air Force was sending the KC-97 to the boneyard in Arizona and that we would be reassigned to fly either the C-124 in the Military Airlift Command or the C-130 in the Tactical Air Command. Again Air Force logic ruled. On my assignment dream sheet, I had chosen MAC. Air Force Personnel sent me to TAC.

My first assignment orders were for Dyess AFB in Abilene, Texas. Not a dream assignment for me. But I must have inadvertently had that as a dream location as it was changed just one week before I was to leave for Sewart AFB, near Nashville, Tennessee. I arrived at Sewart in October 1965.

Nashville & the C-130 Hercules
Sewart AFB, Smyrna, Tennessee
October 1965 – March 1970

In late September 1965, we spent our first two weeks in Tennessee in our Holiday Rambler camping trailer in Cedars of Lebanon State Park, about 30 minutes from Sewart AFB. Our time was balanced with searching for a new home, getting the kids in school, and beginning my training and checkout to fly the C-130 Hercules. We finally settled in a new community called Edge O'Lake subdivision in south Nashville at 2740 Mossdale Drive. It was a short drive to the base and only two blocks from an elementary school. Our kids considered this their hometown as they went to Nashville schools from grade school to high school.

Edge O'Lake subdivision was near Percy Priest Lake, which was planned to come within blocks of the house. The Corps of Engineers Lake stretched from Nashville to south of Smyrna, flooding thousands of acres of limestone and cedar tree pasture land. When we moved in, the only water was in Stones River – the name of a major Civil War battlefield area.

Stones River became our go-to fishing area. It was full of smallmouth bass and panfish. Elaine would drive us to a bridge near the base where we would launch our Jon boat with a 3-horsepower Sears's motor and head with the current to another bridge not far from our house. This would take a full day to navigate all the bends in the river. Later, when the lake came in, we could get from one end of lake to the other in about an hour in our Bass Pro Shop Bomber powered by a 65-horsepower engine.

Tennessee was loaded with major lakes renowned for bass fishing. Most of my free time, and that of the family, was spent on the waters of Kentucky Lake to the west, Center Hill to the east, and Dale Hollow to the north, plus the rivers in between. By the time I left Sewart AB, I was toying with the idea of becoming a professional bass fisherman and guide.

Sewart Claim to Fame
Four Horseman Acrobatic Team

Sewart was well known for being the home of the 'Four Horsemen.' They were a U.S. Air Force aerobatic display team that flew four C-130A Hercules transport aircraft using the same maneuvers flown by the Air Force Thunderbirds. That was made possible by adding an oil sump pump at the engines' top to allow inverted flight. The team's pilots were Captains Gene Chaney, Jim Aiken, David Moore, and Bill Hatfield.

The team's first public demonstration was at Sewart before the newer C-130E transports arrived at the base. Soon after this demonstration, Tactical Air Command gave the team official status as an aerial demonstration team. The team's crew included two pilots, a flight engineer and an observer. The navigator's seat sat empty during the shows. The crews came from within the squadron, but the 'Four Horsemen' pilots always tried to fly with the same flight engineers.

The 'Four Horsemen' demonstrated the aircraft's short takeoff ability in a diamond formation. Because of the downwash from the propellers, each of the following aircraft had to fly slightly higher than the one in front. Each pilot would try to fly 'right on top of the bubble.' The slot airplane would be the highest in the formation. The 'Four Horsemen' flew in close formation, separated only by about 10 feet. After the demonstration, all four Hercules aircraft landed in a diamond formation again.

C-130 Hercules Training

My first assignment at Sewart was as a student aircraft commander undergoing classroom, simulator, and C-130E flight training with the 4442 Combat Crew Training Wing. Classroom instruction was during normal daytime hours, while flight training involved day and night. My simulator training was usually at 2–4 a.m., which was good experience for my future flying. Our saying in the combat squadrons was that we were like bats: we sleep all day and only go out at night to fly.

Things got interesting that December. The Defense Department announced the closure of several bases in the United States, including Sewart AFB, set for December 1971. This placed the base in a controlled decay status for five years. That meant no new construction projects and limiting repairs and upkeep for hazardous status only.

I completed the training and was assigned as an aircraft commander to the 62nd Tactical Airlift Squadron as a line pilot in late December 1965. My instructor pilot pushed my training hard. He succeeded in having his student finish at the top of my class 66-E-34, the official course number.

Crew assignments in the C-130 were not fixed as they were with the KC-97. Everyone flew interchangeable and put together for each mission from a pool. The crew on the C-130 consisted of an aircraft commander, a co-pilot, a navigator, a flight engineer, and normally two loadmasters.

Sewart AFB C-130 Flight Line

We flew low-level training missions locally at 1,000 feet above ground level. We supported airdrop missions with the 101st Airborne at nearby Ft. Campbell on the Tennessee/Kentucky border and the 82nd Airborne at Ft. Bragg, North Carolina. To get navigators training in celestial navigation, we flew missions for the Military Air Lift Command to Europe, the Caribbean, and the Pacific. In a nutshell, our job was to support the U.S. Army by developing assault airlift operations and participating in aerial demonstrations, exercises, maneuvers, and joint operations. Many of my flying missions were to substandard airfields in Europe, Asia, and the Middle East. I flew lead of formations drops of equipment and paratroops twice during NATO joint exercises in Greece and Turkey.

Several times we had missions to provide paratroop training for units based in Germany. We normally would fly out of Wiesbaden AB using low-level penetration techniques. Then, we'd pop up to drop altitude over a designated landing zone in the sugar beet fields of Rheinland-Pfalz near Kaiserslautern. At Wiesbaden, I had my first experience with wine. There was a neat, small piano bar downtown of this spa city called 'Der Eimer' (the bucket). They offered tastings of 1/8th of a glass to sample. We thought that was for children. So we ordered standard 1/4th glasses and worked our way through the menu. We went home singing.

We had a morning drop scheduled, and I was mission commander. When I woke, I was in bad shape. But I made it to the 5 a.m. weather decision briefing and cleared the crews to arrive for 7 a.m. takeoffs. As mission commander, my job was to get the crews and aircraft into the air. I was not scheduled to fly. I knew the flight shack had a bed, and my target was to get the flights launched and then sack out.

As the flights were taxiing out, I got a radio call. One of the co-pilots was sick. That meant I had to replace him. My recovery plan was dashed. I was a novice wine drinker, and it became a lesson learned the hard way.

I was also tasked to head the Air Force press center for the joint exercise 'Exotic Dancer' in Puerto Rico. We used Ramey AFB in Aguadilla on the northwest coast for this center. We operated out of a tent city, adding more realism to a combat mission exercise. The exercises involving Air Force, Army, Navy, and Marine forces were directed by the Joint Chiefs of Staff and conducted by the Atlantic Command. Our major part involved airdrops at Viejas Island northeast of Puerto Rico.

The weather was stifling hot and muggy. I cheated on sleeping in tents when I learned that the obstetric rooms in the air conditioned base hospital were vacant at night. I took advantage of that to sleep on an examination table with my feet in the stirrups.

It was a time of turmoil at Sewart as the 314th Tactical Airlift Wing, one of the two wings at this large base, was transferred with everyone assigned to Kung Kuan AB Taiwan. (*Sidebar story: Actually, the name 'Kung Kuan' in Chinese means Air Base. So that makes it Air Base Air Base. The name of the base used in the Tactical Air Command official orders was CCK or Ching Chaun Kang AB effective January 22, 1966.*)

My squadron at Sewart became part of the newly activated 64th Tactical Airlift Wing. We performed global airlift and medical evacuation missions, including several deployments to South Viet Nam. Our missions in Viet Nam were flown from Kadena AB and Naha AB in Okinawa or Clark AB and Mactan AB in the Philippines. Altogether I flew 49 combat missions in Viet Nam during five military campaign periods and was awarded both the Air Medal and the Bronze Star.

On July 1, 1966, I became the Wing Executive Officer to the new 64th Airlift Wing Commander Col. Earle Mac-Donald. I still flew C-130 missions with the 62nd TAS to maintain flight pay, including flights to Europe, the Caribbean, and the Pacific.

One of the most interesting missions in Europe was flying Embassy missions from Copenhagen, Denmark to Warsaw, Poland, and Moscow in the then Soviet Union. We had to be in place two days before the flight and two more days in Copenhagen on return. This allowed adding a Soviet 'navigator' as an augmented crew member, and allowing Soviets detailed inspection of the aircraft to ensure no spy equipment was aboard. On return we had another two days in Copenhagen. This time, we ensured the Soviets had not place any espionage equipment on the aircraft. That gave my crew four days to explore Copenhagen.

But now I could select the flights I wanted to take. If it was one I didn't like, I could claim I was too busy in the office. However, when there was one of interest, I could tell my boss, "Sorry, I have to go fly!" Best of all worlds.

Director of Public Affairs Again

In the fall of 1966, I was still dual-hatted – serving as Executive Officer to the wing commander and flying with the 62nd Tactical Airlift Squadron. I was going through the morning mail and overnight message traffic as usual. But one message jumped out to me. The Commander of the Tactical Air Command had sent out notice that public affairs offices at the base level would no longer be assigned to base commanders – but would now be under wing commanders. I gave Colonel MacDonald the message and said I would like his support to become his public affairs officer. It worked, and I was now the Chief of the Information Office at Sewart AFB while still flying in combat or simulated combat conditions.

My office was about a block away from the Wing Headquarters and about the same distance from the Division Headquarter headed by Col. Wayne Matson. He turned out to be pivotal to what I was able to do in this new job. Colonel MacDonald was much more interested in his flying unit and not so much with the broad aspects of public and community affairs. Matson was. So I was on the books as working for Colonel MacDonald, but in reality, working for his boss.

Nashville and central Tennessee were wonderful locations for working in public information. It was a media center, a major banking and insurance center, home of the Grand Ole Opry and the country music industry, multiple colleges, and a location easy to get to with the intersection of three interstate highways.

The public affairs mission had not changed from what I was doing at Harmon AB. The four pillars of public information, community relations, internal information, and history were still in place. But there were no Radio/TV station management requirements and no Air Force Band to be concerned about.

Like at Lincoln AFB I got considerable staffing support. I had three assistant public affairs officers, a senior experienced NCO (MSgt. Chuck Wills who I joined later at MACV Headquarters in Saigon), three airmen for the base newspaper, one broadcaster, two junior sergeants, and a historian slot. I was not able to find a qualified civilian to become a historian. I took that job for one year until I got the right person for the job. My journalism training got me through this problem, and I was even selected by Tactical Air Command for being Historian of the Year for a six-month report in 1966 and another six-month report in 1967.

Then, the Air Force added a new manpower slot at the base level. Those serving overseas as members of Armed Forces Radio & Television lost their positions as AFRTS exists only overseas. The new slots allowed them to remain broadcast orientated while awaiting another assignment overseas. My gain was TSgt. Dan Driscoll, who had been with AFRTS in Taiwan.

Dan began a weekly radio show about Sewart aired on Mary Reeves' station in Murfreesboro, Tennessee, about 12 miles south of the base. Mary was the widow of country music Hall of Fame star Jim Reeves. Eventually, Dan decided to retire and became a full-time morning drive-time disc jockey. At this time, Dan was stopped for speeding by the Tennessee Highway Patrol. Dan pulled over, took out his Tennessee Highway Patrol press card, and gave it to the officer. After looking over the press card and Dan's driver's license, he asked, "Are you the Dan Driscoll I listen to every morning?" Dan replied that indeed he was. The officer then asked' "Gee, Mr. Driscoll were you in a hurry?" Dan said he was. The officer said, "Well, I'll write the citation as fast as I can."

Media interface

Our primary interface with media in the Nashville area was with the *Nashville Tennessean*, the *Nashville Banner*, and *Rutherford County Journal* in Smyrna just outside the gate, WSM radio and TV, plus 17 regional radio stations. All the print media had beat reporters assigned for reporting on the base. WSM was special, as it was the station that owned the Grand Ole Opry. WSM-TV had a unique noontime public affairs show appropriately called *The Noon Show*. Guests frequently were on from the base – and the one they liked best was the Magic Chaplain. He was assigned at Sewart as a chaplain but did magic in his youth ministry. His best trick was levitating his wife on camera in the station parking lot.

Our interface with the Grand Ole Opry was to present Roy Acuff with an award for base support during a live performance and having many of the 'stars' out to the base for golf tournaments. Mrs. Henry Cannon (Minnie Pearl) was a regular.

The print beat reporters covered base activities and on occasion deployed with us for firepower demonstrations and live drops of paratroops and equipment. This happened at Fort Campbell, 50 miles north on the Tennessee/Kentucky border, and Fort Bragg in North Carolina. They also accompanied us on missions to the United Kingdom,

Germany, and Turkey. One disk jockey in Nashville aired on one of my "Halbertisms" by adopting my POETS day in place of TGIF for Fridays (Piss On Everything, Tomorrow's Saturday).

Most regional print and broadcast media were provided orientation flights that involved airdrops and low-level flights. Mason Tucker of the *Rutherford Courier* in Smyrna deployed with us to Incirlik AB, Turkey. Tucker had been a Baptist minister and was highly excited to be in the biblical areas of eastern Turkey. He even went on a base tour to Ephesus. He asked his bus seatmate, the navigator on this deployment, "Do you know what Ephesus is famous for?" The Nav replied, "Sure, it's the first place where Marc Anthony and Cleopatra shacked up." A year later, Mason flew with me to RAF Mildenhall in England. Both trips resulted in sections in the *Rutherford Courier* detailing his impressions.

Internal Information

The primary vehicle for communication internally was the base newspaper, which was published weekly. The contract printer was in Murfreesboro, which meant the editor would drive 15 miles south each Thursday to supervise layout and make any instant changes.

The other vehicle was the monthly commander's call program. As at Lincoln and Harmon, we would assist unit commanders in providing topics, slide briefings, and select films for their individualized programs.

Community Relations

Our community outreach program was expanded. Most of our C-130 flights were on designated low level routes designed to avoid major populations. But we still excited a wide swath of people throughout central Tennessee, southern Kentucky, and northern Alabama. We instituted a speakers program to reach schools, civic clubs, and local government organizations. Our speakers would be C-130 crew members or combat controllers (the guys that are dropped in behind enemy lines to establish drop zones and direct airdrops).

As we approached the closure of Sewart AFB, now planned for 1970, I personally gave 75 speeches in the metro area to civic leaders and business groups. I served as 834th Air Division protocol chief and briefer for distinguished VIPs from all over the world. Our base tour program drew more than 2,000 visitors per year.

The base was selected by DoD to conduct an orientation for 130 teachers as an Aerospace Education Workshop. In the summer of 1969, I doubled as aircraft commander and public affairs officer at the Milwaukee Aerospace Expo, providing a static display of the C-130. The Expo drew 250,000 visitors.

We established an annual concert at the community music hall in Nashville of the Air Force Academy Band in Colorado Springs conducted by Capt. Terry Heymeyer. Highly appropriate for 'Music City USA.'

Base Brochure

Because we had access to C-130s that hold 100 para-troopers, we had lots of passenger space aboard. We made Civic Leader trips to places like Cape Canaveral and Sea Survival School at Homestead AFB, Florida; Nellis AFB, Nevada; The Air Force Museum at Wright-Patterson AFB, Ohio; and the twice-yearly joint firepower demonstrations at Pope AFB and Ft. Bragg in North Carolina. We made two of these trips each year. The civic leaders were from a cross-section of Nashville, Davidson County and Rutherford County where the base was located. We included educators, mayors and business executives, the 'thought leaders' of the community. Always just men.

One additional touch. With the help of a graphic shop, I created a 'Certificate of Degree' awarding a 'Bachelor of Airlift' to every community leader that participated in an orientation presentation or a civic leaders flight.

My boss at the time was Col. Wayne Matson. He was the second commander I worked for who was public relations savvy. At his retirement party held by the Chamber of Commerce in Nashville, he was roasted when one of his wing commanders said, for him, it was the first time he had ever been at a base with two wings assigned to an information office. I took it as an accolade.

Colonel Matson was an unusual boss. He would show up on the flight line after midnight unannounced to talk with the ground crews readying aircraft for missions. He would spend time educating young airmen on how to save money for college painlessly and show up at my office two blocks away from his to chat. (All commanders that I had worked for in the past usually just called saying, "Halbert, get up here!")

At one of those sessions at my desk, he sought feedback about a civic leader trip we had just taken to Cape Canaveral and the TAC Sea Survival School at Miami. That allowed me a chance to comment that we have never taken an integrated group on our civic leader trips. He was puzzled as he always ensured that the pilots for these flights were Black and those chosen for invitations were White and Black. My pitch then focused on, "We have never taken a woman on these trips." I hit a nerve. Not missing a beat he said: "Do it!"

Okay, great. Now I had to produce. I had no real community knowledge of who women civic leaders might be in Nashville. But I did know Nashville was the seat of state government, a huge center for insurance and banking, the home of the Ford Glass Company and the entertainment industry. I began making calls.

At first, I would ask what woman holds the most prestigious title. The response was a puzzled, "Huh?" Then I would ask what woman had the largest office. The response was, "Huh?" Then I would ask what woman gets the highest pay. The response again was, "Huh?" But all agreed to research it and call back. After about three days, I began getting names. And that gave me a first cut list to run by Colonel Matson. He picked 40 names to make sure we had a significant group, knowing we would run into calendar conflicts. In the end we took a group of 30 women on the orientation.

Now I had to start the process to get Air Force approvals. I had another option as my sensing was the 'guys' in D.C. weren't ready for this concept. Colonel Matson was a division commander, meaning he was boss of both Sewart AFB and Pope AFB in North Carolina. Since he 'owned' both bases, Colonel Matson could approve such flights without Air Force level review. Thus we set up a trip to the next firepower demonstration at Pope AFB/Fort Bragg, North Carolina.

We made it a one-day trip. We left Sewart early in the morning, saw the show, and returned that evening. Everything clicked. It happened. Bottom line: for men, every orientation trip we took was what I called a two-day trip. Meaning that they would talk about it to their friends for the next two days. We found out for the women it became at least a six-month trip. Nothing like that had touched their lives before, and it became a long-lasting memory. Mission accomplished.

In November 1969, I was tasked to be the Tactical Air Command and senior DoD representative for Moratorium activity planning in Washington, D.C. The massive Moratorium march was Saturday, November 15, 1969, and attracted over 500,000 demonstrators against the war, including many performers and activists. Locally I was appointed to the Governor of Tennessee planning committee concerning the future usage of Sewart AFB following planned closure in 1970.

Authoring Wing Histories

My first history was written several months after Sewart had its only combat loss in Viet Nam. (Air Force histories are written six months after the end date of a six-month period to allow for the acquisition of backup documentation and the time to write one.) On May 31, 1966, a Sewart C-130E and crew, led by Col. Thomas Case, was shot down while attempting to lay magnetic mines in the Song Ma River along the demilitarized zone. Their goal was to destroy the Thanh Hóa Bridge, spanning the Song Ma River. The bridge was situated three miles northeast of Thanh Hóa, the capital of Thanh Hóa Province in North Viet Nam. It was one of many attempts to destroy the bridge attempted in various ways between 1965 and 1972 when the bridge was finally destroyed by aircraft bombing efforts.

It was the second attempt by this crew to destroy the bridge. The day before, and based on surprise, the crew flew under antiaircraft fire to lay the mines. The Pentagon directed that they fly the mission again, and this time the antiaircraft defenses were prepared. We lost an aircraft and crew. Other crew members lost were Lt. Col. Harold Zook, Major William Edmondson, Major Emmett McDonald, Captain Armon Shingledecker, CMSgt. Bobby Alberton, SMSgt. Elroy Harworth and SMSgt. Phillip Stickney. They were all people I had flown with at Sewart.

I would later add this tragic bit of history to the 64th Tactical Airlift Wing histories I compiled. I was honored as the Outstanding Historian of the Year for the Tactical Air Command. In December 1967, I was presented my awards by General Gabriel P. Disosway, commander of the U.S. Air Force Tactical Air Command at Langley AFB in Virginia.

My Officer Effectiveness Reports during this time were in the 'Absolutely Superior' range, the highest rating. The citation noted that Major Halbert's "initiative and dedication and is ideally suited for the field of public relations, doing this while maintaining his combat proficiency as an Aircraft Commander in the C-130 and can drop bundles on target with the best of TAC aircrews." I was promoted to Major, effective on January 25, 1969.

With great pride, my office and my team were selected the best public affairs office in the Tactical Air Command in 1969.

Viet Nam Combat Missions

During the Viet Nam War, tactical airlift provided unparalleled logistical support that surpassed that provided during the fabled Berlin Airlift, the World War II Hump, and the Korean War combined. The workhorse was the C-130 Hercules. All of this support came from bases in Okinawa and the Philippines used by crews and aircraft rotating from C-130 bases throughout the United States. At the peak of the effort, C-130s transported four million troops and passengers to and within the war zone annually. That is the equivalent of the combined population of Boston, Cincinnati, Dallas, Oklahoma City, Omaha, and Honolulu.

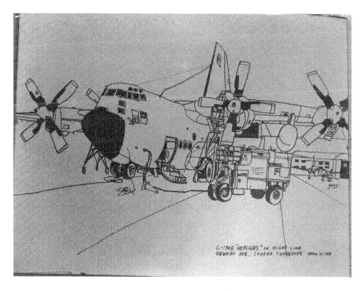

Air Force Art Program Etching of Sewart C-130

The C-130s operated out of bases, dirt strips at firebases, and even dirt roads in the countryside. The number of actual landing strips in Viet Nam exceeded 150. We delivered everything from supplies, weapons, and munitions to the *Stars & Stripes* newspaper. Many times,

C-130 crews responded to urgent calls for help, particularly where there were no ground roads or other means of responding. There were no front lines in this war. Urgent requirements could pop up anywhere. When landing was feasible, we could also be directed to change the aircraft's configuration, and become a medical air evacuation aircraft to get wounded to hospitals.

Some of the notable chapters were at Khe Sanh, a firebase near the Laos border. For 77 days, C-130 crews kept the Marines' cupboard full of ammunition, food and fuel. Or the A Shan Valley, where the Army's 1st Air Cavalry was pinned down and could only be supplied by parachute. Or Kham Duc, where the camp was completely surrounded. C-130s took fire during a four-hour evacuation of 500 Vietnamese and Americans.

The 1965–1969 Viet Nam era was when it was a full-scale war. It was when we not only flew things and people across the Pacific but when we put our C-130 combat training into actual wartime missions. We air-dropped munitions and supplies and slid pallets pulled by drogue chutes on runways without landing at remote firebases, like Khe Sanh. We infiltrated road watch teams along the Ho Chi Mihn trail using high altitude, low opening parachute techniques.

(*Road watch teams would jump out of the C-130 at 10,000 feet and open their parachutes at 1,000 feet under cover of darkness. Their mission once on the ground was to act as combat controllers who directed F-4 Phantom attacks on targets they could mark by lasers. We recovered the teams snagging a cable attached to a helium balloon and tied to the team member, jerking them into the air and winching them back aboard the aircraft.)*

The other mission was to drop 20,000-pound bombs. They looked like a corn silo, corrugated metal strapped together with a long probe on the front of the bomb. They would be loaded on a pallet, drug out by a drogue chute. The bomb was designed to explode above the ground, using the probe to set it off. The purpose was to destroy a large area of the jungle and create instant helicopter assaults pads without prior warning.

We also experimented with spraying silicon on the Ho Chi Minh Trail on the downhill side of mountain roads. The concept was that the North Viet Nam trucks would not have brakes and would be destroyed by crashing on curving mountain roads. It didn't work.

The C-7 Caribou

Another Pentagon arrangement occurred at Sewart when the twin-engine de Havilland C-7 Caribou fixed-wing cargo aircraft was transferred to the Air Force. This happened following a purported poolside agreement at Ft. McNair in Arlington, Virginia, between the Chief of Staff of the Army and the Chief of Staff of the Air Force. The Army gave up the Caribou, and the Air Force transferred its combat helicopter mission to the Army. The Caribou unit flew out of Sewart for training before being flown to Viet Nam for missions there. The Caribou was extremely valuable for supporting isolated Civilian Irregular Defense camps with very short landing strips carved out of the jungle.

Two things of note: The intense training at Sewart involved ways to extend normal flight time. The aircraft were to be flown island-hopping style to get across the Pacific to Viet Nam. The second was that the Caribou soon earned the reputation of having a major safety issue with bird strikes – from the rear.

Assassination of Dr. Martin Luther King Jr. April 4, 1968

My longest flying mission ever started just hours after the assassination of Dr. Martin Luther King Jr. The assassination occurred at 6:01 p.m. Central Time on April 4, 1968. The famous Civil Rights leader was hit by a sniper's bullet. King had been standing on the balcony in front of his room at the Lorraine Motel in Memphis, Tennessee. He was shot without warning. The .30-caliber rifle bullet entered King's right cheek, traveled through his neck, and finally stopped at his shoulder blade. King was immediately taken to a nearby hospital but was pronounced dead at 7:05 p.m. Violence and controversy followed. In outrage of the murder, many Blacks took to the streets across the United States in a massive wave of riots.

By 9 p.m., every available crew and aircraft were ordered to fly to Army bases throughout the Southern U.S. to load military police, support troops, communications, and command units. These were to be delivered to Andrews

AFB outside Washington D.C. The mission lasted three days without any sleep. It was the first time I had ever taken flight surgeon-issued green 'go' pills that kept us awake until the emergency airlift was complete. We then got red 'stop' pills and dropped off to welcome rest.

Each of the multiple times I landed at Andrews with troops and equipment, we could see large sections of Washington burning. At Andrews, our aircraft were refueled, giving us time for hot meals, a chance to use normal creature comforts (bathrooms), and make phone calls to update our families.

Hurricane Camille – August 17, 1969 Gulfport, Mississippi Press Center

Hurricane Camille was the most ferocious hurricane ever to hit the United States. But it was an event planned for and for which almost instant support would be sent within hours. Sewart AFB, like all airlift bases, had prepared missions for the movement of portable hospitals, medical and military police personnel, water purifications, cadaver sniffing dogs, vehicles, and engineering equipment. You name it. We had it. And we had practiced during training exercises to react with little notice.

Camille was a Category 5 when it hit land between Bay St. Louis and Pass Christian, Mississippi. The coastline was hit with waves up to 70 feet high causing destructive flooding. This, coupled with 150 mph winds and embedded tornadoes, had pretty much wiped out everything from the coastline to the railroad barrier about six blocks inland where the flooding was contained. The wind and tornado damages extended north for miles.

Nearby Gulfport had a U.S. Coast Guard base with runways useable by C-130s. The base had some damage but was pretty much intact. We were alerted to begin to load our C-130s to bring our part of the pre-determined disaster package to Gulfport.

I was tasked by the Director of Information at Tactical Air Command headquarters at Langley AFB, Virginia, to set up a disaster press center at the Coast Guard base as Chief of the TAC information team. MSgt. Dan Driscoll and I boarded one of the first C-130s to leave for Gulfport, and two hours later, we had a press center established. We were joined the next day when Captain Bob Carroll. He was the information officer for the Tactical Operations Center at Eglin AFB in Ft. Walton Beach, Florida. He found his way in a military vehicle to get to our center. He added an Eglin photographer he brought with him to our team.

Communications were basically non-existent with the outside world. The only thing moving was the C-130 flights to the base and emergency vehicles on the roads. No one in a private vehicle was allowed in the disaster zone. A few enterprising reporters did make it to the press center by flying in on the C-130 armada that continued for about five days.

We found office space and converted rooms for sleeping areas. We were able to scrounge two military jeeps for our use in obtaining coverage of the disaster relief operation. Bob Carroll had the military vehicle that he drove to Gulfport. Our vehicles were used to drive on base. All traffic off-base was limited to convoy only.

Bob and I were creating news releases and taking photographs. Dan was doing the broadcast reporting shooting 16mm film, and doing voice reports on audiotape. There was no electrical power, telex, or any other then-modern means to get our stories out. Our 'workaround' for written copy was to create message traffic using the official Air Force communication forms. We addressed it to Headquarters TAC for dissemination and gave the forms to departing pilots with instructions to get the information to the nearest base communication unit wherever they landed. Raw film and audiotape would be delivered the same way to the nearest base they were heading for. It was a shot in the dark. And it worked. Once we got basic communications restored, we found that our work had indeed been received and disseminated.

This experience and effort would lead me to be dumbfounded when Hurricane Katrina wiped out New Orleans on August 25, 2005. I was struck that there was no Air Force response, even days after the disaster. Apparently, no contingency support, as was provided during Camille. I have never found out why, but assume that the disaster mission we had in 1969 was quietly deleted from the military budget somewhere along the way. Very short-sighted as undoubtedly many of the 1,200 deaths during Katrina might have been prevented.

Debi Asserts Her Bricklaying Role

Oldest daughter Debra Elaine Halbert began to understand her role as first-born and being the bricklayer for
her siblings. Nashville was where Debi found her first
and longest-lasting love - horses. She rapidly grew from
having her first pony to becoming a rider who participated in horse shows with her five-gaited mare. Her
horses were purchased from Gina Peay, who lived about
a mile away. Before Debi got her first horse, Debi began
working at the Peay stables that provided her first lessons in riding and care. She was 10 years old. It quickly
led to her competing in horse shows around Nashville
and beyond. Now we needed a horse trailer. We also
needed to be available to take her and her horse to shows
on weekends. And this was also where Debi met Gina's
son Grady.

Our four kids were focused on fishing on newly formed
Percy Priest Lake and visiting Opryland amusement park.
They camped in our Holiday Rambler trailer from the Kentucky Lake region to the north and Six Flags over Georgia
to the south. Also, they started Scout group activities and
elementary school a block away and later in Antioch by the
Nashville Airport.

This would become their hometown – the place where they
lived the longest, created lifelong friends, and where they
acquired their Tennessee accents.

LPN Elaine Halbert

About 1968, Elaine got the bug to get a job. The kids had reached ages where they didn't need full-time supervision. She found out about an opportunity to become a licensed practical nurse. The course was free and included pay during the on-the-job training portion. Her education was sponsored by the State of Tennessee. However, it required a commitment to work in a hospital following graduation. It was Elaine's first paycheck since leaving Moultrie (excluding her stint as a TV show moderator at Harmon AB). It was a great boost for her self-worth. Still, in reality, her pay was just enough to move us into a higher tax bracket – and it came out as a minus in a net income decrease in our joint tax return.

On the positive side, it gave her a skill that she used into the late 1990s. She used those skills in Nashville and later when she remarried and worked in Thomasville, Georgia.

Onward to Viet Nam
Saigon & the Peanut War

In late 1969, I got orders for reassignment to HQs 7th Air Force at Tan Son Nhut AB in Saigon. We knew that we would be reassigned. In 1965, they announced that Sewart AFB would be closed in 1970. During those five years, Sewart facilities were in 'controlled decay' status. Only emergency work was done on base buildings during that time. The base officially closed on March 7, 1970, shortly after I had arrived in Saigon. The 64th Tactical Airlift Wing was originally to move to Blytheville AFB in northern Arkansas – not a popular base in the Mississippi River cotton-growing region. However, the gods of happiness prevailed when the unit assignment was changed to metropolitan Little Rock AFB, Arkansas. Like Sewart, Little Rock AFB was adjoined to the state capital.

Assignments in Viet Nam were unaccompanied (meaning no family members were sent with you, but a few had their wives join them for periods of time). We elected for Elaine and the kids to remain in Nashville, where they were already settled in with school and friends. My year in Viet Nam would be extended involuntary, keeping me there for 13 months instead of the normal 12.

The assignment was worked by Lt. Colonel Don Burggrabe. He was the information field personnel specialist at the Air Force Personnel level. It was curious to us who served in Viet Nam that Lt. Colonel Burggrabe was the only Lt.

Colonel in Air Force Public Information who never served in Viet Nam.

HQ 7th Air Force – Tan Son Nhut AB, Saigon March 1970 – April 1971

My first job was to be the senior officer in media relations of the 7th Air Force. This branch of the 7th Air Force Office of Information totaled me as chief, three captains (Alan Schreihofer, Jim Ragan, and Bob Fuller), and two sergeants. The expected job would be to work with the news media and keep them abreast of what the Air Force was doing in this war. The reality was the 4-star general that commanded 7th AF provided us strict guidance: "I don't talk to the press – you don't talk to the press." We were allowed to respond to questions as long as the answer had been cleared for release by the press office at the Military Assistance Command headquartered nearby. That left us a lot of time on our hands.

It was an age when there was no Internet, no social media, and telephone calls were expensive. Our primary official communication sources were message traffic filed by local communication offices, or telex. We did have military phone capabilities, but calls were handled one-on-one with base operators. All calls were prioritized, and public relations was way down the priority scale.

My senior bosses were Colonel Irv Breslauer as Director and Lt. Colonel John Barbato as his deputy. Irv was short, and the running gag was that he was the only Colonel in the Air Force that could buy clothes directly off the rack in Saigon. John was the affable Italian. One day, Irv decided to make Major Shirley Bach his executive officer. He moved her desk into his office – sending his deputy Lt. Colonel John Barbato to an outer office. John came back later that day and found his desk moved. He asked for the enlisted guys to help him and he moved his desk outside into the parking lot. Irv returned from a staff meeting and found John sitting outside. Before Irv could speak, John looked up and said, "Just let me in when it rains."

My counterpart for Internal information was Major Rick Solander. He was responsible for the 7ᵗʰ *Air Force News*, a weekly published by Stars and Stripes in Tokyo. Many of us tried to grow mustaches. Rick was blond. You could hardly see it. But it was visible enough to be noticed by the Vietnamese secretaries. They could barely keep from giggling when they saw him.

My mustache came in as a tri-color, red, black, and grey. Our Executive Officer Major Shirley Bach stopped me one day and said, "Tom, your mustache looks terrible." I replied, "I can't see it – so that's your problem." I kept this personal protest until I got back to my new base in Florida.

Our work hours were from 7 a.m. to 7 p.m. daily, and we would take a long break at noon for 'exercise' on a football field near our hooch. The hooches were two-story dormitory buildings with individual rooms and a communal bathroom and showers. The rooms were single occupancy (if you didn't count the geckos sharing space with you). The geckos were welcome as they were more effective than bug spray in keeping you mosquito-free. Great pets. They were quiet, and didn't require feeding or walking.

Jogging was in, but it was also the time when you would stretch out working on your tan and listen to the daily newscast featuring Paul Harvey. The newscasts aired over Armed Forces Radio were much more important than the disc jockeys of *Good Morning Vietnam* ilk. We also had the *Stars and Stripes* newspaper daily, but it was published in Tokyo and flown into Saigon. It was the equivalent of getting a day-old paper, useful and interesting, but not up to date.

We discovered South Vietnam had four seasons – summer, winter, monsoon and dry. We didn't expect winter, but we had a hint all summer. Our Vietnamese secretaries all were knitting sweaters during lunch breaks. Someone in civil engineering got the idea that the base needed a playground for the children of the Vietnamese Air Force who resided on base. So a wonderful, elaborate American playground was installed. No one had considered the impact of the hot summer sun on metal slides. Many young Vietnamese boys and girls ended up with 3rd-degree burns.

Vietnamese children's major recreational choice was the readily available rice bugs. They were larger than crickets. Always available. And did not cost anything. It required finding a large stick to draw a circle as you would for playing marbles. The two boys would stand outside the circle with their rice bug. They would forcefully blow toward the head of their male rice bugs and their wings would fluff out. (Female rice bugs were more demure and did not 'fluff.') This apparently was the rice bugs' way of settling territorial conflicts. The rice bugs would be put in the circle, and a fight till death ensued. Besides the 'fun' of the fight, money was frequently waged in the equivalent of a rooster cockfight.

A major rule that you learned rapidly is if there is a line at the Base Exchange – get into it. It always meant they had something today they hadn't had for a long time.

Mail was the big event. There were no cell phones, hard lines, or Internet connection. It was mail call where your day was made … or unmade.

The Fleener/Davis Court-Martial

I was busy from the moment I got to my desk in April 1970. It was the beginning of the Fleener/Davis court-martial and drew considerable media interest. Majors Fleener and Davis were C-54 pilots who flew large VIP delegations of congressmen and government leaders to locations in the war zone and Asia from Bangkok to Hong Kong. I became the public affairs advisor to assist the media attending, ensuring they had access daily and provided answers to their questions. The trial drew about 15 media representatives daily.

The background on this case begins on a flight returning to Tan Son Nhut from Bangkok. It had been a long day for the crew, and they were heading home. A navigator was aboard who was not a crew member. He knew there was a crew bunk in the aircraft and planned to use it on this leg of the flight. When he got to the bunk, he saw several cardboard boxes on the bed. He began to move them to the aircraft floor and was amazed at the heavy weight of these small boxes. He opened one and found compact bricks inside. He took one brick and then curled up for a nap. Getting back to Saigon, the crew departed the aircraft, mission complete.

Three days later, the navigator took the brick he had removed to the Office of Special Investigation office at Tan Son Nhut. They identified that brick as being cocaine. That day they conducted a raid on the hooch rooms of both Fleener and Davis. They found the boxes in Davis's room, arrested and charged both pilots with transporting drugs for profit. The charges became public. The media interest intensified.

This was a trial with twists and turns. The night before the court-martial was to begin, someone broke into the OSI office and stole all the boxes of cocaine. That left the prosecutors with only photographs and witness testimony as evidence. That led to one humorous challenge by the defense. The witnesses said the bricks all were stamped with the symbol 999, the symbol used for cocaine. The defense challenged that by saying, "Are you sure it wasn't 666?" The defense position was the pilots had no idea the boxes were on the aircraft. But the question as to how they got into Davis's room couldn't be answered. The trial lasted five days, and both Fleener and Davis were found guilty.

Chief of 7th Air Force Media Branch

Now I was back to being Chief of Media in my one-room office. My assessment was that we were fairly useful to the media, despite restrictions imposed. The networks (U.S. and other nations) delivered all news film to this office. From here, it went aboard the nightly flight from Tan Son Nhut AB to the nearest satellite uplink in Hong Kong. The film came in orange grapefruit sacks labeled by networks. My sergeants would drive the film to the aircraft, and the crew took it from there. Basically, any news footage from Viet Nam in the U.S. came through my office. Viet Nam was the first televised war, and we were keenly aware of our mission to get network footage from Saigon to the satellite uplink in Hong Kong. The aircraft for this mission was an executive T-39 Saberliner normally used for distinguished visitors such as congressmen and very senior officers. The aircraft identification was Scatback.

One trial effort that did not do well was giving a weekly press update at the 7th AF commander's staff meeting. We had access to most major papers in the U.S. as they were provided to the base library. My office began collecting the old copies, as they would be thrown out after being in the library after more than two days. Since this was a visual presentation at the staff meeting, we focused on explaining how the war was being viewed at home by showing political cartoons. My sensing in doing this was to give the staff a look at how media impacted our mission – and very little of it was good. It wasn't warm and fuzzy. That approach died after about 30 days of presentations and went down in my 'nice try' historical file.

I was also involved with planning and executing many on-the-record and off-the-record press conferences for 7th Air Force, President Nixon's fact-finding group of government leaders led by Presidential Communications Director Herb Klein, Secretary of State William P. Rogers, and numerous groups of senators and congressmen.

We did get requests from the wartime press corps. One of note for me came from Steve Bell, then the ABC bureau chief in Saigon. He asked me for a photo of Angkor Wat in Cambodia, which was becoming a hot news location. (Steve had been news director of one of the Omaha TV stations for which we shot new film for while at Lincoln AFB.) I went to our photo-reconnaissance office and asked if they had any shots of this historic location. They did. But all were marked classified confidential. I asked what was classified in the photo, and they told me nothing was. It turned out the classification markings were for convenience, not secrecy. It was easier to handle large batches of reconnaissance film with a batch classification at the highest level on the film than to identify each photo. I noticed that the 'Confidential' markings on the photo were all in the margins. So I took the copy to a cutting board in my office and removed the markings. I then took it to the Air France office and had them stamp the back of photo 'Photo Courtesy Air France' – then gave it to Steve.

Another weird occasion was when an accredited foreign newsgroup was making a commercial recording of the sounds of war. He wanted to go out to the runway at night when things were very quiet and capture the pastoral sounds of the frogs and crickets. This peace would then be punctuated by the blast of an F-4 Phantom jet hitting the afterburner on takeoff. Great! Can do! This was a job for my sergeant who delivered the news film on the flight line every night. But as fate would have it, he missed a checkpoint in the dark, and as they were parking to set up, they were surrounded by flashing red lights on armored vehicles with machine guns.

A bunch of combat air police jumped out and demanded to know what this group was doing. My sergeant was reported as stammering, "We are, are, are out here to tape record the sounds of crickets and frogs and jets taking off…" The lead combat cop then asked, "Are you from 7th" Air Force?" My guy said he was – and the combat cop said, "It's a strange war," and the group disappeared again into the night.

I got the job of being an escort for an artist who was documenting the Air Force in Viet Nam. Miriam Schottland was associated with the New York Society of Illustrators. Along with artists in the same organization in Chicago and Los Angeles, they donated paintings to the Air Force Art Program annually. The purpose of the program was to incorporate the language of art to show the actions and deeds of Air Force people in ways that words alone could not tell. Radio and TV had a shelf life of interest in terms of hours, newspapers by days and magazines by months. Art is permanent.

We had met when I was at Sewart AFB flying C-130s. She visited the base to fly on a low-level training flight over parts of Kentucky, Tennessee, and Alabama under the Air Force Art program.

Now she had an opportunity to fly with Vietnamese Air Force Major Nguyen Quoc Hung, vice commander of the VNAFs 23 Tactical Wing at Bien Hoa AB in a two-seat combat F-5 based nearby. She had met Major Hung during an Air Force Art visit to Williams AFB, Arizona, in 1967, where he received his F-5 Skosh Tiger flying training. (His sister was on my staff as a secretary in *Combat News*).

Everything was fine and normal on this combat mission until they returned to the base. It was the major's 'fini' flight – the final flight he would take in that assignment. On landing, he was met by base fire trucks with sirens blaring. They got out of the jet and were immediately hosed down by the firemen. She got soaked. But being a good trooper, she went back to the aircraft, took out a dry flight suit, stripped down to bra and panties, and put on the dry flight suit. The maintenance crew went nuts seeing an attractive 'round eye' change her outfit exclaiming, "I just had three air bursts and a rim job."

Chief 7AF Combat News

I was barely in month three of this assignment when I changed jobs and became head of Combat News for 7th AF. This was the center of information production at 7AF. I had a newsroom with 20 Air Force professional writers, photographers, and broadcast specialists. We produced lots of features that were disseminated to targeted media – much of it hometown-based. (Capt. Jim Reinhart was responsible for electronic news and Capt. Bob Hyatt was in charge of print. Bob was the first public affairs officer to obtain a Master's Degree in polling. This was his first assignment after graduating from Southern Illinois University.) Everything we produced had to be cleared at MACV before releasing. We got a lot of help from the office that was now being run by MSgt. Chuck Wills, the leader of my enlisted staff at Sewart AFB.

Also helpful was that Col. Jerry Dalton was now executive officer to the head of the MACV Information office. Major Randy Randolph, my first crew navigator at Lincoln AFB, was now commander of the 834th Air Division office at Tan son Nhut. Randy spent a lot of time when we had 'booze-burger' time at 7th AF during 5–7p.m., before we would adjourn to the Officers' Club for an evening of entertainment.

One night at the club, we had a group of attractive female Australian musicians. Our table was right next to their makeshift dressing room. It was just the corner of the dining room with dividers made of strips of plastic to provide privacy. While the group was singing and the dressing room was empty, one of our young, shy lieutenants, Bob Hyatt, grabbed a rather large red brassiere from a makeup table. The next day early, he mounted it above his desk at Combat News. His stock really jumped with the enlisted staff.

Most of the club entertainment was from Asian groups. They did well with American pop music, including singing the words – although with unique accents. For example, two popular songs were *Lolling down the Liver* and the *Gleen Gleen Glass of Home* as they couldn't pronounce the letter 'r.'.

As the junior officer at 7th AF, Bob got stuck being responsible for one of the buildings in the headquarters complex.
It happened to be the communal bathroom. But he was
forced to sign for it and thereby was responsible for anything missing. The building had always been open 24 hours
a day. He decided that since he couldn't monitor coming
and goings day and night, he would lock it at 11 p.m.
nightly and open it again at 7 a.m. The door lock was constantly being broken by those whose urgency outweighed
finding another location. Each morning Bob would duti-
fully report a break-in at his building now known as the
Hyatt House. The security police would have to investi-
gate. And this led to the following discussion:

Investigator: "Do you think anything was taken?"

Capt. Hyatt: "Yeah – probably a shit."

Many evenings were spent at the Vietnamese Air Force Officers' Club where the treat was Shrimp Noodle Soup. A
bowl was a full meal. Bar time was at an Army club made
from old railroad cars where we learned to drink wine we
knew as Peanut War – better known as Pinot Noir. On base,
the favorite was the Korean-operated Mexican Restaurant.

Saga of TSgt Tommy Rowe – 7th AF Public Affairs NCO Elephant Hunter and Tenacious Father

This sidebar story should have become a book or a movie.
TSgt. Tommy Rowe was the non-commissioned officer in
the Media Branch of my original office when I got to Tan

Son Nhut AB in Saigon. It was his third tour of duty in Viet Nam. The first two were as a soldier in the U.S. Army. He was unusual in this regard as the normal assignment policy was to limit assignments to Viet Nam to two tours. He got around that restriction by separating from the Army and then enlisting in the Air Force.

His first assignment in Viet Nam was from January through December 1962, assigned as an Army Security Agency direction finder plotter with the 3rd Radio Research Unit housed in an empty warehouse at Saigon Airport. According to the Southeast Asia ASA Veterans Association 'Old Spooks & Spies' website, the 92-man unit were required to wear civilian clothing and use U.S. Passports for identification.

His second tour of duty in Viet Nam began August 31, 1966, as a public information specialist with the 25th Infantry Division in Cu Chi. The very next day, he was given the 'news beat' of the 1st Battalion of the Division. He was taking part in a search and destroy mission when the armored personnel carrier he was riding in hit a mine, causing minor injuries that caused him to limp for a few days. He was pulled from field duty and assigned media liaison duties working with the Saigon international press corps. He extended his assignment making his return date August 1968.

His third tour of duty in Vietnam was with 7th Air Force assigned to the Public Information Division at Tan Son Nhut Air Base in Saigon in 1970. Tom really knew his way around the city. He was the driver for the director and deputy director of Public Information, and one of the guys who delivered the network news film on the Scatback flights to Hong Kong. Tom was also an elephant hunter that the senior staff called upon many times.

Elephant hunting in Saigon is a bit different. Elephants were a hot item. Tom knew where to get them and have them delivered safely to anywhere in the U.S. These were the porcelain elephants that in the 1970s were common decorations in homes throughout the U.S. Tom's reputation of being a top-notch elephant-hunter even reached to the highest level in Washington, D.C. The Secretary of State, Henry Kissinger, asked Tom to send a pair of porcelain elephants to movie star Jill St. John in Hollywood. The neat thing about mailing an elephant is that you never wrap it. Just stick a mailing label on its back. Everyone could see it was fragile, so they were handled with care in shipping. By the end of 1970, Tom lost count of the number of elephants he had shipped to dignitaries and senior officers in the U.S.

The second and most important factor for Tom involved becoming a father during his second assignment to Viet Nam. His girlfriend Tuyet (Le Ngoc Lan) gave birth to his daughter on February 6, 1968, in Saigon. The little girl was being raised by her grandmother. Since Tom was not married, the daughter was not a military dependent. The U.S. government rules did not allow the use of government transportation of persons in this status. Tom tried everything he could to get a Department of Immigration exception. When I arrived, it was still his top priority and the real reason for his being in Viet Nam for a third tour of duty.

The breakthrough came when Pearl Buck, the famous author, heard about Tom's story. She used her clout to get nearly all of Washington involved, including Congress and political bigwigs. It worked. Tom got a one-time exception to grant his daughter entry into the U.S. and an exception to allow the daughter to fly as a military dependent on military aircraft. There was still one hurdle. The daughter had to pass Viet Nam emigration checks at the Tan Son Nhut Airport. With a little help from the U.S. Embassy, that show stopper was avoided. Tom and his daughter were taken in a U.S. Embassy vehicle directly to the aircraft – bypassing emigration checks.

Tom and his daughter eventually settled in San Jose, California, where Tom earned his Bachelor's degree and his Master's degree at San Jose State University. It is where his daughter grew up, married and became a mother of three Californian daughters. Tom, in later years, became a lecturer on Viet Nam at San Jose State and later Western Civilization classes at universities in his home state of Massachusetts before finally retiring in Salt Lake City, Utah.

HQ MACV – Tan Son Nhut AB – Saigon September 1970 – April 1971

And then that 3-month adventure ended. I was transferred to a compound away to HQ Military Assistance Command Viet Nam. I became the Air Briefer at the 'Five o'clock Follies,' as the daily press briefing in downtown Saigon was known. That label was attributed to Richard Pyle, one of the Associated Press Saigon Bureau Chiefs during the war.

He described the briefings as "the longest-playing tragi-comedy in southwest Asia's theater of the absurd."

I was one of four briefers who took the stage at 4 p.m. each day at the Rex Hotel in downtown Saigon. The others were spokesmen for our State Department, the U.S. Army, and the U.S. Navy as experts on policy, the air war, the ground war, and the black water war on the rivers of Viet Nam.

The Viet Nam War was run by the State Department, not the Department of Defense. The daily press briefing was held in a 200-seat auditorium on the ground floor of a former hotel. The military briefers came to work around 5 a.m. and would go directly to the war room and find out what had happened overnight. We would then return to the office and generate our first cut for (1) our presentations that afternoon and (2) our list of questions and answers we thought might come up. The Q&As were in a thick 3-ring notebook that we could refer to on stage if we needed backup information to answer questions. Our deadline was 11 a.m. Saigon time. Our individual briefing and Q&As would then go to the Department of Defense and State Department in Washington for final clearance.

At that time, 450 news correspondents were 'accredited' by the US Embassy in Saigon. Being accredited brought support privileges to use military facilities, access to flights on military aircraft, and for the television networks a daily flight to Hong Kong to deliver news film to be sent by satellite to the U.S. My assessment was about 40 reporters attended the daily Five O'clock Follies with about 20 representing U.S. media.

The Rex Hotel – Site of the Five O'clock Follies

Media coverage was open and unrestricted without censorship. Politically, the Washington policy was to rely on reporters and bureau chiefs' judgement and sense in place of censorship. The impetus for this policy was because there was no volunteer military – it was an era where the draft was relied upon for maintaining desired force levels. Open coverage was viewed as being critical to retaining public support for the draft. The Viet Nam War was a time of casual intimacy between soldiers and reporters.

My golden moment was when I actually gave an answer on the fly, without referring to the Q&A book or guidance, and the one I had the most fun answering. It was the day when we were finally cleared by State Department to announce North Vietnamese Army SAM missiles firings as part of our briefing. As luck would have, it the first SAM (Surface to Air missile) firing after that decision was at a 0-2 Super Skymaster. This aircraft were used to spot and report enemy movements and was flown by forward air controllers (FACs). It was a unique aircraft as it had a prop engine in the front and another at the rear. Their mission was to fly over the same area day by day to become familiar with every foot of terrain. FACs flew low and slow and would use smoke grenades or smoke rockets to mark targets for fast-flying fighter pilots.

The Air Force O-2 Super Skymaster aircraft

State Department approved the following release: "An Air Force 0-2 aircraft flying near the DMZ was fired at by a SAM missile. Both the aircraft and pilot returned safely." End of story. The NBC bureau chief, a news director in a Seattle affiliate, stuck up his hand and said: "Tom, did the aircraft fire back?" I paused dumbfounded, as the 0-2 has no armament. It was a bug smasher – one step up from a Piper Cub. The job of 0-2 was to drop leaflets or deploy speakers. But I recovered to respond, "No – but I have an unconfirmed report that the pilot threw a hand grenade, and it landed 15 miles short."

The long history of government management of media relations by 1970 had taken its toll with both the media and us in media relations. As public information professionals, our only currency was being truthful and accurate. It was a tough tightrope. Those in military public affairs became limited in our responses by using selective truths. We had the briefing book for expansion of responses, but it was only useful if a media representative asked the right question. It was a game both sides understood well. To our professional pride, we were perceived as remaining dedicated to providing evenly balanced information.

The war in 1970 was much different from when I flew combat missions from 1965–1969. It was very apparent that we were at the beginning of a period for drawdown. The fatigue of war, now with drug and morale problems, was escalating antagonism within the military and the American public. The generals in the logistic world began to focus on how to get valuable things out of Viet Nam and back to supply centers in the U.S.

In January 1970, I got my weeklong R&R (Rest and Relaxation) respite. We had several choices for a sanity break location away from the war zone. Probably the most popular was in Hawaii that allowed reunions with spouses. Elaine decided to forgo this opportunity, due to a commitment from her nursing work and not wanting to be away from the kids for a week. So I elected to go to Australia. We flew on commercial contract flights at government expense from Saigon. It is one hell of a long haul. We had to stop in Darwin on the northwest coast to refuel. January is full summer in Australia, and Darwin was miserably hot and muggy. Then we boarded for an equally long flight to get to Sydney. And Sydney turned out to be perfect for everything.

On clearing customs, we checked in at a U.S. military assistance office to get a place to stay and tickets for events and transportation. I selected a beautiful townhome on the high bluffs with a terrace overlooking the Sydney Harbor and tons of sailboats, the famous 'clothes hanger' bridge and the city skyline featuring the Sydney Opera Hall. It was a whirlwind of beer, koala bears, the famous kangaroos, beaches, bay and river cruises, learning to throw boomerangs, feasting, concerts, and shopping. It was amazing how fast you can adjust to relaxation and fun after months of being stuck in a crazy, unnecessary war.

Lam Son 719 – The Incursion into Cambodia February 8 – March 24, 1971

This campaign was carried out by the Republic of Vietnam (South Viet Nam) armed forces into the Kingdom of Laos. The U.S.'s role in this effort was to provide logistical, aerial, and artillery support. U.S. ground forces were prohibited from entering Laos territory. I was tasked to be the senior officer for the MACV press camp at Quang Tri at the northern edge of the DMZ.

The camp became a beehive of activity assisting accredited news media with updates, transportation, living quarters, and communication links. As always, news film from all networks had to be transported to the satellite uplink facility in Hong Kong. Our office was in a building that was blocked to the North by a minefield. I often wondered if the planners were hoping some of the media might inadvertently stray into this area.

We did have one media casualty in the camp. Gloria Emerson of the *New York Times* went outside our building to the makeshift latrines. She discarded a lighted cigarette into the dug-out waste area, and it exploded. Gloria suffered serious burns and was not able to sit for weeks. (For health reasons, outhouse latrines were 'sanitized' by pouring gasoline into the pit.)

Award of Combat Bronze Star Medal

Col. Irv Breslauer, director of public affairs for 7th Air Force. awarded me the Bronze Star Medal at ceremonies at Tan Son Nhut on April 3, 1971. The citation read: "Major John T. Halbert distinguished himself by meritorious service as Chief, Media Liaison Division and Chief of Combat News Division consecutively, Directorate of Information, Headquarters Seventh Air Force, Republic of Viet Nam while engaged in support of air operations against an opposing armed force for April 5, 1970, through April 3, 1971. During this period, while exposed to extreme danger from hostile bombing and mortar attacks, Major Halbert established and maintained vital long-range programs in support of the United States Air Force information objectives in Southeast Asia. His vast journalistic experience and mature judgment were in producing professional releases for both public and internal media. Through his untiring efforts the quality of Air Force information products increased greatly. The exemplary leadership, personal endeavor and devotion to duty displayed by Major Halbert in this responsible position reflect great credit upon himself and the United States Air Force."

Republic of Viet Nam Armed Forces Honor Medal March 31, 1971

Lt. General Tran Van Mihn, Commander of the Vietnamese Air Force presented me the Republic of Viet Nam Armed Forces Honor Medal, First Class, on the stage of the 'Five O'clock Follies' in downtown Saigon on March 31, 1971. The award cited me for "Sincere cooperation and enthusiastic assistance provided to the Republic of Viet Nam Armed Forces."

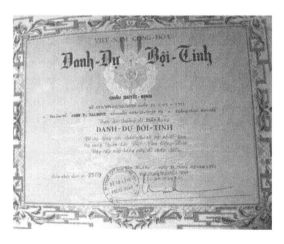

RVN Armed Forces Honor Medal, First Class

Also while on this assignment I became a command pilot on March 14, 1971, meaning I now had a star with a wreath on my pilot wings as I reached 15 years as a pilot and amassed more than 3,000 flying hours. (It was jokingly said the star was because you had a son in the service and the wreath was because your mother-in-law was discharged.)

Command Pilot Wings

Two weeks later, in April 1971, I actually boarded a commercial 'freedom flight' to San Francisco and onward to Tallahassee, Florida, where I would rejoin the family. It took all of 10 minutes to forget my year in Viet Nam. After arriving in California, I caught a non-stop flight to Atlanta, and from there, to Tallahassee where Elaine and the kids were waiting. (Basic rule of the South: If you die anywhere in the South, you have to go to Atlanta to transfer to heaven.)

Eglin AFB, Florida &
a Successful Failure
April 1971 – December 1972

The first item to accomplish at our new base was to find housing. In no time at all, we were living in military housing at 119-B Birch Circle on Eglin AFB. Our household goods arrived and our one story, 3-bedroom bungalow became our new home for Elaine, the kids and me on May 25, 1971. The kids went to on-base public schools. The transition was smooth.

After our reunion in Tallahassee in early April, I began my new job at Eglin while Elaine and the kids returned to Nashville to get everything ready to move to Eglin. We rented out our Nashville home, expecting to return after I retired from active duty on reaching the 20-years of service point. I was fully expecting that this would be my last military assignment.

Our house was one block from the Officers' Club on Choctawhatchee Bay. It included a swimming pool easily reached by the kids by walking through the backyard and not having to cross streets. It was just two blocks to the boat launch on Choctawhatchee Bay, and less than 20 minutes by boat to reach the pass and white sand beaches of Destin for access to the Gulf of Mexico. For Elaine, the big bonus was being less than three hours away from her family home in Colquitt, Georgia.

Just as we were getting settled, I got word that my paternal grandmother Mary Ethel Dillon Halbert had died at the Iowa Soldier's Home in Marshalltown, May 24, 1971. I made a quick trip back to Red Oak for her burial in the family plot at Evergreen Cemetery. She was my last remaining grandparent.

As background, Eglin Air Base is the largest military base in the world, encompassing 640 square miles. Historically it was part of a National Forest until the outbreak of WWII, when a proving ground for aircraft armament was established. The U.S. Forest Service ceded over 340,000 acres of the Choctawhatchee National Forest to the War Department on 18 October, 1940. When the Halbert family arrived, Eglin was a massive complex with several diversified organizations and three major airfields serving Army, Navy, and Air Force units.

The public affairs shop I inherited at Eglin was unusual. Eglin was a massive base loaded with lots of diversified major organizations. While I was in Viet Nam, the Pentagon public affairs planners led by Col. Clay Leyser (my first boss at 7AF in Viet Nam) were attempting to create a single public affairs office for the base. The effort failed. However, the Tactical Air Command at Langley AFB, Virginia, saw merit in consolidation. I ended up as head of the TAC Public Affairs Office – the first (*and only*) consolidated office in the Air Force. I suspect that Colonel Leyser picked me for this position because he knew my capabilities and me.

The success of the consolidation became widely known and applauded locally and throughout the Air Force Public Affairs world. It worked, and not one commander of the units involved ever made an effort to dissemble the consolidation. But shortly after I left, the consolidation died and has never been tried again. The beauty of the consolidation was we could set our own agenda. When working with four commanders, each did not get involved with specific direction. Each thought we were working for the other commander. The biggest problem was ensuring one of the officers attended daily staff meetings held by each commander.

I was assigned on paper as the Chief of Public Information for the USAF Special Operations Command (SOF). The unit history goes back to WWII. The Air Commandos flew missions from CBI (China, Burma, India) bases over the hump. Brig. General James Knight, a very sharp, savvy and modest leader, would write my efficiency report. He had an 'I love me' room, where artifacts and awards are displayed, normally at home. But General Knight chose his office bathroom to display his 'I love me' mementos.

My responsibilities expanded with the consolidation. I was now responsible for public affairs programs for SOF and its subordinate units at nearby Hurlburt AFB and with Air Force Reserve bases throughout the United States and also those of the TAC Air Warfare Center, the 33rd TAC Fighter Wing, the 919th Special Operations Group at Duke Field on the Eglin complex.

My office staff consisted of three other officers (Captain Bob Carroll, Captain Karen Miller and 1st Lieutenant Jack Hesse), two enlisted men, and a secretary. The base public affairs office had the responsibility of the base newspaper. My public affairs sergeant was the beat reporter for providing input to the base paper. We had authority for media interface for our units and community relations programs. We did coordinate all our initiatives with Air Force System Command base public affairs office run by Major Dick Rapp.

Under this umbrella, we supervised open houses attended by 60,000 annually at Eglin and Hurlburt, a POW/MIA Jumpfest viewed by another 10,000, and placing six exhibits at the Pensacola Interstate Fair attended by 100,000 visitors. We conducted a news release program to more than 220 regional and local media outlets.

It was at a June 17, 1971, staff meeting when my boss, Brig. General James Knight said I was "out of uniform," removed my Major insignia, and replaced them with Lt. Colonel silver oak leaves.

My most welcome accolade and value of the consolidation initiative during this assignment came from Colonel Richard Henry, the Commander of the 33rd TAC Fighter Wing that had the motto "Our Mission is to Fly and Fight." His previous office of one officer and one airman had been eliminated as a result of the consolidation. He submitted an attachment to my annual efficiency report that cited admirable support to his organization. His narrative said;

"Lt . Colonel Halbert's initiative, ingenuity and aggressive support through the Consolidated Information Office has brought greater talent to bear in support of the wing information program than was heretofore possible. It has been an effort that benefited my command and its working relationship with the Air Force System Command in the Eglin AFB complex."

One embarrassing event I won't forget is when I wandered into the Officers' Club one Saturday noon, I noted my secretary having lunch with two men. She asked me over and introduced me to her guests. She told them about the many attempts I had made to get her promoted. Because I had been totally unsuccessful and was not happy about it, I blurted out how stupid the personnel system was. She blanched and introduced me to the head of civilian personnel at Eglin and his boss who was head of civilian personnel for the Air Force System Command. All I could think to say was, "See what I mean," and disappear. One month later her promotion was approved.

Special Operations Force (Air Commando)

The Special Operations Force (SOF) was an Air Force organization like the Army's Green Berets or the Navy Seals. Much of what we did was in concert with the Green Berets and Seals and remains classified. We could talk about anything other than operations. The mission was to maintain a quick reaction force using unconventional warfare, counterinsurgency, psychological activities, and civic actions at trouble spots worldwide. We were active in Central and South America, Europe, Africa, and the Middle East. We were also charged with developing combat tactics for numerous combat aircraft and conducted flight training for Air Force and foreign combat crews. (My C-130 training for dropping 20,000-pound bombs in Viet Nam was conducted by SOF.)

SOF was considered a major Air Force command. So, I had supervision responsibilities with information offices at Hurlburt AFB, Florida; England AFB, Louisiana; and another 12 Air Force Reserve bases across the United States.

SOF also trained personnel from Bolivia, Costa Rica, Ecuador, El Salvador, Ethiopia, Guatemala, Iran, Greece, Saudi Arabia, Mali, Nicaragua, the Republic of the Congo, Thailand, the Dominican Republic, and the Republic of Viet Nam. We frequently participated in tactical exercises in the U.S. and foreign nations, mercy missions and humanitarian flights. These missions were not restricted from being acknowledged and publicized. One such operation was our involvement using C-123 aircraft to airdrop sterile screwworm flies in Puerto Rico and the Virgin Islands. This was to eradicate the insects for the benefit of the cattle industry.

One operation in Viet Nam that did become public knowledge was Operation Ivory Coast, the attempted POW rescue from Son Tay prison in North Vietnam. They were extensively trained and rehearsed at Eglin Air Force Base. At the same time, planning and intelligence gathering continued from 25 May to 20 November 1970. The mission failed when it was found during the Son Tay raid that all the prisoners had been previously moved to another camp just hours before.

Tactical Air Warfare Center

Captain Bob Carroll was still at Eglin as TAWC public affairs officer when the consolidation was created. So it made sense Bob would continue to be the primary contact with TAWC and attend their staff meetings. He already had an excellent relationship with Maj. General Dick Cattledge, who commanded this organization.

TAWC's mission was to conduct operational tests and evaluations of new weapons as they were introduced for use by tactical squadrons. By 1971 it expanded to include new programs that dealt with night operations, improved tactical communications, and weapons systems designed to destroy enemy supply lines and troop movements. In 1971, TAWC absorbed the mission of the tactical airlift and tactical reconnaissance centers. It became the Air Force focal point for tactical airlift, reconnaissance, and special operations.

33rd TAC Fighter Wing

The 33rd Tactical Fighter Wing was commanded by Col. Richard Henry and flew F-4 Phantoms. The mission was to be available for worldwide deployment in air superiority and ground support roles. It was the only combat organization at this huge Air Force System Command complex. Also assigned for maintenance support was the 4453rd TTS (T) until it was transferred April 12, 1971, to the Tactical Air Warfare Center at Eglin AFB, Florida.

919th Special Operations Group

The 919 SOG flying C-130 Hercules was located about five miles south of Crestview and 20 miles from Eglin main at Eglin AFB Auxiliary Field No. 3 (Duke Field) and is the only special operations wing in the Air Force Reserve Command (AFRC). Their public information officer was Mr. Ralph Francis, who attended my staff meetings.

Super Bowl VI – Tulane Stadium, New Orleans Dallas Cowboys vs. Miami Dolphins

Super Bowl VI was the championship game between the National Football Conference (NFC) champion Dallas Cowboys and the American Football Conference (AFC) champion Miami Dolphins to decide the National Football League (NFL) champion for the 1971 season. The Cowboys defeated the Dolphins by 24–3 to win their first Super Bowl. The game was played on January 16, 1972, at Tulane Stadium in New Orleans, Louisiana. It was the second time the Super Bowl was played in that city. Despite the southerly location, it was unseasonably cold at game time. The kickoff air temperature was 24° F, making this the coldest Super Bowl ever played in an open-air stadium.

I was tasked to assist network camera crews covering the game, while ensuring they knew where and when the Air Force F-4 Phantom Missing Man formation flyover was timed to happen. It was at the end of the National Anthem at the start of the game. It was a tough assignment. I had to stay in a hotel in the French Quarter and had to be in place three days before the game. I was in the stadium with the camera crews as they set up for game coverage giving the directors in trailers outside the stadium ideas for camera angles. It was also practice time for the halftime show that featured the Kilgore Rangerettes. The weather pre-game was warm and comfortable.

The Kilgore Rangerettes Precision Dance Team

The Rangerettes were lifesavers during the game. After my stadium top vantage for the flyover, I was able to huddle with the Rangerettes during the game to keep from freezing.

North Florida Press Club

The North Florida Press Club was a professional organization encompassing Central Time Florida communities. (All of Florida, except the Northwest corner, is on Eastern Time. Panama City to Pensacola is on Central Time.) In 1971, I was elected Vice President of the North Florida Press Club, a position I held until my transfer to the Pentagon.

Secretary of the Air Force – Office of Information
December 1972 – July 1975

During a visit by Air Force Director of Information Major General Robert Ginsberg to Eglin, I was invited to dinner at the Officers' Club with him. I was wary and did everything I could to make a bad impression using everything but a lampshade on my head. But it was all for naught. He advised me I would be joining his staff in the Pentagon as Chief of the Civil Branch. Even today, you can probably find heel marks on the highways from North Florida to Washington, D.C.

Decision Time II – What Now

At this time in my career, I was planning to retire from the Air Force and was focused on returning to Nashville. I would be eligible for retirement in 1975 when I reached the 20-years of active duty point. We were also concerned about giving our kids a more solid sense of place. So, we agreed that the family should return to our home at Nashville. I would go to Washington unaccompanied. I settled into an apartment at the Crystal House in Arlington, Virginia. The Pentagon was close by, and I frequently used my bicycle for transportation to my office.

My new job was Chief of the Civil Branch in the Community Relations Division of the Office of Public Affairs assigned to the Secretary of the Air Force. I arrived just as my branch had a 100 percent turnover, a complete lack of continuity, and had to 're-invent the wheel.' I knew I was responsible for liaison with national organizations, and responding to letters to the Air Force on a wide basis, including the hot issues of the day. These included the Air Force using Beagle dogs as laboratory animals, Unidentified Flying Objects, the fur used on parkas and many, many others.

Our primary liaison responsibilities involved 28 national aerospace organizations, 16 national defense organizations, and four Society of Illustrators groups who were part of the Air Force Art Program. Our national organization interest was ensuring appropriate cooperative support was provided. Some of those organizations were the Air Force Association, the American Legion, The Veterans of Foreign Wars, the Boy Scouts of America, Girl Scouts of America and tons of others. Additionally, we arranged for judges for the National Science Fair and Military Wife of the Year programs.

My office included four captains (Fred Gebler, Doug Jacobson, Richard Sheffield and Angelo Cerchione) and Terri Sprinkle as secretary. It was a great team. We didn't have an officers' club nearby, but many evenings we got together socially at Matt Kane's Irish Bar off Thomas Circle. Another occasion was my annual silent 4th of July fireworks party in my high-rise Crystal City apartment. I had a great view of the mall, but sealed windows blocked the city noise. That is why it became known as the silent 4th of July party.

Angelo was a hoot. Brilliant but blunt. He held two advanced degrees, one for a hot button item – environmental issues. He was the go-to guy on environmental issue after issue. One time, during a briefing at the four-star level, he was in the back of the room. As a colonel was going through his rehearsed slide presentation, lights dimmed, and Angelo exploded, loudly saying, "You're using the rain coat approach!" With that, the briefing stopped, lights came up, and Angelo went on to say, "You know, you meet a girl, you like her, you invite her on dates, and with time, that may lead somewhere. But you guys are working this like you are wearing raincoats, and opening them up full frontal and expecting to score!" It was another of the calls I got from my front office, "Halbert, get up here."

But Angelo's expertise resulted in save after save to bring enlightened sensing to Air Force initiatives. At Tinker AFB in Oklahoma City, he was one of the leaders in successfully getting more than 1,000 homes removed from the end of a runway. These were built by developers in a normally clear zone. His Tinker project success brought him to the prominent role he would play in the late 1970s as an environmental leader.

We all worked the flood of requests and responsibilities we were charged with and to create a record of continuity for our replacements. The most important addition to the office was a Wang 1200. It allowed Terri to type text on a conventional IBM electric keyboard. When the return key was pressed, the line of text was stored on a cassette tape. One cassette held roughly 20 pages of text, and could be 'played back.' The stored text could also be edited, using keys to Insert or Delete. This device's labor and cost savings were immediate and remarkable: pages of text no longer had to be retyped to correct simple errors, and projects could be worked on, stored, and then retrieved for use later on.

The continuity issue was solved along with the drudge work involved in the coordination process. This was when all paper products were typed with original and carbon copies. Approval levels often went through five levels of staff clearance. Approval was indicated by initialing. (This was where the bureaucratic excuse came about when things went wrong after being approved· "Just because I initialed it does mean I understood it.") Any change at any level required retyping the entire product. The Wang created the first 'computer-like' capability to make corrections, additions or deletions. Wow! For our office, this was as important as the first flight of an aircraft at Kitty Hawk. We became an office with visitors from all over the building who wanted to see our secretaries' Wang.

Since much of our activities resulted from national organization calendars, for example, national conventions. The Wang provided us with a way to just make slight edits to policy letters and other guidance. No more tied to old-fashioned typewriter creations.

Letters from individuals seeking Air Force information came to our office. We gleaned out and forwarded many to other agencies such as Air Force Recruiting. We got another large bunch that we could provide a Wang response to. And we had some that were controversial.

The biggest issue that caused more than 1,000 irate responses resulted when Wisconsin Congressman Les Aspin's press release was made just as the July 4th holiday happened. Aspin charged the Air Force with killing Snoopy due to a laboratory animal test. Because of the holiday, he had a three-day head start on publicity before we could begin to respond. I became the designated response letter signer. Our overly coordinated response was created by committee to 'explain' the test.

In a nutshell, shortly before the test began, a civilian aircraft crashed at Meigs Field in Chicago. All passengers survived the crash, but all lost their lives from fumes from burning seats. That triggered concern by the Air Force, because we also fly military passengers in our aircraft. The test was set up at Wright-Patterson AFB. It involved determining what materials could be used in passenger seats that would not result in asphyxiation death from burning seat coverings. The Air Force response was that Beagles were selected. They were the largest group of animals in puppy mills that did not find buyers and were to be exterminated. They also were the cheapest option. Since it was Beagles, Les Aspin related them to Snoopy.

I got responses back to our committee response. Not unexpected. But the one I liked best was from a woman who sent my letter back with a magic marker response saying, "What manner of mongrel whelped you?" I answered her by writing, "I am a public servant and cannot do anything legally to respond. However, you may want to know that I have sent a copy to my mother, and you may hear from her lawyer."

The hands-down winner of subjects was about UFOs. My office was the keeper of all the independent investigations by the National Academy of Science and Project Blue Book that was closed in 1968. Synopsis of the NAS investigation were: (1) no UFO reported, investigated, and evaluated by the Air Force has ever given any indication of threat to our national security; (2) there has been no evidence submitted to or discovered by the Air Force that sightings categorized as 'unidentified' represent technological developments or principles beyond the range of present-day scientific knowledge; and (3) there has been no evidence indicating that sightings categorized as 'unidentified' are extraterrestrial vehicles. Our bottom line was the Air Force has never stated that UFOs are not real. We have said there has been no identified threat from UFOs. We responded that if individuals have concerns, they should notify local authorities, scientific organizations, or universities.

Another big hit was the wolf fur in parkas used in Arctic locations. Wolf fur had been in use since World War II. But this was the era of demonstrations about women wearing furs. This issue drew hundreds of letters but eventually subsided after synthetic fur was used on the hoods. As a result, only hoods for these parkas made before 1972 have real fur.

For unknown reasons, our five-drawer safes became the home for rocks brought back from the moon. We had no idea how we became the keepers of these rocks. When I left in 1975, the rocks were still in our safe and all attempts to find a proper home for them failed.

This was a great assignment for me. Most of the interface with those in charge of national organizations was in their offices in Washington or lunch meetings. These took place at Maison Blanche across the street from the White House, or other well-known restaurants in Georgetown or the Potomac River Harbor area.

White House MX Missile Planning Committee

Between 1972 and 1979, the Air Force evaluated 40 schemes for the placement of the MX missile. I was chosen as the Air Force representative on the original White House public affairs planning team for gaining public and congressional support for this third-generation ICBM.

It also never took flight, even after President Carter threw his support for full-scale development in June 1979. Congress never liked the concept, and finally, the concept died in 1991. It was killed by President George Bush, citing the collapse of the Soviet Union and shrinking budgets. We realized Congressional support was lacking and even began giving a missile the nickname 'Congressman,' providing a sense it would never work.

Operation Homecoming

Starting on February 12, 1973, and continuing until March 29, the North Vietnamese gave up their most prized war trophies, American prisoners of war, one planeload at a time. The first of the C-141s – which became known as 'Hanoi Taxis' – was a medical evacuation for the wounded, crippled, and sick. The worst cases were carried aboard on stretchers. The passenger lists for the ensuing flights out of Hanoi's Gia Lam Airport always started with the man who had been imprisoned the longest. First in, first out.

When the final freedom flight had touched down at Clark Air Base in the Philippines, 590 men were now former POWs. A German nurse, captured during the Tet Offensive, was the only woman. The vast majority were captured after aircraft crashes; almost 500 were pilots and aircrew. By service branch, 325 were Air Force, 138 Navy, 77 Army, and 26 Marines. There were 25 civilians.

I was tasked to man the DoD pressroom during this period on the midnight shift. It was the one location in the Pentagon that had real-time reports from the cockpits of the freedom flight aircraft while they were on the ground in North Viet Nam. The only person I can recall who came to the newsroom that late at night was Secretary of Defense Elliott Richardson. He was informal and relaxed, with his feet on the desk, as we both listened to the live reports.

Aviation/Space Writers Tribute
May 12, 1974

The AWA presented a certificate of excellence of public affairs activities as a special tribute to the men and women of the Armed Forces who were involved in Operation Homecoming. Lt. General Chappie James, who was Principal Deputy Assistant Secretary of Defense, presented my certificate to me.

Air Force Association Presidential Award September 16, 1974

This award was presented to me at the Air Force Association 1974 national convention at the Sheraton-Park Hotel in Washington by AFA President Joe Shosid. At the ceremony, President Shosid told those attending the award that was to recognize, "The one person in a support role that made the 28th Annual Convention has to be Tom Halbert." He added: "The big thing about Tom is that he doesn't get shook up. And that is the higher tribute than any I could pay you. Of course, some people don't get shook up because they don't understand the problem. You do, and then you go and do something about it."

Air Force Association National President Award Presentation to Lt. Colonel Halbert at AFA National Convention at Sheraton Park Hotel in Washington, D.C.

Death of my Mother Mary Pilkington Halbert March 24, 1975

I was at the annual Air Force Association's Iron Gate Ball in New York City when I got a call from Liz Kentopp. My mother was hospitalized and was not expected to survive. She had been physically restricted for years with emphysema, and her oxygen tanks could no longer assist her.

I left the event and caught a commercial flight to Omaha, where Liz met me, and we went to the hospital. It was our last discussion together. She died that night – March 24, 1975. Liz was a big help and together we arranged for services in Omaha for her University friends and for burial in Red Oak. (Liz remained in Omaha until her death on December 13, 2008.)

The American University – Kogod School of Business Master's Degree in Public Relations – 1975

During my free-time evenings on my Pentagon assignment, I took advantage of the GI Bill and my previous 10 hours of graduate schooling from Boston University to complete my Master's Degree.

It was here that I was mentored by a giant in the world of Public Relations – Arthur V. Ciervo. Art at the time was head of public relations for Georgetown University. After I left Washington for my assignment in Germany, Art moved onto head public relations for Pennsylvania State

University. He eventually founded CUPRAP – a national College and University Public Relations and Associated Professional organization.

Art was on the leading edge as Public Relations changed. It moved from having the main task of sending out press releases and hoping to get a story or airtime, to a more thoughtful approach as primary advisors to leadership.

One approach he incorporated at Georgetown University was to create a contact book of all professors, including their names, phone numbers, and areas of special worldwide expertise. That gave editors and news department heads an instant expert to interview on hot topics of the day. He gained the university President and department heads' understanding and support to the project. This propelled Georgetown University as an authoritative leader recognized worldwide. He did this in a town where most media contact was micro-managed at multiple levels.

He involved us in real-world exercises, providing unique insight into the world of political communication. He opened doors of innovation that he was recognized for when he became a member of the Public Relations Society of America's Hall of Fame.

In classes, we learned and worked together in teams in areas where none of us had any previous expertise. He broke us into small working groups to work on real-world issues for real-world organizations. One of the group projects I was involved in was creating a television promotion campaign for the National Zoo. He directed my thesis that involved grassroots communication by the National Wildlife Federation.

My thesis project propelled me to understand how national organizations expanded their outreach in an era before the Internet, when the telephone was the most important tool in the toolbox. One surprise to me was how phone banks were so important and effective at the state level. It was an era where long-distance calls were expensive, and any call outside of a specific community required payment from the non profit's tight budget.

The workaround was effective and novel. Those making phone calls would just go to local state office buildings in the evening, when the only people present were cleaning teams. They would find an empty office, occupy a desk and make effective calls on 'watts-line' phones that had unlimited long-distance bulk service.

Following graduation, I now had another Union Card to use for job seeking. Over the years, I found that the only question on job applications was, "What is the highest grade level attained?" No one ever asked me what schools I attended or what my degree was in. It was a signal to me that the real interest on education levels was how much discipline you displayed, knowing 'we will train you our way anyway.' My Master's allowed me to be hired by the University of Maryland to teach journalism and public relations in the late 1970s, and become the senior civilian in Air Force Public Affairs from 1980 to 1987.

Uncontested Divorce June 26, 1975
Thelma Elaine Halbert v. John Thomas Halbert

In late March 1975, I drove to Andrews AFB Hospital in Maryland with extreme pain caused by gallstones. The operation involved in a 12-inch incision and a painful weeklong recovery. (Today, that operation is a 2-inch incision and a quick recovery time.) On the day I was released, I got a call from Tomajean. She told me she, Mike and Curtis were home alone. Their mother had moved out. I had no choice; I asked and got approval for emergency leave to go to Nashville to do what I could to get the family together again. Debra was on her own and living in nearby Murfreesboro.

It was an 18-hour drive from Arlington, Virginia, to Nashville. My doctor told me he could not agree to my going as, "If you are in an accident you won't survive." I had no choice and made the trip. When I got to 2740 Mossdale, the kids were there, but our bedroom furniture in the master bedroom was gone. I contacted Elaine the next day, and she told me she wanted a divorce and I could have the kids. I got a lawyer and filed for divorce.

The divorce was finalized by the Fourth Circuit Court of Davidson County, Tennessee (Halbert v. Halbert – File # 77669) on June 26, 1975. I was awarded custody of our three minor children (Tomajean, John Michael and Curtis Charles) with the "right to take them on assignments to such duty stations to which he made be ordered as an active duty military officer." We were directed to divide any proceeds from the sale of our home at 2740 Mossdale Drive in Nashville. Elaine was awarded our 1972 Plymouth. The court concurred with our already determined division of property goods. During the hearing the only objection raised was mine. I thought it unnecessary for Elaine to be required to make child support payments. My salary as an Air Force Lt. Colonel and a Command Pilot would not cause me any hardship in caring for my underage children.

I contacted my boss, Major General Guy Hairston, and asked for his support to have a transfer from Washington to anywhere I could get my kids with me. He was under pressure from the Commander of U.S. Air Force in Europe to send him a qualified deputy of director of information. So it turned out to be a win/win opportunity, and by July, we were all in Ramstein AB in southwest Germany. That ended my plan to retire that summer and return to Nashville.

The new Director of Information at Ramstein was Col. Gerry Hickman. We knew each other well. His wife Ann had been my instructor for being a ballet dancer in the Sugar Plum Fairy at the annual office Christmas party at Bolling AFB. He also was anxious for my joining his team.

I look back on this divorce and believe my decision to have an Air Force career was undoubtedly at the root of our breakup. Elaine spent 18 years of her life with a husband who was frequently not there. She was required to run the household when I was on alert, deployed, and the year-long separation to Viet Nam. Air Force divorce rates had been high for years because of this turmoil. She now was on her own and could rely on her profession as a nurse. We split amicably.

Now I was embroiled in getting orders to a new assignment, having household goods packed and shipped from Nashville and Washington, dividing the proceeds from the sale of our Nashville house, transferring our family car to Elaine, taking over my mother's older car, and shipping it by boat to Germany. Tomi had become an unwed mother, and that compounded getting her son on my travel orders. Got that done too, and Tomi, Mike, Curtis, and grandchild Christopher got ready to fly to Germany. Debi, who was already on her own, remained in Nashville.

HQ US Air Forces Europe
HQ Allied Air Forces Central Europe
July 1975 – August 1979

Once reaching Ramstein AB, my first order of business was finding a place for myself and my family of four to live. We originally stayed in two rooms in the Visiting Officers' Quarters. Cramped living. Colonel Hickman made sure I had help getting settled, and I began a search for rental housing in the Ramstein area. Then came a breakthrough. I was told there was a 3-bedroom apartment available in a high-rise building on the hill in Landstuhl with a commanding view of the base, the rural German landscape below, and the ruins of a castle next door.

We settled into Apt 3-2, Berliner Strasse, Landstuhl, Germany, a three-bedroom, two-bath 'home.' This was the center building of three high-rise apartment buildings. The one to the west housed British families assigned to Allied Air Forces Central Europe, while the one to the east housed U.S. enlisted families. The apartments were furnished by base housing at Ramstein. We had a wide selection of furnishing options. Here is where I ran into what became a prevalent theme of shock. The base housing staff was stunned that a divorced father had four kids being together.

Tomi, Mike, and Curt would begin their school year at Department of Defense Schools in nearby Kaiserslautern. I hired a combination cleaning lady and nanny to be home with the kids when I was working or traveling. Now that we had housing nailed down, I focused on my daily work routine.

The military community provided almost all of the kids' friends and activities. None had an interest in learning German. They did take an interest in Volksmarches on weekends and enjoy skiing trips in Bavaria and Switzerland, trips to museums, and attending Volksfests. At home, they had Armed Forces Radio and Television and base theaters for US films and entertainment.

Deputy Director of Information US Air Forces Europe

My new job was to be an Air Force major command Deputy Director of Information with unique duties of assisting the director of information of Allied Air Forces Central Europe and coordinating with U.S. Embassies throughout Europe. Specifically, I was charged with developing and implementing active programs based on full professional knowledge of all methods of communication tempered by understanding foreign media and cultural sensitivities.

As deputy, I was deeply involved daily with the USAFE/ Public Affairs staff of 27 and with the supervision of 400 public affairs personnel at 35 bases and broadcasters at Armed Forces Radio and Television facilities stretching from the Azores Islands in the Atlantic to Tehran in Iran and from Scandinavia to Africa. That included two bases in Greece, two in the Netherlands, three in Spain, three in Italy, three in Turkey, 10 bases in England, and 15 in Germany. In 2020, USAFE had one base in Italy, one in Turkey, two in England, and two in Germany. The broadcasters brought local and U.S. news and entertainment to airmen in dormitories and families living on base or on the economy, as living in German communities was termed. That service included one television channel, one AM radio and one FM radio station. (This included managing all manpower resources and an annual budget of $893,000.)

Other responsibilities included daily interface with foreign governments at the 'state' and national level, embassies, ministries of defense, news media representatives, senior military leaders, and community leaders.

This was a great team, one where we had meaningful accomplishments on the one hand and fun on the other hand. We had all the public affairs elements you would expect: media relations, community relations, internal information (employee communication in people talk), and long-range planning. What we had in addition that exists only overseas was a Community Advisor. That job was held by Traudl Karolyi, the highest-paid German employee in the command with responsibilities for advising the Commander on community and political interests in all European and Middle East nations impacted by U.S. Air Forces Europe.

Baader–Meinhof Terrorism Attacks
US Military Bases in Germany

U.S. military personnel and their families based in Germany came under the threat of bombings from the Baader-Meinhof terrorist group beginning in 1970 and continuing until the mid-1980s. Scores were wounded in these attacks against the U.S. military, and 10 were killed by this anti-imperialist, antiwar, anti-capitalist gang. Their targets also included German politicians and industrialists. The result was psychological fear and facing increased security measures that impacted daily living for most U.S. service personnel.

Baader-Meinhof was responsible for the bombing of the U.S. Air Forces in Europe headquarters at Ramstein AB, wounding 18, and the Rhein-Main AB Officers' Club twice (1981 and 1985) resulting in two deaths and 20 wounded. It also resulted in the military license plates changed to black and white plates matching standard European plates. Our previous green license plates probably assisted base guards but 'shouted' to the Meinhof gang, "These are Americans!"

U.S. Army locations bombed included the I.G. Farben Building in Frankfurt, the Headquarters of V Corps on May 11, 1972, killing one and wounding 13. Two weeks later, at Headquarters U.S. Army Europe at Campbell Barracks in Heidelberg, two car bombs resulted in three deaths and five wounded. U.S. Army Europe commander Gen. Frederick C. Kroesen luckily survived when his armored

Mercedes was hit by a rocket-propelled grenade and automatic rifle fire in September 1981 on the way to a dentist in Heidelberg, Germany.

The Baader-Meinhof gang engaged in a series of bombings, assassinations, kidnappings, bank robberies, and shootouts with police for three decades. Their activity peaked in late 1977 when we were living in Landstuhl, Germany. Altogether, the gang was held responsible for many injuries involving 296 bomb attacks, arson, and other attacks killing 34 persons while losing 34 gang members.

The impacts on me were very small when I was in Germany on temporary duty or assigned to Ramstein AB with my family. We were caught frequently in temporary roadblocks on local highways. The roadblocks caused deviation from the highway to a single-file line to complete checks of cars, drivers, and passengers. Both sides of the deviations were lined with armored vehicles with armed German police. The Baader-Meinhof gang was thought to have made attacks in Germany and then retreated to France. Our area was only 20 miles from the French border, making it a constant area under surveillance. The rural border crossing and sparse population of the Pfälzerwald (a national park area between Kaiserslautern and the border) presented easy border crossings due to limited traffic.

Bert Tavender

Bert Tavender was an Air Force civilian employee who headed the war plans shop. He was a retired Air Force vet living with his British wife Monica in a village west of Ramstein. At one time, he had been a reporter for the *European Stars and Stripes* daily newspaper. We had known each other professionally when he was a senior civilian at Wright-Patterson AFB in Dayton, Ohio. Bert was more Brit than a Brit with his trademark full mustache. Bert had a fantastic dry wit. My absolute favorite Bert life quote: "There comes a time in every man's life when he can't take yes for an answer."

Off duty, Bert Tavender was a partner with Traudl, Tomi, Mike, Curtis, and myself on weekends when we would Volksmarch at communities throughout southwest Germany. As a newcomer to Volksmarching, you are told, "It's a great way to learn about Germany." But you really find out that one German woods looks like any other German woods. The first problem is to find the 'Starthalle' where the walks begin. Flyers about area Volksmarches were available at several locations on base. Each would have a map showing where the community is. Not as easy as it sounds. German highway signs are infrequent. It was easy to get lost by missing turns that were poorly marked or not marked at all.

The Starthalle is the start place and is where you basically check-in and meet your friends and chat while eating or drinking a bit. The well-marked trails meander through woods, hills and towns. You have a choice of distances of five kilometers, 10 kilometers, or 20 kilometers. You also end your walk at the Starthalle. There you are greeted by live oompah music, get your Volksmarch medal and enjoy the camaraderie of a real party going on.

Volksmarch Medal Collection

Mark Twain's Horrible German Language

I had taken Spanish for two years of high school and two more years of college Spanish. I got good grades, became proficient in conjugating verbs and reading, but I never mastered speaking. I took Spanish as I was told Spanish was an easy language, especially when the only other language offered in Red Oak was Latin.

Shortly after settling in Ramstein, I began night courses in speaking German. I ended up completing 120 hours of classes and was able to communicate in social or travel opportunities. With that background I enrolled in University of Maryland German classes to learn grammar with a Dutch instructor. Bingo! It was a great way to learn a language. Get the vocabulary down first and then learn why you say it. My reaction was we teach language backwards. Get the vocabulary, then learn why. Do not try to do both at the same time.

I didn't have any goal when I began German, only an interest in being able to speak with my new neighbors and friends. But it enabled me to bring English language cable television to U.S. Army, Air Force and Embassy locations. It also led to eventual employment with Deutsche Telekom to negotiate cable access for programing from U.S. networks and the Hollywood film industry.

About a year after arriving at Ramstein, I began dating Traudl Karolyi, the community relations advisor for the Commander of the U.S. Air Forces in Europe. Traudl was from the Sudetenland that was part of the Austrian-Hungarian Empire for centuries. Traudl tried to help me learn German, but it was like trying to teach your spouse to drive. It was a very frustrating experience for her. But little by little, I improved with the help of my instructors and using German radio and television to begin an immersion process. German TV sets aside a 30-minute block from 6:30 p.m. to 7:00 p.m. for nothing but commercials. That allowed primetime TV to be advertisement-free. Commercials are simple, and pictures aid in gaining understanding and pronunciation of new and strange-sounding words.

Romancing Waltraud (Traudl) Fritch Karolyi

Traudl grew up in Franzensbad, a spa city in the Egerland area of what was known as Sudetenland (now part of the Czech Republic). She was born in Franzensbad on December 14, 1928. Her mother, Mare' Fritch, lived through WWI and WWII. Traudl attended public schools (Volkshochschule and Bürgerschule) in Franzensbad, followed by college (Handelsschule) in nearby Eger. Franzensbad was one of three very famous spas in the Czech Republic that catered to European Royalty and the wealthy. The other two spas were Karlsbad and Marienbad. On graduation from college, she began working for an insurance company in Franzensbad to assist spa visitors in getting specific health benefit treatments.

World War II became a time of turmoil and German occupation. Like many other young women, she became a forced laborer on farms. At the end of the war, the Sudeten veterans were murdered by the Czechs in large numbers as they arrived by truck in their hometowns. Or, they became refugees by being sent from their homes aboard freight trains or forced marches. They lost everything they had, except for jewelry that the women had sewn into their dresses. In December 1945, Traudl's mother arranged for Traudl to be smuggled across the border into Bavaria and out of Soviet-occupied Egerland. She crossed the Eger River by swimming into U.S.-occupied West Germany, where she had a girlfriend. She later went to a refugee camp on Lake Chiemsee in Bavaria, living in an old castle with only straw for a bed.

Traudl Karolyi and Frau Fritsch

Several months later, she found that her mother and grand-mother were at a refugee camp between Salzburg, Austria, and Berchtesgaden, Germany. They united, and Traudl, her mother, and grandmother moved to Munich. Her mother got a job as a waitress in a restaurant near the famous Munich Rathaus. Traudl had learned some English by reading Shakespeare in school. That was enough to qualify her for a job with the Allied Reparations Government working for the U.S. section at McGraw Kaserne in Munich. After the Reparations Government shut down, she got a job with the U.S. Air Force nearby Neubiberg AB with the 86th Fighter Wing.

It was at the time when all Air Force bases were being moved west across the Rhein River. One location was Landstuhl AB (renamed later as Ramstein AB) near Kaiserslautern. Landstuhl was listed as a spa location. That did it, and she moved there with the transfer of the wing.

While at Ramstein AB, she was at the forefront of arranging for Air Force support to a widely dispersed community in the West Pfalz along the Weinstrasse. The support included the construction of the first paved road in Ramstein Village, and numerous soccer fields that assisted the Air Force in maintaining training requirements. She was the official hostess of the annual International Woodland Golf Tournament in the 1950s and 1960s at Ramstein AB. Dignitaries included participants from the United States and Europe, including the King of Belgium.

She was at the forefront with all senior commanders, first at Ramstein and then at U.S. Air Forces headquarters. She served as a translator at formal receptions and official meetings with government officials, including visits by German Chancellors Willy Brandt and Helmut Schmidt. At USAFE, her responsibilities expanded to coordinating Host Nation/Community Relations advisor support at 25 bases extending from the United Kingdom to Iran.

Her service was recognized by former Ramstein City Mayor Peter Pfeiffer in his 60-page book detailing his 12-and-a-half years as Mayor from 1957 to 1969. A chapter in his book was titled *Frau Karolyi: the Soul of the Community and the Air Force and NATO Organizations Working Together*.

She married Franz Karolyi, a Hungarian engineer and Cold War refugee working at Ramstein. The marriage lasted three years before Franz died from cancer. Traudl was raised by a family with a history from the Austro-Hungarian Habsburg Empire. She was aware of the importance of royalty in Europe and that names gave clues of any connection to nobility.

Karolyi is just such a name. As the prefix 'Von' in German or 'Van' in the Netherlands signified a 'royal' connection, Hungarian names ending in 'yi' do the same.

Traudl was a widow for more than 20 years and treasured the Karolyi ('yi'-ending). We met in the fall of 1975, and the rest became history. She took the name Waltraud Karolyi Halbert when we married. For years after, she began to wish that she hadn't. Especially when signing official documents or checks.

Bi-Centennial Commemoration – 1976

The Bi-Centennial of the founding of the United States was a major project for arranging speaking engagement of U.S. Air Forces in Europe commanders and community relations events throughout Europe, the Mid-East, and Africa. But the one we gave the most effort was for the USAFE Band to conduct concerts in Moscow. It began a diplomatic war of sorts, and the Russians threw up all kinds of roadblocks to cause our effort to fail.

In the end, we were restricted from flying band members to Moscow. We were allowed to fly their instruments, however, as diplomatic baggage. So when the time came, we loaded the aircraft with the band members and their gear, and flew to Helsinki, Finland. The band members got off the plane, and the plane continued to Moscow. The band members then boarded a train for the remainder of the trip to Moscow.

A great workaround – we thought. So now we had the band members in Moscow at U.S. Embassy facilities, but the instruments were being held in Soviet hands until July 5. So the band proceeded on to the Embassy-planned venues and performed by singing.

General Chappie James
Disastrous Visit to Bitburg AB

Chappie James was the first black Air Force officer to become a four-star General. He flew 78 combat missions over North Vietnam. Chappie was 8th Fighter Wing Director of Operations under the command of a famous World War II, Korea and Viet Nam combat pilot. His commander at Ubon Royal Thai AB in Thailand was triple ace Colonel Robin Olds. He had credits for 17 aerial victories in World War II and Viet Nam. Together they became a legendary team known as Blackman and Robin.

Chappie was a giant of a man. Born in Pensacola, Florida, raised in an area without paved streets, he graduated from the famous Tuskegee Institute in Alabama. When you first met him, you wondered how he ever got shoehorned into the front seat of the cramped F-4 Phantom. When I first met him, he was Principal Deputy Assistant Secretary of Defense (Public Affairs) in the Pentagon.

While I was at Headquarters US Air Forces Europe, I was tasked to lead a public affairs support team for a visit he made to Bitburg in early 1975 to be a banquet speaker for Black History Month. Most of the team was in place three days in advance. We set about arranging for both US and German media, and coverage by Armed Force Radio and Television. Things went smoothly to handle media with the cooperation of base leaders and agencies. The coordinated plan was to have him arrive at 5 p.m. for a cocktail hour to meet guests from the base and local communities, the banquet at 6 p.m., and the speech following. We did three dry runs to establish unobtrusive camera positions, media seating, and roving camera teams locations. We thought we had nailed it. Everyone knew where and when and what they were to do.

Chappie arrived early in the afternoon, was taken to VIP guest quarters to work on his remarks and rest. He arrived punctually at the club and was greeted by commanders and selected guests. However….

Ten minutes after he arrived and 50 minutes before dinner, he announced he wanted to give his remarks – Now. The reception ended. Everyone was escorted into the dining area. He took the podium and began speaking. Within minutes there was a loud explosion. The power failed. But his strong voice continued as base engineers scrambled to restore power. The cause was a power surge overload. The TV lighting, the building lighting, food warmers at the reception, stoves and kitchen requirements for dinner were all turned on simultaneously.

His deviation from the plan created a power demand no one could envision. The abandoned reception food became snacks for the troops at the enlisted and non-commissioned officers' clubs. The banquet meals were delayed until the kitchen could finish cooking and plating. AFRTS coverage was minimal. However, the guests and the media were courteous and understanding, and Chappie finished his remarks unabashed.

Luckily, the bar provided some assistance, and beer from on tap or in coolers was still drinkable. Ice was still available for mixed drinks as we recovered from a disastrous head-scratcher.

President Carter's Visit to Berlin
July 15, 1978

On July 15, 1978, President Jimmy Carter visited Berlin. On the flight to Berlin were the Carters, their aides, and the White House Press Corps members. The U.S. European Command tasked me to head the press center at Tempelhof AB for this event. I had a team selected by EUCOM to join me. We were provided considerable support from Major William Hubbard and his information office at Tempelhof. It was especially useful to learn to get around in a maze of corridors and underground tunnels in the complex.

Tempelhof and Berlin were not new to me. I had flown C-130 missions there many times since the mid-1960s. From 1975 to 1980 I had conducted several inspections of the information office at the base.

There were only two ways to get to West Berlin, by aircraft or the nightly troop train from Frankfurt, Germany. While based at RAF Greenham Common we made many fights to Tempelhof. We had to become familiar with procedures for the three flight corridors over Soviet-controlled East Germany and emergency procedures if radio contract was lost, recognizing Soviet attempts for spoofing (purposely trying to get you to deviate from the corridor), and Brass Monkey procedures. 'Brass Monkey' was the code word to immediately turn around and depart East German airspace.

The only ground access was the troop train that left Frankfurt Hauptbahnhof late in the evening and arrived in Berlin at daybreak in the morning. There was no normal seating on the train. You were assigned to a room, sharing two bunk beds. Windows were covered in your room and the hallways. The train engine was changed at Fulda to one operated by East German crews. Return to Frankfurt was a similar nighttime experience.

Our team began forming three days before the visit. It gave us a chance to get to know each other, learn how to get around the labyrinth of Tempelhof, set up our press center, ensure they had communications to file stories, and set up the press area at the Airlift Memorial. We became tourists on the Ku'Damm (the Kurfürstendamm), the Fifth Avenue of Berlin. Berlin was highly noted as being a center for Cold War spies. We took advantage of that perception by occasionally speaking into our pens or lapels at restaurants and bars.

President Carter hit the ground running to hold meetings with the Berlin leaders, the military commanders in Berlin. (Berlin was an occupied city, divided into four sectors under the jurisdiction of military organizations from the United States, England, France, and Russia.)

His major public event was a speech at the Airlift Memorial just outside the gates of Tempelhof AB. Our EUCOM team was responsible for media accreditation and access for the Tempelhof portion of the President's visit. This included White House reporters traveling with the President, media from Berlin, European nations, and those based in Bonn (then the capital of West Germany). Things went very smoothly – except:

Unknown to us, Barbara Walters of NBC news had taken off on her own and was no longer with the press corps group. It wasn't until Carter and his entourage pulled up to Air Force One on the tarmac that I got a radio call that Barbara was at a closed gate by the Air Field. I gave authority for her entry, but we had no vehicles handy to pick her up, nor was any vehicle allowed on the Air Field. The ramp was locked up tight because of security precautions.

She knew that Air Force One was sitting on the ramp, engines running and ready to close the door and taxi to the runway the minute Carter was aboard the aircraft. My assessment was she would not get to the aircraft in time walking from the far gate. Carter got out of his limo and began walking to Air Force One. As he reached the stairs, he turned around to wave at the crowd. Then he returned to the ramp to shake hands with all of the 'White Mice,' as the ceremonial West Berlin motorcycle police escorts were called. That deviation was a game saver for Barbara Walters as she barely made it aboard ahead of President Carter.

Coloring Book of Air Planes and the MAD Campaign

General Rees Coloring Book

Two projects for our Internal Information and Community Relations programs were pets of USAFE Vice Commander Lt. General Clifford H. 'Ted' Rees, Jr. We knew each other quite well as General Rees' last job was as Director of Legislative Liaison for the Air Force, and I sat in on his daily staff meetings. Both of us were also on the overseas trips taken by the Secretary of the Air Force.

His community relations coloring book was aimed at young German school-age kids in response to more and more protests and noise complaints, particularly in Germany. The product was a 20-page coloring book featuring aircraft of the United States as one of 16 NATO nations protecting freedom in Germany and Europe.

The other was to create an award he could personally hand out to individuals in the command as he traveled around the command. We came up with a 'Make a Difference' campaign. The award was an eagle pin, small enough to carry for him to award at his pleasure. Unfortunately, the manufactured pin looked more like a chicken than an eagle. And on top of that, the troops quickly reacted to the concept calling it the 'MAD' campaign. As a result, the program never got off the ground.

Deputy Director of Public Affairs
Allied Air Forces in Central Europe (AAFCE)

My final two years on active duty came when I was Deputy Director of Public Affairs for the NATO Command, also headquartered at Ramstein. Now I was working on a NATO staff for a German General. Most of my role was as an advisor. But the job also included participation at NATO military meetings in Mons, Belgium, and NATO governmental meetings in Brussels.

Our major public relations event was the NATO Music Fest held every other year at the Fritz-Walter-Stadion. This is a soccer stadium on Betzenburg hill in Kaiserslautern and is the home of the 1st Fussball Club Kaiserslautern. The 1st FCK was a national team, equivalent in status to a National League football team in America. The Music Fest was held at the end of May or early June of odd-numbered

years and featured military bands from multiple European nations. The first Music Fest was held in 1965 and the
event continues today.

Each fest involved 300-500 musicians in a three-hour televised event. Military bands represented England, Scotland,
France, the Netherlands, Germany, Denmark, Norway, Italy, Greece, Turkey, and the U.S. Army Europe Band. Military bands from Switzerland, Latvia and Estonia have been
added in recent years. The host band was the U.S. Air Force
European Band based at Glenn Miller Hall in Einsiedler-
hof between Ramstein AB and Kaiserslautern.

NATO Music Fest Rehearsal at Fritz Walter Stadium

Tomajean & Mike Leave the Nest

Before my retirement, both Tomajean and Mike elected to
return to the United States. Both went to join their mother
in Thomasville, Georgia. Tomi later married and moved
to reside with her husband in Alabama. Mike began trade

school and became a welder working for a defense contract business in Thomasville that was making parts for NASA Spacecraft. Mike was given his grandfather's fishing cabin on Lake Iamonia, just north of Tallahassee, Florida, following Clyde's death. He has remained there since, although the old cabin was torn down and replaced by a modern Jim Walter's home on stilts. Elaine had purchased the cabin when her father became restricted by heart problems when we were residing in Nashville. Lake Iamonia was noted for both flooding at times and then being nearly drained in times of drought. But it continues to be a top Florida bass and crappie fishing lake.

Retirement Awards

Legion of Merit Citation

On July 12, 1975, USAFE Director of Information Col. Gerald Hickman nominated me for the Legion of Merit. The citation reads:

"Colonel Halbert distinguished himself by exceptional meritorious conduct in the performance of outstanding service to the United States while assigned to the USAFE Directorate of Information from 27 July 1975 to 31 August 1979. During this period he served as Deputy Director of USAFE/OI and as special assistant to the Public Information Officer of Allied Air Forces Central Europe (AAFCE).

Colonel Halbert has been a mainstay of the information program, playing a key role in transforming a non-productive operation into what DoD has called 'the model information program for the entire Defense Department.' In helping effect improvement Colonel Halbert obtained additional resources. Command-wide information manning improved from 70 to 100 percent; and broadcast manning from 55 to 96 percent.

He initiated financial reviews that ensured that OI (Office of Information) reviews at all levels budgeted realistically. The headquarters operating budget was significantly improved. He consolidated the directorate's administration saving manpower dollars and increasing productivity. He procured cost-effective, yet efficient products. He was largely responsible for DoD's increase in TV satellite programming that went from eight events per year to 39. His management initiatives helped bring satellite broadcasting to Spain, FM radio to the Kaiserslautern military community, and Mini-TV to remote sites.

Colonel Halbert also developed the highly effective public affairs plans such as the 30th Anniversary of the Berlin Airlift, that resulted in USAFE receiving the Public Relations Society of America Silver Anvil award in 1978; a 'Helping Our Own' plan when the US dollar declined and an Air Force Assistance publicity effort that helped USAFE exceed its goal by $100,000.

Under his guidance OI planning helped gain public assistance of command readiness initiatives such as reopening RAF Fairford. He prepared plans for the visits of senior American and NATO officials, including President Carter, Vice President Rockefeller, German Chancellor Schmidt, German President Scheel, and Secretary of Defense Brown.

The White House staff singled out Colonel Halbert for special recognition for President Carter's visit to Berlin.

Colonel Halbert developed field visits to evaluate productivity and quality of field information efforts, and to render headquarters assistance when indicated. He has demonstrated exceptional dedication to mission accomplished throughout four years of service to the command and America's NATO allies. The singularly distinctive accomplishments of Colonel Halbert culminated a distinguished career of service of his country and reflect great credit upon himself and the United States Air Force."

Marriage of Waltraud Karolyi and John Halbert
Miesenbach, Germany – February 15, 1979

On February 15, 1979, Traudl and I were married in Miesenbach, Germany, in a ceremony conducted by the city mayor. It was a small wedding with about 20 German and American friends attending, including Traudl's mother, Maria Fritch, and my son, Curtis Halbert. The ceremony ended with the Mayor saying, "Jetzt müssen Sie für die spass bezahlen," (Now you must pay for the fun). I was escorted to an office to pay for the properly stamped documentation. The ceremony was followed by a reception at the Ramstein Officers' Club with 150 German and American guests.

Our first wedding night was spent at Traudl's apartment at Burgstrasse 9 in downtown Kaiserslautern. We left early the next morning for Frankfurt International Airport for a flight to the island of Madeira in the Atlantic off the coast of Portugal. Curtis remained in Landstuhl with friends and would join us when we returned to our new home in Rodenbach.

It was a great location for a honeymoon. Remote, semi-tropical, and beautiful. Our hotel on the outskirts of Funchal had a balcony with a panoramic view of banana and avocado plantations and the Atlantic. The weather in Funchal was wonderful in the mid-70s – a welcome break from the cold winter in Germany. We could walk to the city center's famous wine restaurants and shop for local handicrafts. We rode a two-person basket sled down a steep street from the hilltop to the city center.

Traudl & Tom Honeymoon in Madeira

One day we took a rental car excursion around the island on roads that hug the sea coast with terraced fields above, drove under waterfalls with stops to enjoy the lava pools for swimming on the northwest corner of the island. Our expense for the trip was $20.

Madeira was a special location for Traudl because of her Austrian-Hungarian Empire heritage. Atop the high hill was the last home of Austrian Kaiser Karl, who was displaced from his monarchy in the aftermath of WWI. For her, it was like visiting Mecca. Like almost every young girl with an Austrian background, she was fascinated by Sissi, the legendary beautiful and powerful wife of Kaiser Franz

AN AMERICAN GYPSY

Joseph. I began to call her Traudl von Habsburg, because of her attachment to the Austrian-Hungary dynasty that created the world's first United Nations in Europe by marriage where 56 languages were spoken empire-wide.

On return from the honeymoon, Traudl, Frau Fritch, Curtis and I moved into a single-family home on Kirchenstrasse 13 in Rodenbach half-way between the base and Kaiserslautern. The house was directly across the street from a church. German churches ring bells at all hours during the week and on weekends. It reminded me of living in Red Oak, where we had the Burlington tracks on the south side of town and Highway 34 with trucks grinding uphill. You get used to it.

Getting married was complicated by the Department of Defense and State Department's requirements. Our paperwork adventure began October 26, 1978, when I initiated the formal 'Application for Authorization to Marry.' This included proof of citizenship, medical examination certificates including X-Rays, and a statement of legal freedom to marry. Approval was received on January 9, 1979. We set our marriage date for February 15, 1979, as Traudl didn't want to marry on Valentine's Day. It was the first time I had ever won the lotto. It was a loving marriage that lasted until Traudl's death in September 2001.

Retirement from
US Air Force Active Duty
Ramstein AB,
Germany – August 31, 1979

My formal retirement was conducted by General John W. Pauly, Commander of U.S. Air Forces Europe and Allied Air Forces Central Europe at Ramstein AB, Germany. My retirement was after 26 years, 10 months and 2 days service, including 8 years and 2 days service at overseas locations.

Traudl, Frau Fritch, Curtis and I remained in Germany following my retirement, residing at Kirchenstrasse 13 in Rodenbach, Germany. I continued to teach for the University of Maryland and to teach basic survival German language courses to US Army troops at bases around the Kaiserslautern Military Community.

University of Maryland Instructor
Journalism and Public Relations:
September 1977 – May 1980

I became a part-time instructor with the University of Maryland (European Division), teaching courses in the upper levels of undergraduate classes in News Reporting and Writing, Public Relations Theory, and Public Relations Techniques. Classes were held in military facilities within a 50-miles radius of where I was living. My supervisor was Dean of the European Division, Dr. Larry Hepinstall, based in Heidelberg. My responsibilities included creating lesson plans, recruiting students, and conducting classes.

My classes drew about 25–30 students, most of whom were not yet focused on educational goals. My goal was to teach basic simple declarative writing and some insight into the world of Journalism and PR. I thought that would serve them well wherever their future careers would take them. The pay was low, but the psychic income was high. There is almost no better feeling than seeing a student's lightbulb go on.

I also taught conversational German at US Army bases in the Kaiserslautern, Mannheim & Heidelberg areas in a 'Headstart' program. This aimed to acquaint newly arrived soldiers to be able to order from restaurant menus, read road signs and use public transportation. It was fun and a great program to explain the culture surrounding them. The US Army was the only service to have such a program for new arrivals and did much to open community doors. It helped soldiers not become 'barracks rats,' who feared exploring their communities and remain on base and watch Armed Forces Television in their barracks rooms.

In addition, I wrote weekly columns for *SuWe* Publication in Mannheim and the *Wochenspiegel* in Kaiserslautern on a freelance basis.

Assistant Director of Public Affairs
Office Secretary of the Air Force
April 1980 – September 1987

In January 1980, I was contacted by my former boss at Ramstein, Col. Gerry Hickman. He asked me to apply for the Assistant Director job – the senior civilian in Air Force Public Affairs. Gerry was deputy director of public affairs for the Air Force and Brig. General Jerry Dalton was director. They both knew my background and me for more than 20 years.

I was pretty much happy with my retirement in Germany. I instructed for the University of Maryland and also taught basic German to newly-arrived Army troops in the Headstart Program. The offer arrived on a day when Traudl had a bad day at the office in U.S. Air Forces Europe, where she was senior advisor to the Commander for command-wide community relations. We discussed it and what the move would entail, and to my surprise, she said I should apply. Then the reality hit a few days later after I had completed the formal application forms.

She spent weeks after that going to church lighting candles, hoping my application would be turned down. In March, we got the word that an independent civil service panel had selected me to be the senior civilian in Air Force public affairs in the Pentagon. Also, during this time, I had made it fully understood that my coming to the Pentagon would be as a family. Traudl's 80-year-old mother was a member of our household, and we would need to have her accompany us. Mothers-in-law do not count as blood relatives to the U.S. Immigration Service, which created a major obstacle.

We had an M-Day (the term for recalling Reserves for wartime duty) AF Reserve Brigadier General by the name of Joe Shosid working for Jerry Dalton. Joe, in real life, was the political advisor to the Speaker of the House, Jim Wright of Texas. Jim Wright wrote a personal letter to the head of Immigration that he wanted an exception granted for Frau Maria Fritsch (Traudl's mother) to be allowed access to the U.S. and accompany us to Washington. Things went along like it would happen, but no official response from Immigration had been made. Informally we were told it would happen. Joe Shosid and Speaker Wright were successful, but Immigration created a weird restriction (at least to us) that she could come to the U.S. in parole status.

Confirmation of our obtaining approval for Frau Fritch to be admitted to the United States was received on June 7, 1980, in a letter signed by David Crosland, acting commissioner of the U.S. Department of Justice, Immigration and Naturalization Service in Washington, D.C. Crosland's letter said the indefinite parole status was approved for humanitarian reasons and in the interest of family unification. The letter authorized her accompanying us on a flight to the United States without a visa. The approval came one day before our flight from Frankfurt to Boston. I had returned to Germany on June 2. I was prepared to not return to the U.S. if we did not get approval for Frau Fritch to accompany us. It was six days of nail-biting right up to the day before we were scheduled to fly to the U.S.

Now we had to get Mama on the plane. Friends recommended cognac before the flight. However, no help was needed. She walked out of the terminal onto the closed ramp to the aircraft, entered the door and was seated. We had window seating with extra legroom. She had lots of stewardess attention, and she loved it. Worries resolved.

What made the immigration policy weird was Frau Fritch was already a military dependent of mine. She had an official dependent ID card, with coverage for medical costs, and shopping in military Exchanges (stores) and Commissaries. She could fly with me on military aircraft. Those things already existed.

We later found out her parole status was even weirder than we thought. Her access to the US was for one time only. If, for example, we made a family trip to Niagara Falls and saw it from the Canadian side – she would not be able to reenter the US. Every time Frau Fritch was required to visit the Immigration office in Washington, I noted how dispassionate and obnoxious the staff was to everyone, including myself. (I am convinced that if this was 2020 and we went through this process during today's political turmoil – the answer would not have been for approval.)

Traudl and I made a preliminary trip to Washington in early April to look for housing. We found a floor plan we liked just as it went under contract. We found out from the builder that another home with that plan was available in Vienna, Virginia. That became our home at 9920 Courthouse Woods Court in the Vienna/Oakton area. She then returned to Ramstein to prepare for packing our household goods, herself and her mother and Curtis to come to the U.S. in June. Traudl then resigned from her job USAFE and started to prepare for the move to America. I went back in June to accompany them on the flight to America. We elected to fly from Frankfurt to Boston to make the flight as short as possible for Frau Fritch. We stayed overnight in Boston and then drove a rental car to Virginia with one overnight stay en route. The move went smoothly, and Frau Fritsch ended up very pleased with her new home, especially having a bedroom with her own bathroom. Curtis also had his own room and bathroom in our new house and began his senior year at the local high school about four blocks from our house.

The new job as the Senior Civilian In Air Force Public Affairs

My primary job as Assistant Director was to be the primary public affairs advisor to the Secretary of the Air Force and a member of the traveling team with the Secretary on trips throughout the U.S. and overseas. The political appointees of President Carter and President Reagan were Dr. Hans Mark, Verne Orr, Russ Rourke, and Pete Aldridge. I was also the designated 'usually reliable source' for off-the-record disclosures to Pentagon press corps members. My bookcase decoration was a metal bucket with several holes in it.

By now I was firmly into my new job. I replaced retired Air Force Colonel Herb Wurth, who was looking forward to less responsibility. Herb did just that by becoming a motorcycle delivery person in downtown Washington. That lasted for about month, when he decided the job was too dangerous.

My responsibilities were to plan, schedule and arrange public affairs activities for both military and civilian Air Force leadership (Secretary, Chief of Staff, Vice Chief, Undersecretary, and the assistant secretaries), to provide advice and counsel on public affairs matters to the leadership, participate in planning, organizing and implementation of worldwide public affairs programs, evaluate results of programs and participation by leadership, represent the Secretary of the Air Force and Director of Public Affairs in communication with national and international news media, distinguished legislative representatives, and civic leaders.

Secretary Hans Mark

Hans Mark was a NASA scientist, the son of a German scientist that immigrated to the U.S. just before the start of World War II. Mark's father worked at I. G. Farben in Ludwigshafen and held the patents for synthetic rubber – a major break for the Allies during the war. Mark was the professor who had a blackboard in his office and delighted in measuring the depths of people's knowledge by taking the other side of any argument. He was the one who brought the Air Force into the space age despite the kicking and screaming of fighter and bomber pilot generals. Mark was nominated as Secretary by President Jimmy Carter.

The worst incident during my time as public relations advisor to Secretary Mark occurred on September 18, 1980. I had been on the job six months. A Titan II missile exploded within the launch duct at a launch site near Searcy, Arkansas, at about 3 a.m. It blew the 740-ton duct closure door 200 feet in the air, with a nuclear warhead landing about 100 feet from the manned complex entry gate. One person died, and 21 others were injured by the explosion or during rescue efforts. By 4 a.m., I was in the office and crafted the first public announcement for Secretary Mark and the DoD Press Desk, and our busy news day began.

Secretary Verne Orr

Verne Orr was raised in Des Moines, Iowa, and began his business career in Pasadena, California, becoming a prominent car dealer. He was California Governor Ronald Reagan's head of the Department of Motor Vehicles. It was Reagan that picked him to be Secretary of the Air Force. His tenure was the longest of any SECAF since the position was instituted. We had a great rapport.

One of my most satisfying moments happened on a trip to McConnell AFB just outside Wichita, Kansas. I got a call from the base commander that a young woman was at the gate and wanted to speak to Secretary Orr. I offered to meet with her – and it was a life-changer. For two hours, I listened to her story of losing her husband in a traffic accident in Louisiana, and becoming a widowed mother.

She lost her military benefits when the military determined his death was 'not in the line of duty.' He was intoxicated after going to dinner off base while on temporary duty at the base. She lost her widow benefits totally. She was most concerned with starting over and wanted to enroll in college under her access as a military widow. That, too, was denied. I told her I would inform Secretary Orr of her situation and get back to her. Two days later, I could tell her that her VA benefits were restored. Her plight had resulted in a permanent change of 'line of duty' determinations which would no longer result in denial of benefits to military widows.

Memorable major trips included a swing through the Middle East and North Africa. It began with five days in Riyadh and Dhahran, Saudi Arabia. Riyadh is the capitol and largest city in the Kingdom. Secretary Orr's visit to the Kingdom was to assist in military-to-military cooperation agreements. Dhahran was a huge logistical airbase on the Persian Gulf with a physical layout that resembled Tinker AFB in Oklahoma (one of the largest USAF logistical bases in the United States). This base was the center for USAF operations in the Middle East.

That next stop was a visit to Israel. That made the trip unique, as we traveled with diplomatic passports – one for Saudi Arabia and one for Israel. Each country restricted visitors who entered with a passport stamp for the other nation. Both visits were primarily to assist ambassadors and military attaches with concerns about joint military agreements and operations. There was no contact with media during either visit.

Our next stop was Ankara, Turkey, continuing discussions on military-to-military international agreements. The trip also included a stop at Izmir, a U.S. Air Force Base, and a NATO headquarters. It also allowed us to visit Ephesus, considered one of the greatest outdoor museums of Turkey, in fact perhaps of the world. I found it more impressive than the pyramids of Egypt.

The original site of ancient Ephesus was established on the Aegean coast, on the shores of that sea which today is located eight kilometers away from today's archaeological excavations. Very little of Ephesus has been excavated. Today you can see a long road where homes once stood. Their mosaic tile floors and foundations still remained, as well as a very elaborate sewer system, a huge amphitheater, plus docks with metal tie-downs for mooring boats. On a hill above is the final home and grave of the Virgin Mary.

Library & Hill Where the Virgin Mary is Buried

Our next stop was Cairo, Egypt, with the same agenda. We stayed in a large Marriott Hotel in the city's center, along the Nile River. Most places where we went for official meetings were by police escort, necessary as the roads were clogged – even worse than in Saigon. The only way to cross a street by the hotel was to hail a taxi. In Egypt, as well as all the countries we visited on this trip, we took leads from the senior Air Force Flight Surgeon who was part of the group. Those rules included never drinking water, beer being safe everywhere in the world, only eating peeled vegetables, and brushing your teeth with Bourbon or Scotch.

We were escorted by the Military Attaché for visiting the pyramids and getting our photos atop a camel. After the tour, he took us to his home in the Embassy compound for dinner (and a chance to hear the Washington Redskins and Dallas Cowboys came on shortwave radio). His gracious wife Gloria prepared a wonderful American meal and hospitality. I later met Gloria Grenier again when she was a member of the board of Sarasota Sister Cities and created a close friendship that has lasted since 2002.

Our last stop was five days in Morocco, beginning in the capital of Rabat for further discussion on joint military cooperation. More travel in police escort with business coupled with stops at historical sites. We ended up for a break in historic Marrakesh at the edge of the Atlas Mountains at the Hotel La Mamounia. The travel team was divided into rooms with balconies overlooking a pool and luscious gardens in the city's center. The photo shows the balcony and each was enjoined. So, when you opened the brown door dividing the balconies, we were able to gather each evening for booze burgers while enjoying the fabulous garden view.

We were surprised at sunset when a bat flew out above us, then another and another. This became an evening ritual and involved betting (1) what time would bat lead depart, and (2) would bat lead turn right or left to avoid the adjacent palm tree.

The pool was inviting and secluded. The hotel was a favorite of French tourists, which led to one of my famous goofs. Many of the ladies at the pool enjoyed swimming and sunbathing topless. One time on the way out to the pool, a young French lady was returning to her room. She was topless. So I used my best French as I said: "Au revoir." Suddenly, I realized I should have said "Bonjour," and stumbled outside, leaving her perplexed.

One of the days, we made an excursion into the Atlas Mountains, about an hour east of Marrakesh. We ended up at an outdoor garden Berber restaurant that featured roast lamb. At that time of the year, wood storks migrated from Europe to Africa for the winter. About a dozen storks were wandering around the garden, watching us eat and hoping that for a moment, we might forget they were there. The 'musical' entertainment was a combination of Berber chants and storks' 'clacking' beaks.

Another major overseas trip involved the Philippines, Japan, and Korea. We began at Clark AFB in the Philippines. It was the largest base in the Pacific at some time. (Years later, the base was evacuated. On June 10, 1991, two days before Mount Pinatubo began the summer-long series of eruptions, Clark Air Base was completely destroyed.) While in Luzon, we had an opportunity to visit historic Corregidor Island and the military resort in the mountains of Baguio.

Corregidor Island is a Pacific War Memorial focused on numerous coastal artillery batteries and the Malinta Tunnel. When Japan invaded the Philippines (December 1941), Gen. Douglas MacArthur chose Bataan and Corregidor Island as his major defense positions. Bataan fell on April 9, 1942, and Corregidor Island became the last outpost of organized resistance in the islands. Lieut. Gen. Jonathan M. Wainwright and his forces repelled the invaders for 27 days until May 6, 1942.

The Malinta Tunnel was impressive, not just because of its short roadway excavated through a ridge. The four tunnels dug deep into the ridge in both directions served as a supply depot, hospital and Gen. Douglas MacArthur's headquarters. Only one of the tunnels was protected by iron bars. That was the tunnel that housed the hospital nurses.

Baguio was a mountain resort that served U.S. military forces as a rest and recreation facility during the Viet Nam war and after. The golf course was very hilly, requiring rope tows as an aid to get to the tops of hills. There was jungle vegetation on both sides of the fairways. Everyone used a caddy, knowing their score would be greatly improved. The caddies were known for finding balls in the jungle rough that somehow would be on the edge of the fairway when you got to the ball. It was also the best location to buy the wood carvings of Air Force wings or batik paintings.

The next stop on this trip was to Japan, visiting Yokota AB, near Tokyo and Misawa in northern Japan. The primary meetings were held at the Japanese Defense Command in Tokyo. Again traffic was a nightmare. We went everywhere by helicopter. That gave us a birds-eye view of the city and Mt. Fujiyama. The multi-story golf driving ranges, used day and night, were most impressive.

In Korea, we visited the capital of Seoul, Air Force bases, and the DMZ. It was also a time to buy obligatory cloisonné and silk beads gifts. And then the long flight home, non-stop, 18 hours, and even losing a calendar day as we changed time zones.

The last major trip was to South America for meetings with governments and the military concerning joint relationships. The first stop was Brazil with meetings in Rio de Janeiro, São Paulo, Manaus, and the District Federal (Brasilia), the nation's capital. The most important visit involved a possible contract selection for purchasing the Embraer EMB 312 Tucano. This was a low-wing, tandem-seat, single-turboprop, basic trainer with counter-insurgency capabilities. In the end, Secretary Orr chose the Beechcraft T-6A as the replacement for the T-37 Tweet.

While in Rio, we wedged in time to go to the top of Sugar Loaf and enjoy the sands of the beach a block away from the hotel. In Manaus, we visited the famous opera house and enjoyed an excursion on the wide, relatively clear Amazon where the black waters of Rio Negro merged. Modern Brasilia was much like Washington, D.C., with rows and rows of government buildings – but where the streets were empty before 9 p.m. The flights over the Amazon were spectacular, with clear sky above and the dense green jungle below punctuated by flocks of parrots and water birds.

After leaving Manaus, we landed at Bogotá, Colombia, situated in the Andes at an altitude of 8,660 feet. When they say it takes your breath away, they are not kidding, as you begin to gulp air to get oxygen. We were guests of the Columbia Air Force during this stay. We enjoyed the open-air market across from our hotel and the special outing to Colombia's famous Salt Cathedral.

Colombia's Salt Cathedral is located about 600 feet underground, in a former salt mine in Zipaquirá, just outside Bogotá. It's especially busy during Easter, with thousands attending services marking the crucifixion and resurrection of Christ.

But the cathedral is also an architectural wonder, built in the caverns and tunnels left behind by miners, who extracted millions of tons of rock salt starting two centuries ago.

At the bottom, the temple opens up to reveal three naves representing the birth, life, and death of Christ. There is a basilica dome, chandeliers, and an enormous, floor-to-ceiling cross illuminated with purple lights.

Our hosts also introduced us to another highlight of Bogotá at Restaurante Santa Clara, even higher up on a mountain overlooking the city. Great view and ambiance, even tougher to catch your breath.

Our third stop was Lima, Peru. We were hosted by the Peruvian Air Force, sweltering in the December heat of the South American summer. The hotel bar provided my introduction to Pisco Sours, using a coupon in a welcome to Peru package in my room. The heat, the long drive from the airport all combined to make this welcome libation really welcome. One Pisco Sour led to another before taking a nap break before an Embassy dinner at a Pacific Ocean beachfront restaurant. I remember being woke up by knocks on the door, but the rest of the evening was fuzzy. I have no recollection of the dinner or how we got back to the hotel. Consider this a warning if ever offered Pisco Sours. The official part of the trip was spent in conferences and viewing Peruvian Air Force facilities and skipping alcoholic drinks.

During one of those base visits, we had lunch in the tourist city of Pisco, located on the Pacific Ocean. It was a beautiful city. Unfortunately, it was destroyed by an earthquake in 2007 that registered 8.0 on the Richter scale.

We began our homeward flight and headed for a stopover in the Caribbean island of Barbados. When we departed, our pilots headed south to stay low-flying over the Nasca Lines, a World Heritage site of geoglyphs etched over miles of the stony desert surface. It is best seen from the air. The site was discovered in 1939, the creation and meaning remain a mystery.

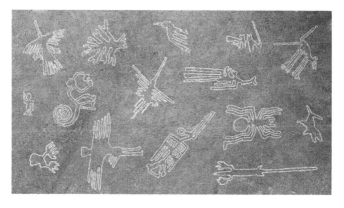

Compilations of the Geoglyphs of the Nasca Lines

Our last stop homeward bound turned out to be a welcome pre-Christmas break. We landed at the airport and were taken by a hotel bus to the Sandy Lane Resort on the island's southwest side. The memories included having Christmas calypso music on the bus, the lush hillsides, and breakfasts at the hotel. The restaurant was semi-outside with open views to the beach. Besides the tourists, breakfast guests also included birds. Usually a small black bird and a larger black bird worked as a team. The little bird was cute as he hopped around the table, drawing your attention to him, and the larger bird would sneak in and steal food off your plate.

Sandy Lane Resort al fresco dining

We finally came home to Andrews AFB on a cold December day. It was so cold that we were actually towed into a heated hangar to unload, collect our belongings and head for home.

Secretary Russ Rourke & Secretary Pete Aldridge

Things went downhill when Secretary Orr left. His replacement was Russ Rourke, a Marine Corps Lt. Colonel who was on the White House staff. I had worked with him earlier when he headed the MX missile White House planning board. He was also a real estate broker in Annapolis, Maryland. He was noted for being in the office on Tuesday, Wednesday and Thursday as Air Force Secretary and being in his real estate role on Friday, Saturday, Sunday and Monday. He was secretary for just four months when he resigned after announcing in his last staff meeting, "This job is no fun."

Rourke was replaced by Pete Aldridge who had been long-time Under Secretary of the Air Force. This happened just two months before I returned to U.S. Air Forces Europe for my final stint in Air Force public affairs.

Air Force Public Affairs Leadership

Brig. General Jerry Dalton retired after 30 years of active duty on August 1, 1980, five months after I arrived in the Pentagon. Jerry was the first director of public affairs to have spent his entire career in Air Force Public Affairs. He was replaced by Brig. General Dick Abel, who remained director until he retired on April 1, 1985. He was replaced by Brig. General Mike McRaney, who was director when I returned to Ramstein AB in 1987.

One of the first new efforts General Dalton designated to me was the interface Air Force legislative liaison that included participation in their daily staff meetings. I formed a public affairs working group that included trip planners for the senior Air Force leadership, their public affairs advisors, and representatives of both the House and Senate legislative affairs offices. We meshed Air Force legislative initiatives with leadership support by arranging media availabilities, speeches, editorial boards and on-the-air interviews in communities across the nation in districts where congressional support was being sought.

My other key duty was as the Air Force representative for the Department of Defense Stars and Stripes Armed Forces Radio and Television Service advisory boards.

Brig. General Jerry Dalton's Mantra

General Dalton made sure that all of us assigned to his office and all those who were visitors to the office would fully understand his mantra. It was a large, framed document next to his office door that read, "Learn to think of the press as the way you think of foul weather. It can make you uncomfortable; it seldom does what you expect; you can't control it, and it only makes you look silly if you try." This quote was written by noted Washington columnist William Raspberry. He also penned an additional sentence to this quote sagely noting his view, "And no matter how often we rain on your parade, remember it's not personal."

Public Affairs Alumni Outreach

General Dalton charged me with creating a listing of public affairs alumni to keep them informed of current issues so they could assist locally in public outreach and support. It began with a Christmas card list of about 100 former PIOs (Public Information Officers) that he had compiled over the years. Within six months, I came up with a list of 700 former public affairs professionals. Using that, I created a monthly newsletter to initiate the program. The newsletter was published by our internal information center.

Eventually, due to budget restrictions, we learned this approach could no longer work.

The solution was creating an Air Force Public Affairs Alumni association with dues as a way of funding programs. So began the AFPAAA that still exists today with a membership of about 600. AFPAAA has held annual conventions at Air Force bases for 're-blueing' and camaraderie ever since.

The Bureaucratic World of Washington, D.C.

In 1982, Dr. James H. Boren, a State Department executive and brother of Senator David Boren of Oklahoma, published a 195-page book titled *Fuzzify*. It became my fun read as a satirical guide for bureaucratic success. Rereading the book today in the Trump era suggests that perhaps Trump used this book as a bible throughout his real estate, television, and political career.

The book was chock full of 'Borenwords' (such as fuzzify) and 'strategies for bureaucratic success.' His basic guidelines were (1) When in charge, ponder, (2) When in trouble, delegate, and (3) When in doubt, mumble.

Fuzzify is the key to becoming a bureaucrat. That means a bureaucrat must be able to present information in a manner that seems clear and precise, but which is characterized by optimal adjustivity of interpretation to build a statement preplanned for adjustivity of interpretation for both present and future interpretation.

Favorite Borenwords include:

- Bladderate: To prolong a meeting in a room with locked doors until everyone agrees due to the pressure to accommodate the physical needs of participants.
- Frumpet: To trumpet or tout a policy in a sloppy manner.
- Halljog: The practice of taking a document out your inbox, purposely stride down the hall until you find an office with no one in it, then place the document into any inbox handy.
- Hunkerfy: The ability to mentally crouch or psychologically spring in whatever direction may be best for one's career.
- Kneequake: The state of being when one realizes the error of his or her position on an issue.
- Loopistic: A lawyer's search for or development of loopholes to be able to pull a client to legal escape.
- Mount Hokum: Capitol Hill in Washington, D.C.
- Pregoose: To give someone a slight physical or verbal nudge as a warning that something bigger is about to happen.
- Snoopify: To prowl for whatever useful information may be found using random rock turning, bedroom bugging and other imaginative practices that might result in leveraging information to your advantage.
- Squattle: To pass through a crisis or difficult situation by sitting it out in order to survive in your job.
- Thunderate: To speak in loud, roaring terms as most arguments are won by thunderation rather than from the quiet voice of logic.

Boren's career checklist seems to fit current times to a tee:

- Have you postponed some activity today?
- Have you sought advice you know you can accept?
- Have you praised your boss in front of someone who you know will pass along the praise?
- Have you set goals you know you nearly met?
- Have you organized a conference or made a dozen phone calls?
- Have you mumbled pretty words without revealing what you think?
- Have you served on some committee that will issue no report?
- Have you helped create a form that millions will complete?
- Have you drafted regulations that will hopelessly confuse?

Borenisms of note include:

- Subsidies are the accepted way of redistributing wealth to those with the most political clout.
- Whistling may be nice at home, but whistle-blowing can be dangerous to your career. Beware of politicians who want you to toot your whistle. A pat on the head may turn to a kick in the pants.
- Bureaucrats rarely have sex with one another. They prefer to do that to the public.
- There is nothing like responsibility to kill a career.
- Bureaucrats and insurance salesmen have all the answers – to their own questions.
- In a bureaucracy, authority dominates, responsibility vacillates.

- Being creative on demand is like gargling underwater. The first 30-seconds are the hardest.
- Recognition of one's own ignorance immediately disqualifies one from becoming a congressman, a college dean, or a bureaucrat.
- A committee meeting is where bureaucrats are born, ideas are killed, and the status quo preserved.
- When a bureaucrat makes a mistake and continues to make it, it usually becomes new policy.
- Nothing is impossible until it is sent to a committee.
- If a bureaucracy were expressed in music, it would be three bars of Chopin, four bars of Gershwin, 10 bars of punk rock and a finale of blues.
- Red tape is mightier than the sword.
- Bureaucracy is the epoxy that greases the wheels of government.

His guidance in time of crisis (which were frequent) included:

- Residuate! Keep a low profile and don't move.
- Fuzzify, profundify and squattleiate (sit it out).
- Intervoid! Practice interface avoidance; avoid confrontation.
- Postpone all decisions!
- Write nothing, say nothing! If forced to write, scribble. If forced to say something, mumble. A scribble can never be pinned down, and a mumble can never be quoted.
- Meet all deadlines to avoid attention.
- At staff meetings be prompt, quiet and subservient!

- Bear no ill tidings! Bearing ill tidings places you in the bull's-eye and the bull's-eye is pulsating red.
- Stay in the middle of crowds, philosophy or policy.
- Wear clothing that matches the wallpaper.

Lawyer Shopping
In the Pentagon

One lesson every action officer (usually a Major assigned to husband a specific issue or program from inception to completion) learned early on was lawyer shopping. This was especially useful for those on the Secretariat side of the house. Since we worked for both the Secretary of the Air Force and the Chief of Staff of the Air Force, we could choose to get a legal review of projects with the legal staff of either side of the house. Action officers learned quickly to pick legal review that they knew leaned toward the action officer's position or not. That was a bonus when you sought either approval or disapproval on the issue at hand.

Action officers often felt that the lawyers were not their friends, echoing the sentiments of the story of two balloonists attempting to set a speed record in a cross-country flight from the West Coast to the East Coast. They launched, and all went well until crossing the Rockies. They then ran into violent Midwest thunderstorms, getting tossed around and losing orientation. Eventually, they ran into a break between storms, looked down, and saw someone along a road. They shouted down, "Where are we?" The response that came back was, "You're in a balloon." And with that, the weather closed in again. One of the balloonist asked,

"Who was that?" His partner responded, "I don't know – but he had to be a lawyer. What he said was totally accurate, but of no help at all."

Sidle Commission –
Ft. McNair, Washington, D. C.
Invasion of the Caribbean Island of Grenada

News media were restricted from the Island of Grenada during the October 25, 1983, incursion. This was seen by the media as a major change in policy. Previously, the press corps had the freedom and responsibilities of open war coverage. The media complaint centered on restriction about an invasion that occurred at 5 a.m. They only learned about it four hours later, when President Reagan's press announcement was made public. In their view, reporters were restricted from accessing the island for 48 hours. Attempts by reporters to get to Grenada by boat or plane 'were scuttled' by the military. The first small press pool reached the island on October 27. The pool was kept on the ground and not taken back to an area where they could file stories until after President Reagan's speech about the incursion was over. Full media unlimited access to Grenada happened on October 30.

The news media at all levels were irked. They demanded immediate changes in the way the media could handle combat coverage. The Chairman of the Joint Chiefs of Staff, General John Vessey, took notice and created a joint media and military commission known as the Sidle

Commission. Retired Major General Winant Sidle was named to chair the panel with former CBS President Dick Salant (then head of the National News Council) as co-chair.

The media representatives included: Keyes Beech, Pulitzer prize winner and retired war correspondent; Bud Merick, retired *U.S. News & World Report* correspondent and Saigon Bureau Chief; Jack Langguth, University of California journalism instructor; Scott Cutlip, former dean of Journalism at the University of Georgia; and Barry Zorthian, former U.S. government spokesman in Saigon. The military representatives included three senior military officers representing the Army, Navy, and Department of Defense and one Air Force government civilian that was myself.

I was selected to be the Air Force representative on this panel. We deliberated and held hearings for five days in February 1984 at Ft. McNair in Washington, D.C. Our final report made 20 recommendations. The one that the media focused on was to have embedded reporters woven into future wartime planning. This took into account reporters' claims that they had been censored and the military's insistence that it had to protect the secrecy and security of the Grenada mission. The commission concluded by affirming the right of reporters and photographers to report on combat. They recommended that the Defense Department start planning for news coverage as military operations were being planned. Also, pools of reporters should be created to protect both operational security and the safety of journalists while ensuring coverage in depth.

Murder Boards and Media Training

By the time I settled into the senior civilian position of Air Force Public Affairs, I had gained a reputation based on my long-term Air Force background as being head of the 'Recall Division.' This was based on constant questions that always began with "Tom, can you recall...." It also placed me into being a member of 'murder boards' used to prep both Air Force military leaders and Presidential appointees for their appearances before Congressional hearings.

Another aspect involved media training for these same leaders that included prep for on the air, planeside interviews, ambush interviews, media availabilities and press conferences. This initiative began within the media branch of Air Force public affairs by then Lt. Col. Terry Hemeyer. It became very popular and, within a year, was adopted by the other military services.

The guidance and interview tips provided in this program included:

1. Attitude is important – TV *is* impressions. You are a guest in their home. Be friendly and conversational. Use the reporter's name.
   a. Key points up front, answer in headlines
   b. Keep answers short and concise, approximately 45 seconds.
   c. Audience: be a translator and interpreter. Remember, "What's in it for them?"
2. Microphone check: give your name, title, organization and brief positive point.
3. Anticipate and rehearse difficult questions.

4. For 'think time' - Pause, use reporter's name, re-state the question addressing the <u>issue</u>.
5. Be alert for reporter's techniques:
   a. Multiple-part questions – answer the best or easiest one.
   b. Hypothetical – do not speculate.
   c. Forced choice – use your own words, make your own choices.
6. Ambush or surprise interviews:
   a. Be pleasant and cooperative.
   b. Set time limits.
   c. Ask for reporters affiliation.
   d. Keep a slow pace, but don't play traffic cop.
   e. Offer to hold a press conference.
7. Appearances:
   a. Light weight clothes – solid colors, no loud patterns.
   b. Posture: lean forward on edge of chair, 45 degree angle, no distracting items or jewelry.
   c. Gestures: hands resting lightly on legs, facing slightly up, don't grasp chair or knees.
8. Three ways to make positive points:
   a. Puff ball – easy question or compliment.
   b. Pause – assert yourself during pauses.
   c. Acknowledge – answer question, bridge to your own positive point and end with a 'sparkler' (quote anecdote, statistics, analogy example).

It was not unusual that I would be Gen. McRaney's replacement at the early morning Secretary of the Air Force staff meetings. Most of those occasions were when Mike was traveling, but some were spontaneous requirements as 'things came up.' He had some of the most unique reasons for missing the meetings: "I can't make it this morning because the dogs are in heat. I can't make it this morning; the garage door is frozen shut. I can't make it this morning because the car won't start."

Another highlight was Pearl Harbor Day. SMSgt Harvey Innoye was from Hawaii, and he had worked for Mike in the past. Every December 7th, in remembrance of Pearl Harbor Day, Harvey would call Mike's home at about 2 a.m. When Mike answered, Harvey would yell, "Tora! Tora! Tora!" and hang up.

Traudl's Class Reunion – September 1983 Schirnding, Bavaria, West Germany

The trip began with applying for visas to Czechoslovakia at the Czech Embassy in Washington, D.C., in the spring of 1983. The Embassy was located along Embassy Row in the District of Columbia. It stood out from the myriad of embassies in the area that were set in park-like beauty with lush gardens and beautiful established trees. The Czech Embassy was surrounded by high chain-link fencing, bare gravel lawns, and no trees. The stark embassy building was lined with cameras along the fence-line and rooftop. There was no access to the embassy building for obtaining a visa – just a window outside where you passed your paperwork and payment through a slot. Two weeks later, we were advised we could return and pick up our visas.

In September, we flew to Frankfurt, stopped in Koblenz to see Traudl's cousin Gitta and her husband Seppl, made a second stop in Kaiserslautern to see old friends, and then drove a rental car to Schirnding, the border-crossing town on the Bavaria-Czech Border. It was a 3-day class reunion that included a Saturday bus trip across the border to Eger (now Cheb) and onward a few kilometers to Franzens-bad (now Františkovy Lázně). We climbed aboard the bus before sunrise on a cool September morning. We were stopped by the German border police on the Bavaria side of the border, who wanted to know if anyone on the bus was not German. I was the only American aboard. They made a copy of my passport, they said, "Just in case I was not on the bus on the return trip."

We were cleared to proceed and began crossing the barri-cades into the 'no man's zone' – about a two-mile ribbon of land that ended at the barricades on the Czech side. We reached the Czech border crossing about 5:15 a.m. The Czech border police collected our passports, and we waited in the bus. It was two-hour wait – a real burden for those who had drunk early morning coffees.

The train line between Bavaria and Czechoslovakia ran through the brightly lit crossing point. The morning we were there, a long freight train carrying coal was checked through. There was a walkway bridge across the track with guards standing over the tracks with long sharp metal poles. As the train inched through, the guards would shove the poles into the coal wagons, making sure that no one was under the coal trying to escape into Germany. As we gained daylight, we could see Soviet Tanks in the no man's land.

They kept an eye on harvest machine operators, ensuring they stayed in the fields and did not attempt to escape into Germany.

After the long wait, we were finally cleared to go into the border crossing building for bathroom breaks and to exchange $100 for Czech currency (which could only be used in Czechoslovakia and had no value at Western European banks).

We then re-boarded our bus and headed into Eger. The area between the highway and that railroad tracks was lined with well-maintained, attractive garden cottages called Schreber gardens (Schrebergärten). These were small, rented plots of land (200–400 sq. meters) usually found on the outskirts of towns, used by private individuals for growing fruits and vegetables or simply for relaxation. However, in Eger and Franzensbad, it was more like uncontrolled decay and neglect everywhere. Gutters were missing, facades were not maintained. Everything was covered by coal furnace soot. It was Saturday morning, and the streets were empty.

When we got to Franzensbad, the entire busload immediately scattered in different directions. The goal of each person was to see their old home first. Later they would explore the town, visit what used to be their family cemetery, view the empty shop windows, and have coffee at the cafe where Frau Fritsch had been a waitress to support her mother and Traudl. This was a Saturday morning, and you could have thrown a bowling ball down the main street and not hit anyone. You would know if a store was actually open, as there would be a line to get in even though no one was sure of what was available to purchase.

Traudl visited her family home, where she lived from childhood until fleeing to Bavaria at the end of World War II. She boldly knocked on the door and explained she would very much like to see inside one more time. The homeowner was visibly scared because she feared Traudl would somehow claim ownership due to the Czech government expelling the Germans at the War's end. But Traudl pulled an ace from her deck and asked if she could use the bathroom. She knew the bathroom was on a landing between the first and second floor. She was reluctantly let it, and could see much of the house. She left amazed at how small the rooms were, even though no changes to the home had been made. It was an example of how everything in the past is larger and more beautiful in your memory than in reality.

We did a walking tour of the Kur (spa) hotels, took to the waters (drinking water that smelled like rotten eggs), saw numerous springs in the extensive parks, and saw the lake very close to her former home that she ice skated on as a young girl.

But the most impressive to me were the ruins of the former Sudetenland German cemetery that goes back to when the area was part of Austria. It was basically a bare grassy field. Most gravestones had been removed. Those that were damaged as they were being removed lay in a mound in the center of the former cemetery. There were trees, one tall monument in the center, and a few concrete mausoleums that could not be moved or easily destroyed. Because of a few standing structures, Traudl and others could triangulate to find approximate locations of family plots.

Across the road was a new Czech cemetery for Franzensbad. Many gravestones taken from the original cemetery were now in place at the new Czech cemetery. It was easy to determine which of the stones had been 'recycled.' Those stones all had the backs covered in cement and the former reverse side engraved with Czech family names. A former children's cemetery was now converted into community garden plots.

Following this experience I wrote about my impressions in Traudl's family history. I called it 'Tribute to Hate.' This impression has even more meaning considering the world politics of today. Lessons from Traudl's family's 300-year heritage in Egerland as part of the Austro-Hungarian Empire could easily translate to the United States.

My concern when I wrote this addition to her family history was, "Could it be possible that some time in the future we might have a war where Russia was the victor and claimed that the lands that have been a part of the United States since 1867 could be reclaimed and become part of Russia?" Or even considering the current 'bromance' our president today has with Vladimir Putin, those politically blue states could be presented as a gift to Russia?

About 153 years ago, Alaska, Washington, Oregon and Northern California were part of Russia. While England, France and Spain were colonizing the eastern side of the Americas, Russia was doing the same along the Pacific Ocean. The colonization of the Americas by Russia began in 1732. That is 44 years before the American Revolution. It lasted until 1867, two years after the end of our Civil War. Russian America began with Alaska and extended south to include the States of Washington *and Oregon plus parts of California areas 50 miles south. The end of that era was capped by Seward's Folly when our congress approved the 'purchase' of Alaska for $7.2 million.*

Alaska and the Pacific Coast region was of interest to Russia because of the fur trade involving the sea otter. The French exploration was driven by the beaver fur trade in Canada and the northern United States. Proximity was also a central reason. The distance across the Bering Strait was only 50 miles. That is equivalent to the distance between my hometown of Red Oak, Iowa, to Omaha, Nebraska.

The capital of Russian America was known as New Archangel in Alaska when it was created in 1808 after being moved from Kodiak Island. The Russian colonization extended south to Fort Ross in California in 1812. Today a small wooden, onion-domed, fairy tale Russian Orthodox church remains as a National Historical Landmark. The name Fort Ross is an Americanization of 'Russ' from the word Russia. By the 1850s, the fur trade was in decline. Competition from the British Hudson's Bay Company brought the sea otter to near extinction. In addition, the population of bears, wolves and foxes were also nearing depletion.

That resulted in Russian Emperor Alexander II offering to sell Alaska to the United States. At the time, the landmass of Alaska was one-fifth the size of the rest of the United States. It was not a popular decision. The purchase was ridiculed by the press as 'Seward's Folly, Seward's icebox, or President Andrew Johnson's Polar Bear Garden.' It was a slow start for the American settlement of Alaska. It took the discovery of gold in 1898 to bring a rapid influx of people.

That brings us to today. At the time, I originally had the thought of Alaska, Washington, Oregon, and northern California being returned to Russia, it was a 'wow!' If this could happen to Traudl's homeland, could it happen here. It was just a wild thought – at the time. But today, we are aware there is a 21st Century resurgence of Russian ultra-nationalism that has spurred regret and recrimination over the sale. There are now periodic mass media stories in Russia that Alaska was not sold to the United States in 1867, but only leased for 150 years, a lease that expired in 1966.

Another takeaway from this visit behind the Iron Curtain was having a feeling of being watched everywhere you went. Government loudspeakers were on every corner. No Czech would speak with you. It was weird. After about four hours, it was apparent that the group had seen enough and gathered at the bus for an early return to Bavaria.

End of Medical Benefits in Washington for Military Retirees

A major blow happened in early 1986 with a public announcement that military dependents in the Washington area would no longer have access to medical benefits at military medical facilities. For most, it only meant that they would switch to community medical services and would not have any out-of-pocket expenses. For Traudl and me, it meant that her mother would have no medical benefits at all. At that stage, she was provided medical care as a dependent of an Air Force retiree. Frau Fritch was now in her 80s and still in good health. We recognized this was a critical change because we could be rapidly bankrupt if anything serious happened to her. After long consideration, we determined we would need to return to Germany, where we all would have full medical coverage.

So with the help of General McRaney, I was able to get a civil service position at HQ USAFE at Ramstein AB. I would be demoted from a GM-15 as the USAFE position was for a GS-12. But I did have salary protection to continue my pay at my current level. It also meant I would have no future opportunity for pay increases. Everything clicked, and we arrived back at Ramstein in July 1987.

Lessons Learned from 10 years in Washington, D.C.

Working in the Pentagon and living in the Washington area during two different eras in the 1980s and 1990s provided key observations and insights into this unusual world. The four most important facts learned were:

1. Happiness is the Pentagon in the rearview mirror;
2. All problems in Washington can be traced to zippers;
3. Everyone in Washington is going to die of seriousness;
4. The Eleventh Commandment: Never commit truth in Washington.

U.S. European Command War Planner Executive Manager AFRTS Europe July 1987 – October 1997

My first responsibility after returning on getting back to Germany was to find a home for Traudl, her mother, and myself. We began exploring Kaiserslautern and the villages near Ramstein AB. After viewing many possibilities, we focused on a single-family home at In der Nasserde 26, in Weilerbach, halfway between Ramstein and Kaiserslautern.

At the time, single-family homes in Germany were rare. Germans were just beginning to change the rules of living. In the past, hardly anyone would take a job more than 10 kilometers from their home. Homes were normally tri-generational. The purchase was made thinking the buyer would live in the home, their children would also live there, and their future children would also. Most Germans were just getting their first car. The car was the new deal-breaker. By the time I left Germany in 2002, most German families had two or three cars. They would have no problem traveling 90 minutes for employment.

The home was perfect for us: four bedrooms, a kitchen with a breakfast area, a living room, and two and ½ baths. Plus, an attached garage with a large garden room, a sauna, laundry room, basement storage room, oil-burning furnace, an outdoor heated swimming pool, a huge porch with awnings overlooking the pool, and pine trees providing backyard privacy.

That gave us an upstairs bedroom for Frau Fritch with her own private bathroom and a door opening to the huge porch. The other upstairs bedroom became our office. The half-bath was right at the front door as it is in every German home. (It's like they expect any visitor to enter the house and need to use the bathroom immediately.) Downstairs was our bedroom that had a door to the backyard, a guest bedroom, a large bathroom and a sauna.

Everything was great, and we proceeded to close on the purchase. Then came Monday, October 19, 1987, now known as **Black Monday**. The dollar and the **Dow** shed nearly 22 percent of their value, as a worldwide financial meltdown came as an unpleasant surprise. Unfortunately, Black Monday was the very day we would close on the purchase of In der Nasserde 26 in Weilerbach.

We took a big hit but went through with the purchase and enjoyed the home for 15 years.

Adjusting to our new home

Our house was spacious, which allowed Frau Fritsch to easily move from room to room on the first floor and enjoy private access to the huge porch. The steps to the lower level where our bedroom and sauna were located did not cause an issue. But to our surprise, Frau Fritch frequently descended the stairs to talk to Traudl. No issue arose, as it took her some time to come down the stairs, each step loud enough to hear. One time, when Traudl's cousin Gitta and her husband Seppl were visiting, Traudl complained about privacy concerns. Gitta told her the answer was simple. She turned to me and said, "Next time, when you hear her coming down the stairs, slip into the bathroom and strip naked. Once she is in the bedroom with Traudl, just step out of the bathroom and enter the bedroom."

I took Gitta's advice, and the next time I quickly changed into my Adam's costume in the bathroom and acted surprised when I entered the bedroom. Frau Fritch never came down the stairs again.

The family member that adjusted immediately was our Yorkshire, Sussi (German for sweet). She loved the run of the house, times on the porch, and exploring the backyard. One time she became extremely excited, barking loudly at the door to the porch. She ran out to the edge of the porch, still barking. I looked in the pool, and there was an Igle (hedgehog) swimming for its life. I fished it out and placed it safely in the yard. The Igle must have been totally exhausted, as it took nearly 30 minutes before it had enough strength to move into the pine tree thicket.

Weilerbach was about the size of Red Oak. It was a twin city with Rodenbach where we first lived following our wedding in 1979 – separated by the main highway that provided easy driving access to Ramstein AB or the city of Kaiserslautern. We made many German, American, European and Middle Eastern friends. We got involved early on with the Weilerbach German-American club and with the community's twinned cities of Isigny-Sur-Mer in Normandy, France, and Kingsbridge in Devon, England.

This provided quick access to new friends and neighbors during get-together events at restaurants and bus trips to wine fests, Christmas markets, and special concerts, including the Mai Markt and Oktober Markt in Kaiserslautern for oompah music, wine and 'Gigelas' (roasted capon chickens). I was honored by the Mayor of Weilerbach at a special farewell party in early January 2002, just before I began my move back to the United States.

Traudl, Drake fraternity brother Colonel Rod Bricker,
German Air Force Captain Konrad Freytag, his wife Ingrid and
myself at local fest in Kaiserslautern

Weilerbach Air Show

Every evening during the spring and summer months, we had a unique air show visible from our porch or when in the pool. Weilerbach was home to 'Rauchschwalben (smoke swallows) that nested in the high school building, just one house away. The Rauchschwalben is a rare species that draws bird watchers to Weilerbach from throughout Europe. At the same time, Weilerbach was home to large numbers of bats. Both species were remarkable in keeping us mosquito-free. The swallows also became our best weather forecasters. When they were flying high, the next day would be sunny; if they were flying low, the next day would bring rain. The bats normally flew low, especially when they would come over the pool just above water level. The best 'seat' for this event was to be hunkered down at the west end of the pool at sunset. With our noses above the water, we could watch the bats doing acrobatics just inches away.

Weilerbach was also noted for having a herd of American buffalo just outside town. The buffalo were being raised by a local farmer who created a business for providing specialty meat to restaurants. And just around the bend was our favorite historical country inn named Landgasthaus Pfeifertal (Whistle Valley) with outdoor and indoor seating. Their specialty was goose that they raised along a creek behind the building. Inside the restaurant were all kinds of stuffed animals and birds in rafters. One was a stork. You learned over time that no woman would sit at the table with the stork overhead.

Chernobyl Nuclear Disaster Impact – 1986

This disaster happened on April 26, 1986, at Chernobyl in the Ukraine (part of the USSR). However, its impact was still being felt throughout Europe when we were at

Ramstein in July 1987. It and continued to be felt for years after. Chernobyl is still considered the worst nuclear disaster in history. It is recognized for causing 4,000 deaths and the evacuation of 68,000 people in the area of worst contamination in three former Soviet states and for another 9,000 to 16,000 fatalities in the continent of Europe.

The prevailing winds did provide some protection to West Germany. Radiation levels became part of the daily news. For us, as a family, the impacts were light. The most serious problem was that it restricted our search for Steinpilze mushrooms. Each fall, we found these across the countryside in large numbers. Traudl had taught me how to hunt for mushrooms in the woods in the 1970s. Steinpilze were the top prize, but I also learned to pick out Birkenpilze and Pfifferlinge.

Amateur mushroom hunters could go to any German police station to be advised on your harvest's edibility. (The general rule in Germany was you could eat any mushroom you find, at least once.)

But since my job took me from Iran to the Azores and Scandinavia to North Africa, I was frequently in countries impacted much more than Germany. When I was at military bases, I had confidence. All produce, meat and dairy items were inspected by base veterinarians before being made available at commissaries, clubs or dining halls. You were extra careful on the economy, the term for anything off a U.S. base.

Mad Cow Disease: 1986–1999

Mad Cow Disease traces back to 1986 in Britain but wasn't considered a threat to humans until March 1996. It wasn't until August 1999 that the export ban on British beef was lifted after 3 ½ years of being imposed. My job required me to make frequent trips to U.S. bases in the United Kingdom and negotiate TV programing rights from TV satellite networks based in London. When I was at military bases I had confidence as all food items were inspected by base veterinarians before being made available at commissaries, clubs or dining halls. The personal impact of being in the UK in those years meant that I could no longer be a blood donor due to travel in the UK and Europe.

Ramstein AB Open House Disaster
August 28, 1988

The Ramstein Air Show disaster occurred on Sunday, August 28, 1988, during the Flugtag '88 airshow at Ramstein Air Base near Kaiserslautern, West Germany. Three aircraft of the Italian Air Force Frecce Tricolori aerial display team collided during their demonstration, crashing to the ground in front of a crowd of about 300,000 people. There were 70 fatalities (67 spectators and three pilots); 346 spectators sustained serious injuries in the resulting explosion and fire, and hundreds more had minor injuries.

Traudl and I were in Wunsiedel in Bavaria, near the Czechoslovakian border, for Traudl's high school reunion. We were in a wonderful hotel with a stream, waterwheel, gourmet restaurant, and indoor swimming pool. The reunion events were held in nearby Schirnding, the Bavarian border crossing point to her hometown of Franzensbad in Czechoslovakia. We got word of the disaster by television news at the hotel and immediately checked out. We speeded back to Ramstein aided by reduced Autobahn traffic on Sunday (no trucks allowed) and no speed limits on Autobahns. We both went to work at the press center before even dropping off our luggage or changing clothes at home.

One Frecce Tricolori aircraft crashed onto the runway. Consequently, both the fuselage and resulting fireball of aviation fuel tumbled into the spectator area, hitting the crowd. It came to rest against a refrigerated trailer being used to dispense ice cream to the various vendor booths in the area. At the same time, another aircraft crashed into the emergency medical evacuation UH-60 Black Hawk helicopter, injuring the helicopter's pilot. He died 20 days later at Brooke Army Medical Center in Texas from burns he suffered in the accident. The pilot of the aircraft that hit the helicopter ejected, but was killed as he hit the runway before his parachute opened. The third aircraft disintegrated in the collision and parts of it were strewn along the runway. The remaining demonstration aircraft regrouped and landed at Sembach Air Base on the East side of Kaiserslautern.

Of the 31 people who died on impact, 28 had been hit by debris in the form of airplane parts, concertina wire, and items on the ground. Sixteen of the fatalities occurred in the days and weeks after the disaster due to severe burns.

About 500 people had to seek hospital treatment following the event and more than 600 people reported to the clinic that afternoon to donate blood.

The disaster revealed serious shortcomings in the handling of large-scale medical emergencies by German civil and American military authorities. U.S. military personnel did not immediately allow German ambulances onto the base, and the rescue work was generally hampered by a lack of efficiency and coordination. The rescue coordination center in Kaiserslautern was unaware of the disaster's scale as much as an hour after it occurred, even though several German medevac helicopters and ambulances had already arrived on site and left with patients. American helicopters and ambulances provided the quickest and largest means of evacuating burn victims, but lacked sufficient capacities for treating them, or had difficulty finding them. Further confusion was added by the American military using different standards for intravenous catheters than the German paramedics.

Fall of the Berlin Wall – November 9, 1989

The fall of the Berlin Wall on November 9, 1989, was a pivotal event in world history. It marked the fall of the Iron Curtain and the start of the fall of Communism in Eastern and Central Europe. It was a Thursday, and Traudl and I were at home for the evening. German TV news began live coverage of crowds dismantling the Berlin Wall. The Berlin Wall was the barrier that for almost 30 years was the symbol of the Cold War division of Europe.

Celebration of End of Berlin Wall

We were glued to the TV screen as thousands of Berliners mounted the Wall, chipping away with hammers and crowbars to try to take down the constructioon piece by piece. All the time, they sang a German folksong – "*So ein Tag, so wunderschön wie heute* (Such a day so wonderful as today). It was a powerful event shared by television that was on par for me with President Franklin Roosevelt's Pearl Harbor speech. The fall of the Wall occurred on the anniversary of another historical date for Germany – 'Kristallnacht.' On that night in 1938, Nazis in Germany torched synagogues, vandalized Jewish homes, schools and businesses, and killed close to 100 Jews.

It was very special for me, especially as I was part of the Strategic Air Command that provided the deterrent power during the Cold War. To me, that was the reason that the Soviet Union and its East European regimes swiftly collapsed.

It also allowed closure. With all my Air Force combat experience, I felt I had served the entire time, never having been on the winning side. In all the wars I was involved with in my career, we eventually just quit and walked away. Though those decisions were the right ones at the time, my thoughts were akin to those you get from kissing your sister. The fall of the Berlin Wall and the repercussions felt worldwide finally gave me a sense of accomplishment that was missing from Korea and Viet Nam.

By October 1990, Germany was reunified, triggering the swift collapse of the other East European regimes. Thirteen months later, on December 25, 1991, Gorbachev resigned and the Union of Soviet Socialist Republics dissolved.

Failure to adhere to the 11th Commandment

One of the U.S. Air Forces Europe/Allied Air Forces Central Europe commanders I got to know was General Mike Dugan. I was his Deputy PR director. In 1990, President George H. W. Bush (42) selected him to be Chief of Staff of the U.S. Air Force. He met with the European press at Ramstein following his nomination. Dugan said he, "felt like a tortoise on a fence post, not certain how he got there, but aware it was a lofty position."

Unfortunately, he fell victim to violating the 11th commandment in Washington. He committed truth on a flight to the Middle East during the Iraq war. He told reporters accompanying him on the flight that the U.S. military planned to target Saddam Hussein, his family, and even his mistress in the Gulf War. He was dismissed by Secretary of Defense Dick Cheney after serving 79 days as Chief of Staff. He gained the distinction of becoming the third four-star to be dismissed, following Admiral Louis Denfeld in1949 and General Douglas MacArthur in 1951. However, Dugan holds the record for the fewest days on the job.

Contingency Planning Role

Because of my past contingency planning history and experience on the Sidle Commission, I was asked to assist in creating plans for several humanitarian operations that involved U.S. European Command participation. They included:

Operation Provide Comfort – 1991

Operation Provide Comfort was a military operation initiated by the United States and other Coalition nations of the Gulf War. It started in April 1991. Its aim was to defend Kurds fleeing their homes in northern Iraq after the Gulf War and deliver humanitarian aid to them.

Operation Provide Promise/Deny Flight
Caserma Ederle, Vicenza, Italy

I was tasked to join the Provide Promise/Deny Flight planning team at the NATO headquarters in Vicenza, Italy. To get there, I elected to go by train as it allowed me to relax and enjoy Alpine views coming and going.

Operation Provide Promise was a humanitarian relief operation in Bosnia and Herzegovina during the Yugoslav Wars, from July 2, 1992, to January 9, 1996, making it the longest-running humanitarian airlift in history.

Operation Deny Flight was a North Atlantic Treaty Organization (NATO) operation that began on April 12, 1993. It was the enforcement of a United Nations (U.N.) no-fly zone over Bosnia and Herzegovina. The United Nations and NATO later expanded the operations' mission to include providing close air support for U.N. troops in Bosnia and carrying out air strikes against targets in Bosnia. Twelve NATO members contributed forces to the operation until its end on December 20, 1995.

Operation Provide Promise quickly impacted my daily off-duty life as a resident of Weilerbach. I was the American President of the German-American Club of Weilerbach and became involved in providing support to Bosnian refugees from Sarajevo. They were fleeing the Serbian ethnic cleansing campaigns and what became the longest siege of a capital city in modern history from April 5, 1992, to February 29, 1996 (1,425 days). The siege was three times longer than the Battle of Stalingrad and a year longer than the siege of Leningrad during World War II. The siege brought enormous suffering to the residents of Sarajevo (population 400,000 at the time). They were constantly shelled and sniped, and people were cut off from food, medicine, water and electricity. Thousands of civilians were killed or wounded.

The Serbian ethnic cleansing campaign resulted in a flood of 600,000 refugees from Bosnia. Villages, towns and cities were being systematically destroyed. The majority of them fled to NATO countries.

Weilerbach was 30 minutes away from a newly created Bosnian refugee center in a former monastery. Our German-American club immediately jumped in as volunteers to help by being translators, providing family assistance along with food and clothing. We got to know the 200 refugees on a daily basis. We assisted in 'adult' education language classes and acquainting them with their new com munity they did not select but were now residing in.

The refugees chose a young 22-year-old as their spokesman. Damir was fluent in both German and English. He became a refugee during his final semester of getting his university degree as a lawyer. Damir was the son of a father who was an editor of a Sarajevo newspaper and a mother that was a bank officer in Sarajevo. For four months, we were in contact with Damir, his parents and the refugee group. Damir and his family became one who joined a total of 130,00 Bosnian refugees resettled in the United States – the majority going to Chicago and Missouri. Damir ended up in Covington, Kentucky, just across the Ohio River from Cincinnati.

Operation Provide Hope
September 1994

Operation Provide Hope was a humanitarian operation conducted in September 1994 by the U.S. Air Force to provide medical equipment to former Soviet Republics during their transition to capitalism.

Cable Television Delivery of Armed Forces Television Bitburg AFB, Germany Initiative

Cable delivery of Armed Forces Television began as a fluke. A base commander at Bitburg AB in the Eifel region of Germany had contracted to renovate the housing complex on the base. While that construction was ongoing, he attended a reception for civilian leaders in the area. Herr Eckhard Dohm attended as president of RKS Trier (Regional Cable Service, a subsidiary of Deutsche Telekom) in nearby Trier. The base commander got in a party conversation and asked if it would be possible to put in cable for TV during the reconstruction of base housing. Dohm said it would, and they shook hands. Time passed. The renovation was completed with cable added. RKS Trier sent a bill for the cable installation. No funds had been allocated for the installation. I got a call for help from Bitburg AB.

Bottom line: I was able to work an agreement between the Department of Defense and RKS Trier as a government-to-government understanding. It would allow RKS Trier (an entity of Deutsche Telekom) to provide basic cable service to residents who elected to have cable. The satellite transmission of Armed Forces TV would be provided at no additional costs. Control of Armed Forces TV would be by use of BMAC decoders at head ends. RKS got a customer base – residents got Armed Forces TV and basic German and Eurovision programming including MTV Europe, CNN International, and a movie channel. This DoD agreement became the basis of extending the reach of Armed Forces TV to more than 1,500 locations from Saudi Arabia to the Azores Islands and from Scandinavia to North Africa. Because this dissemination was by satellite I became known as the 'Dish Fairy.'

This quickly allowed Deutsche Telekom to extend service to all U.S. military and embassy locations. It also gave impetus for Deutsche Telekom to offer the same arrangements for British and French NATO forces in Germany.

German-American Press Club Speech
Military and the Media: February 20, 1991

On February 20, 1991, I gave a speech on Wartime Public Affairs to about 80 members of the German-American Press Club. At the time, there was considerable discussion about censorship. I was asked to provide the members my experiences on this topic from the viewpoint of a former journalist, wartime spokesman, and wartime planner. These are the remarks I made:

Wartime public affairs and the issue of censorship are topics of broad interest today. I hope I can shed some light on them based on my personal experience of wartime public affairs and long-term public affairs planning. I was pleased to have been asked to share my thoughts and experiences today. I hope my insight, as an air briefer in Saigon, a member of the Sidle commission following Grenada, and my current observations, will be of interest to you as reporters or as a consumer of media coverage.

Let me begin by taking you back 20 years to 1970–1971 in Saigon. Like today, the Military Assistance Command Viet Nam, or MACV as it was better known, conducted daily press briefings. The briefings were held downtown in a State Department briefing room. It was across the street from the hotel that served as headquarters for a mixed bag of 450 accredited media representing media organizations worldwide. Of that total, about 40 would attend the daily briefings. Included in that number were many adventurers or recently discharged military members who acquired letterhead status as stringers. Occasionally, enterprising military wives used accreditation to join military spouses on duty in Viet Nam, where dependents were not provided support. Most observers viewed this era as one of relative harmony and respect between the military and media. The military allowed the press great latitude in reporting, and also rejected military censorship, relying on media promises to maintain security.

Media accreditation was handled by State Department's Joint United States Public Affairs Office in Saigon. The ticket to becoming an accredited media was based on JUSPAO being provided a letterhead document attesting that the individual was a bona fide representative of that media organization. That accreditation allowed US Military Command Viet Nam (MACV) unprecedented access to troops in combat, ground transportation and airlift 'in country.' (*The term 'in country' applied to the war within Viet Nam itself. The term SEA, Southeast Asia, was used for the wider war region that included Cambodia and Thailand.*) At the height of the Viet Nam War (Tet) 500,000 U.S. troops were deployed with a ratio of one reporter for every 1,077 soldiers.

Americans, indeed, citizens worldwide, could now view combat on their TV screens nightly, and the information was only one or two days old. Although not instantaneous like today's, coverage of Viet Nam was groundbreaking. Today's news is formed by images that often move faster than journalists can provide context or explanation.

What did we cover at the briefings? Basically, it was a straightforward rundown for the past 24 hours. The three military briefers included one for the ground war, one for the maritime war, and one for the air war. My job was the air war. We began our day shortly after 5 a.m. Saigon time, going through combat center reports, coming up with a synopsis of important event facts. By 7 a.m., our review would be through, and the important verification process would begin. You learn early on the basic rule that first reports are always wrong. This process was critical. Accuracy is paramount. Guesses and opinions have no place in presentations. Documentation backup of briefing material was a must. And finally and equally important was to ensure mission security of ongoing operations was not compromised.

The briefers would then write their handouts – Memos for Correspondents – and go through a murder board process of review and challenges by superiors. The final draft product was transmitted to Washington before a noon deadline Saigon time, for final Department of Defense and State Department clearance. At 4 p.m., we would join the State

Department briefer on the stage, and the 'Five O'clock Follies' began.

Those media attending would read the handouts, listen to the briefings, and ask questions seeking more detail. More often, reporters would use the event to vent anger in front of the TV cameras. No reporter would ask questions at the 'Follies' that might jeopardize an exclusive unfolding story. Many times, the networks would seek on-camera interviews after the briefing on topics they thought might be valuable for airing on national news shows.

Another unheralded role was getting the raw network news film from Saigon to the nearest satellite uplink in Hong Kong. The Air Force provided a six-passenger executive T-39 jet to get the network film to Hong Kong nightly. I point this out, because in 1970–1971, print media could still compete with television because of logistics. This is a key point to remember when you consider wartime news dissemination today.

But working with the media is only a part of the wartime public affairs agenda. Equally important was the role of internal or employee information. This includes involvement by commanders, all forms of print and electronic communication, and rumor control.

A culture watershed change in the military occurred in 1973. That is when the draft ended, and the military became an all-volunteer force. No longer were citizens required to perform obligatory service. The large cross-section of America that at one time served and then went on to civilian lives and careers, ceased to exist. With the end of the draft, fewer and fewer of America's elite – including journalists – would have firsthand experiences in the military. This cultural gap created an economic and cultural divide that would also be compounded by the influx of women from the baby boom generation going into journalism in large numbers.

Let me jump forward to seven years ago. In February 1984, General John Vessey, then chairman of the Joint Chiefs of Staff took the initiative following media complaints about military restrictions during the invasion of Grenada. He formed a panel to review and make recommendations concerning media involvement in future military operations. Retired Major General Winant Sidle was named to chair the panel with former CBS President, now head of the National News Council, Dick Salant as co-chair.

The media representatives included: Keyes Beech, Pulitzer prize winner and retired war correspondent; Bud Merick, retired *U.S. News & World Report* correspondent and Saigon Bureau Chief; Jack Langguth, University of California journalism instructor; Scott Cutlip, former Dean of Journalism at the University of Georgia; and Barry Zorthian, former U.S. government spokesman in Saigon. The military representatives included three senior military officers representing the Army, Navy, and Department of Defense; and myself as the Air Force member.

The panel heard presentations from 18 news media organizations and accepted written inputs for several others. By the end of April the panel submitted its report that included about 20 recommendations to General Vessey.

The primary finding was, "The American people must be informed about military operations and this information can best be provided through both the media and government." The panel agreed it is essential that media cover military operations to the maximum degree possible consistent with mission security of U.S. forces.

The second most important recommendation was that efforts be initiated to improve media-military understanding and cooperation. The recommendation fits extremely well with the German-American Press Club founded nearly 35 years ago by *Rheinpfalz* Editor, Dr. Manfred Frenzel, and Air Force Colonel Shale Tulin. This organization has been vital in improving media-military understanding since its inception.

The underlying sensing and basic facts uncovered during this panel included (1) Military victory is not determined by putting sufficient boots on the ground and dropping plane loads of bombs; (2) True military victory only comes when an enemy thinks they are defeated; (3) Likewise, the U.S. public does not necessarily equate military victory with the destruction of the enemy's regime or army, and (4) Winning the peace is as important, if not more important, than winning the war.

The Sidle Panel strongly believed the need for such interface between the military and the media to allow focus on contentious issues. The concern stems from a real-world perception of Majors and Captains – future military leaders – that there was more to fear from an uncapped lens than from an unseen enemy sniper. At the time of the Sidle

Panel, many military leaders would have rather dealt with
Herpes than with the media.

It was interesting to note that another panel, sponsored
by the Twentieth Century Fund, came up with the same
findings and results as the Sidle Panel. The Task Force on
the Military and the Media was made up entirely of media
representatives. This task force came up with another major
finding concerning news media responsibility. The group
defined media responsibility consisting as – first – news
media assigning people with military knowledge to cover
military operations; and – second – by insisting on reporting and editing that is fair, accurate, sophisticated and com-
prehensive as battlefield conditions permit. The Task Force
saw media credibility suffering unless journalists have the
skills commensurate with the complexity and seriousness
of their tasks assigned to cover combat operations.

Unfortunately, this recommendation has not received
much emphasis. In spite of what you see at the televised
Pentagon news briefings, there were only 37 reporters that
covered the Pentagon daily. Across America newspapers
that used to have military reporters have not replaced those
advancing or retiring. And in the age of the all-volunteer
military, few reporters have ever had any contact with the
military before becoming 'war correspondents.'

From 1980 to 1987 I traveled with four Secretaries of the
Air Force. This is the individual charged for everything involving the future of the Air Force – including its manning,
its budget and resources, and its weapon systems. It was
rare when visiting a city anywhere that you would find a

reporter who has done homework about the Secretary or issues he was considering. I fault assignment editors, not the reporters. Often, a reporter would hardly have any advance notice of the requirement. The reporter would be chosen not because of interest or knowledge, but because he or she were available at that moment and the editor was primarily concerned to have presence at the media availability.

Even in the Pentagon, reporters many times were faced with challenges when writing stories about complex subjects without background while facing time restraints. Fred Reed, a *Washington Times* Pentagon correspondent, was one who did his homework. He tells about the time he ducked into the Army library in the Pentagon to research tank design. He asked the librarian if he could check out books there. She replied, "Gee, I don't know…no one has ever asked before."

Not only were we seeing a dearth of experience and a lack of interest in having military beat reporters, but also in the 1980s there was an increasing anti-military bias with some editors. Freelance writers told us it was easy to sell an article exposing problems with new weapon systems and almost impossible to sell an article debunking criticism of the same system. For years, you've been reading about high-tech equipment that doesn't work or can't be relied upon. Knowledge of advanced technology working may be lacking. But our adversaries are keenly aware and had a far different picture of our technology.

Now let's come forward to *1991*. There have been geometric changes in military public affairs since I was an air briefer in Saigon. The 450 accredited news media in Viet Nam has now topped 1,600 in Saudi Arabia. That's nearly three battalions of media – more than five times the number covering the Viet Nam conflict. The wartime internal or command information role of public affairs continues, and we do media relations and command information with about 40 percent fewer public affairs professionals in the military than we had in 1970. We foresee that public affairs support will decrease even more dramatically in the future, as U.S. military declines, cutting manpower and bases overseas and in the United States.

The reduction in public affairs support has placed more responsibility on commanders and senior staff. Press center briefers you see on television today are now Brigadier Generals rather than Majors. Another change is the growth industry of the 'military expert.' Since Iraq, no report about the war is aired without a senior retired military officer to explain what has been accomplished or not, and what it all means. Cable News Network had 41 such experts hired as of January 1991.

The one thing that hasn't changed in wartime public affairs is the ground rules. The DoD public affairs charter remains maximum disclosure with minimum delay, consistent with mission security, and safety of U.S. and coalition forces. I am amazed at the detail and combat footage that is released daily, the candid response to questions, the availability of pilots and frontline troops for press interviews and the coordination in handling 20 media pools at bases, at the front lines, in combat aircraft, and at sea.

Let me talk a little bit about censorship. To me this is a non-issue. It has become a 'me too' or herd journalism story. My belief is what we are seeing is a reflection on long-standing culture gaps between the military 'team players' and the 'individualistic' journalists. There is no 'duty, honor, country' counterpart in journalism or the military leader's ultimate responsibility for life, death and the nation's security. Reporters have little responsibility for other people. They are not team players, but competitive people determined to keep up with, or beat, other news organizations and other reporters.

The culture gap is not only between the military and the media, but also between the media and the public. Let me refer to a January 31 *Washington Post* story detailing results on current American attitudes on the media censorship issue. A total of 78 percent of those polled said, "The military is not hiding bad news and is telling the public as much as it can under the circumstances."

The plus side for the press, 80 percent thought the media was doing an excellent or good job of covering the war; 61 percent said the coverage has been reasonably accurate; and 75 percent said newspapers are just covering the same ground as was covered the day before on television. Donald Kellerman, press director for the 'Times Mirror Center for the People' said this is the first time television has a monopoly on war – most felt they were getting enough, or too much, on television. Kellerman indicated that the daily television briefings have fueled public skepticism toward the media. His sensing included, "Some of the questions sound awfully silly and many seemed to be probing too deeply into issues the press has no business knowing about." Kellerman sees this as a potential public backlash for the media if American causalities would increase.

The military today is very sensitive to censorship. The DoD regulation detailing the 'how to' of wartime censorship was eliminated in 1980. No one in the military is a censor. The military understands the reality of a 'free press.' We understand it is unique and essential, that the media cannot be ignored or controlled. The public must be informed and the job of the media is to inform them. It is also noted that the U.S. Constitution imposes no obligation on the media to be responsible – neither does it confer a license to be irresponsible. The military, on the other hand, does have responsibilities, including releasing maximum information with minimum delay consistent with mission security and force safety.

The Sidle Panel's second recommendation for more military/media interface was emphasized to enhance objectivity in reporting, increase sensitivities to legitimate safeguarding classified information, and to further fairness in treatment of complex military issues. Better coverage provides a better educated, a better-informed public providing a common ground on which the military and the reporter stand.

NATO Seminar - St, Martin, Germany
January 17-22, 1993

I was privileged to be the US Air Forces Europe representative to attend a 6-day NATO German language seminar in a conference center in the charming wine village of Sankt Martin that featured 30 speakers. The primary topics concerned "German-French relations, the hunt for and concern about Stasi officers and operatives in Germany and eastern nations, Germany military/political concerns and Russia today."

Looking back, the presentations on "The Situation Today in Russia" and "Stasi — No End in Sight" were the most prophetic. The first was presented by Professor Doctor German Andrewjew of the University of Mainz and was formerly a teacher in Moscow where Boris Yeltsen, then President of Russia, was one of his students. The second was presented by Klaus-Dieter Schlechte from the Office for Disclosure of East German Communist Party Crimes in Berlin.

Andrewjew set the historical stage by saying Russia today (1993) has more to do with history and a population of 150 million people (90 percent Slavic) than it had to do with Gorbachov and Yeltsen. The key to keep in mind, Andrewjew said, is the Slavic mindset is tuned to "What ever our leaders say, we do: what ever our leaders give us, we take, He said in Russia, the general rule of thumb is an individual has no will of his own. When things go bad, an individual can do nothing about it. A Russian has no experience with freedom to organize their own lives. Russian famers, for example, are free to farm, but own no land. They grow what they are told to grow. Farmers are 50 percent of the Russian population.

Andrewjew provided a history of Russian freedom, beginning in 1906 when Russia became a European nation. Political parties were formed for the first time. All individual rights were guaranteed, including freedom of the press and freedom of expression. Farmers were given land.

Then in 1917 fallout from the World War I resulted in a change to "building a new people, free and collective who live for others rather than themselves. An era of no private ownership of homes or land. During this era 100 million citizens were annihilated by the state and another 160 million died from indirect causes. The mentality key in the totalitarian state was "to say one thing, but think another." His example was "Ivanoff, why to you repeat what you see in the party newspapers — don't you have any thoughts of your own"? The answer would be "Yes, I have thoughts of my own, but I don't understand them."

The in 1985 Gorbachov came to power with the beginning of reforms under Perestroika (reconstruction). Russia has had one Perestroika after another. Lenin's was called "New Economic Policy." Stalin's first one was maintaining socialism with a touch of the free market, and his second was reforming collective industry and farms. Gorbachov recognized Communism was falling apart and was driven to Glasnost (openness or transparency) that resulted in true press freedom and the milestone first free election in 1992.

Andrewjew said America was the cause of the change. "It was fear of Regan, the strategic use of space, technological advances and the power of information that drove this change.

There have been many elections before in Russia and Andrewjew said he participated in many of them. It was a time that led to Russian political folklore was if a leader was bald, he will be more liberal; if he had hair he will be more conservative. But most people don't understand that a Soviet ballots then consisted of one name with instructions to put an X by that name. The long standing joke about elections was:

Has there ever been a Soviet type election before in the course of history?

Yes, of course. Adam had the same elective choice when he chose Eve for his wife.

In 1991 there was a coup attempt on Gorbachov — but one driven by the government and not the military. It began as a democratic revolution by political organizations. Real Democracy is still not in-place due to fear of civil war. What exists are acceptable compromises with communism lead by the Citizen Union made up of farmers who fear democracy and free market economics; and the National Rescue Front made up of "old and new communists, chauvinistic writers and scientists, disappointed young people without ideas and old ladies who fear their pensions could be cut.

A second presentation of note was "Stasi — No End in Sight given by Klaus-Dieter Schlechte from the Office for Disclosure of East German Communist Party Crimes in Berlin. The underlying events for the eventual forming of this office began in 1985 with the election of Gorbachov. The sensing by the Soviets had been East Germany was about to fall apart by 1990. That resulted in a meeting in Moscow in the summer of 1988 over what could or should be done.

It was at the same time that Perestroika was falling apart in Russia and Gorbachov was seeking help from the West. President Regan response was "no" and other nations were saying can't help or won't help.

The Moscow the study group came up with three approaches:

1) Dawydow Group —Turn the tanks loose;
2) Falin & Sagladin Group —Replace East German Chancello Eric Honecker with Egon Krentz, using Austria as a model;
3) The Radical Group — Drive the car against a tree and rebuild the car from strewn parts

The radical solution was accepted by the KGB and Gorbachov in September 1988, more than a year before the Berlin Wall fell. Stasi chief Erich Mielke and his generals were briefed in Berlin later in September. Mielke's plan was not to use tanks, but rather target selected enemies (churches and reform groups) and control them from within. Mielke had estimated 50 percent of protestant church leadership was Stasi. He also ordered the critical documents maintained by the Stasi were to be destroyed or removed from Berlin and taken to Moscow, China, Bulgaria and Cuba.

By the end of October 1988 the Stasi was in chaos. Documents and computers were being destroyed. Information in files was randomly scattered in wrong file folders, What was known by September 6, 1992 was the total count of Stasi files reached 206km (130 miles). Files on individuals reached 19.5km (12 miles). Each master document contained about 10,000 pages. A file was kept on every person in the DDR (East Germany). There are 2.5 million files on West Germans.

The hunt for Stasi officers and operatives was tough and boring. What they had found out by 1993 provided some general rules:

1) If no file exists on a person, he/she is suspected of being Stasi.
2) Corroborating evidence many times came from attendee lists at Stasi events, ceremonies and receptions.
3) Clothing reimbursement records even gave Stasi rank information.

Schlechte's group believes around 10,000 Stasi offices began going underground a year before the fall of the Berlin Wall. Another 8,000 were in other nations, and about 400 in Germany. About 3-5,000 are considered elite Stasi and 500 were terrorist trained. It should be noted the Vladimir Putin was a Stasi Colonel stationed at Stasi Headquarters in Dresden (East Germany) at the time, and remained under cover in Germany many years before returning to Russia.

Death of Daughter Debra Elaine Halbert 1996: Springfield, Tennessee

No parent ever expects to have one of their children die before they do. So it was a shock when Debi was diagnosed with pancreatic cancer. She and the medical profession fought long and hard for months until she passed away at NorthCrest Medical Center in nearby Springfield, TN, at the age of 39 on August 15, 1996.

I was still living in Germany but was attending an Air Force Public Affairs Alumni reunion in Hampton, VA. I received a call from granddaughter April that her mother was in her final hours. I had a rental car and left Hampton on Saturday, August 9, to drive non-stop to Adairville, Kentucky. Granddaughter April and son-in-law Grady Peay drove me to the first of many visits to NorthCrest Medical Center.

It was comforting to see and talk with her those final days. And it was especially tough for me to honor her final wish that her mother not attend her funeral. That was the hardest phone call I ever made when I told Elaine that Debi had died. Debi's funeral was held in Springfield on August 19, with burial in the Peay family plot in Madison, Tennessee.

Civil Service Retirement
October 1997: Ramstein AB, Germany

My retirement roast was held at the Officer's Club at Ramstein AB. GM-15 John Halbert was saluted by a team of roasters from United States Air Forces in Europe and NATO's Allied Air Forces Central Europe at Ramstein; the U.S. European Command at Stuttgart, Germany; and Armed Forces Network at Frankfurt, Germany.

General Michael Ryan, commander of USAFE and AAFCE, led off the evening by reading a message he was handed just before the event from Washington, D.C. It read "Dear Tom … Hillary and I want to wish you a wonderful retirement following 46 years of Air Force service as a combat pilot, officer, and as one of our top civil servants. Enjoy your evening and your future endeavors with our best wishes." The message was signed Bill and Hillary Lieberman of Falls Church, Virginia.

It went downhill from there. Moderator Major Jeff Baker noted this was going to be a "rotor rooter evening where we don't know what will be discussed, but chances are it won't be good." Jeff went on to say that when he first met me, he was impressed with my knowledge of public affairs. He quoted me as saying public affairs is lot like sex – you don't have to be good at it to enjoy it.

Another expression noted was my belief that seeking to be in public affairs is a lot like asking to be on the Titanic. I was also accused of being the only pilot he knew who wasn't named Ace, Buzz, Zippy, or Moose. Following the pilot theme he said no one has ever met a shy, quiet pilot and that if over-confidence was an Olympic event he was sure I would be the American representative.

It was a fun evening complete with hard-roll throwing when I spoke and ending with being awarded a Hymn. That is a chant the goes back to the Viet Nam years when bosses would be 'honored' at go-away parties with a chant that goes "Hymn, Hymn, Fxxk Him." Go-away parties were normally held the day after the boss left.

Euro-American Public Relations
1997–2002

I now was an unemployed American living in Germany. So I did what any unemployed American would do – I became a consultant. While I had official German government approval for living in Germany (an *Aufenhaltsgeneh-menigen* stamp on my passport), I did not have approval for employment. If I had been from any European nation, I would have qualified. But being an American, I was officially lumped into the category of 'all others.'

I legally formed and registered my company Euro-American Public Relations in Tennessee, a tax-friendly state where I still had an address. I was paid in dollars which were transferred to my Tennessee bank account by the multiple organizations I assisted, including Deutsche Telekom, French and British Forces in Germany, and the governments of Malta, Greece, Turkey, Italy, the Netherlands, Belgium, and the United Kingdom. My work centered on obtaining programming rights for cable distribution to NATO forces and embassies in Europe, the Middle East, and Africa.

Being a consultant had major benefits. I could take on tasks or decline them. I had a secure income from my Air Force retirement, my civil service retirement, and had just qualified for Social Security payments. Traudl had her retirement pay, and both Traudl and her mother were fully covered by German health insurance.

It was a happy time that allowed us to travel locally and internationally – mostly to the Alpine areas of Germany, Austria and Italy. We were still involved with the German-American Press Club, the German-American Club of Weilerbach, and the Egerland Gmoi in Kaiserslautern. We still spent many weekends Volksmarching and attending wine fests.

Serious Genealogy Research Time

Driven by the life-long question of "Who am I?" and now having three family groupings to research (Halbert-Pilkington, Haas-Murphy, Fritsch-Turba), I began to dive into research at the Kaiserslautern Mormon Church Genealogy Center and the Internet. My grandfather Marion Halbert, a county clerk in Red Oak, had created a handwritten family history on yellow legal papers attached to a clipboard. At one time, I had looked through it with limited interest. And over the years, it was lost. The only thing I remember from it was my grandfather detailing the Halbert family connection to Pocahontas after the first Halberts arrived along the Potomac in Virginia in the late 1600s. He also was proud that the lineage could be traced to most famous Americans who were early settlers in Virginia, including George Washington and Thomas Jefferson.

My Halbert Family Tree

My grandfather had shared his family history in handwritten form in the mid-1900s. As a result, his research began showing up on the World Wide Web. I began a quest to recover the family records that had been lost somewhere in our family moves.

Within months I was able to recover his work and more. The Kaiserslautern Mormon Family History Center allowed me to gain hundreds of other records that resulted in actual documentation and even corrections. You learn early in genealogy research to take any records from the Daughters of the American Revolution with a grain of salt. Some may be factual, but many records have been fabricated to allow those seeking membership in this group to show a tie to the Revolutionary War. (That is exactly how the Halbert relation to Pocahontas was forged, a connection that cannot be proved.)

This branch of Halberts immigrated to Virginia in the early 1600s, settling along the Roanoke River. The first immigrant was thought to be of Scottish descent, who settled in Saint Anne's Parrish in Essex County sometime before 1709 when his oldest son Joel was born. My Halbert lineage comes from Joel and his son William Anson Halbert, who was a Colonel in Washington's Army. After the Revolutionary War, William was given a land grant in Anderson, North Carolina. His son Joel migrated to Shoals, Indiana, around 1816. He had three children with his first wife, who was killed by a bear. My great-great-grandfather, Elihu Halbert, came from his marriage to his wife's sister.

Elihu's son, William Halbert, and his new wife, Sarah Amelia Morgan, moved from Illinois in a lumber wagon to begin farming in Pilot Grove Township in Montgomery County, Iowa in 1869. This was between the towns of Elliott and Grant. Their move came one year before the mass migration of pioneers that began in 1870.

William was my great-grandfather. His son, John Marion Halbert, was the father of Russel Dillion Halbert, my adopted father. Marion was the youngest of four brothers and sisters. They grew up as members of a pioneer family. Their schooling was in the one-room Botts School in Pilot Grove, with social gatherings involving spelling bees, literary societies, and church box social programs.

Both my grandfather and my father were born in Elliott, Iowa, 12 miles north of Red Oak on the 'North Branch' rail feeder that ran from Red Oak to Elliott and Griswold. It was the only reason Elliott sprung into existence. One historical report tells of a trip up the Nishnabotna Valley on December 19, 1879, from Red Oak to Elliott on the CB&Q. It noted that, just 10 years before, "it was a wild, undulating plain, dotted with homesteads here and there, now there were homes by the thousands." It was a ride of

12 miles and Elliott was a little town with the stir of a city. The cribs of Elliott held 15,000 bushels of grain, making it one of the largest grain stations in the state. New stores were springing up, including two saloons, with plenty of home lots available at $50 to $150 each.

Arbor Lodge, Nebraska City, Nebraska

It was in park-like setting, complete with a carriage house and a shop for selling memorabilia. April got her first University of Nebraska Cornhusker's sweatshirt. From there we drove to Omaha, passing Offutt AFB where I was based in late 1950s. We saw her mother's second home in South Omaha, and my home around Hansom Park where I lived while in fifth grade. We had dinner in the warehouse district of Omaha where I had loaded produce in the Red Oak Wholesale Fruit truck. Then on to my hometown where she saw our family homes, my schools, the Carnegie Library, the fabled Courthouse, the location of the former Halbert Seed Corn center, the Nishnabotna river, the family plots in Evergreen Cemetery, the bayous around town, and the original Halbert family homestead farm near Elliott.

At the former Halbert farm the only things that indicated that someone lived there were trees planted as a windbreak and spring bulbs in bloom. Everything else had been removed to ensure every square foot possible was now plowable. Agriculture had moved on to where you now need a minimum of four sections of land to be profitable as a farmer. She also saw the home of 'Halbert's Hair Restorer,' a patent medicine created by my grandfather's brother in his drug store.

C. B. Halbert's Store, Elliott, Iowa, 1896

My Haas Family Tree

In the 1970s, I was living less than two hours away from the community where my birth mother's family emigrated from in the principality of Baden, across the Rhein River from Strasbourg, France. This was after a 30-year search to find from where in Germany my Haas line originated. I had found family records on the web that had the name 'Kirk' handwritten on the document. But there is no such place or word in German that references Kirk. There is 'Kirche' (Church) or 'Kirchen' (Cherries) but no Kirk. I had hired a professional genealogist along the way, but none of us broke the code by trying to replace the 'i' with either a, e, o or u. Doing that finally led me to the town of Kork in Baden and a family history of shoemakers that goes back to 1630.

My maternal great-grandfather had legally immigrated to Illinois on a boat leaving Le Havre, France. He was a young man and about to be mandatorily conscripted into the Prince of Darmstadt's army. It was the time of the revolution in 1860 that led to the foundation of Germany as a nation. Wilhelm Georg Haas applied and was given permission to immigrate by the Prince, as he was an 'orphan.' It was a time when one became an orphan if your father had died, even though your mother was still living.

Once I found out about Kork, I made several trips to the town and got to know the mayor. He took an interest in my family quest. By the time I made my second trip, he had gathered the complete Haas family history for me from city records created during the Adolph Hitler years. Family history was big to Hitler, as that is how the Nazi regime determined the family was not Jewish. The year 1630 is important for genealogy in Europe. In 1630, the Swedes invaded Western Europe during the 30 Years' War. The Swedes destroyed everything they passed, including Churches where birth, marriage and death records were kept. The only family histories in central Europe that survived the 30 Years' War were those of royalty.

My visits to Kork, including one made with Gayle in 2004, were very revealing, The Protestant church in Kork had survived the centuries, and the town square, the market area and cobble stone streets were still the same. Many of the half-timbered homes still survived from my great-grandfather's era. Genealogically speaking, the families in the Haas collection were from Kork or communities not more than seven kilometers away. It was an age of limited public transportation. Most people were too poor to own a horse. I surmised that a suitor would walk seven miles, at the most, to find his wife-to-be.

The mayor had fun with me when I mentioned that my great-grandfather's name of Wilhelm was very common at the time. I had the feeling if I was in the market square on a Saturday in 1850 and yelled out, "Wilhelm," several hundred men would turn their heads to respond. He enlightened me by saying, "Oh, you poor dumb soul, don't you realize that boys were named for whoever the Prince was at the time?" That accounted for why there were so many Wilhelm's and Wilhelmina's in my great-grandfather's era.

Then, I innocently asked why there were so many half-timbered houses? And he replied, "Oh, you poor dumb soul, don't you realize that these homes were the original house trailers in Europe? When wars or other bad times came, the homeowners could load the timber part of the home onto wagons and head for safety. The straw and mud to rebuild the home could be found anywhere."

My final question was, "Why was it so hard to read church records handwritten by parish priests or ministers?" And he replied, "Oh, your poor dumb soul, don't you realize that the oldest son always inherited the farm and the dumbest son always became a priest?"

Kork was along the Rhein River, located a couple of miles east of the river flood plain. It was the location of the only bridge across the Rhein that far south. Thus it was the escape route in troubled times, such as the 30 Years' War. The residents of Kork fled over that bridge to reach Switzerland. The Haas family was one of many who ended up in Basel until they felt safe enough to return to Kork.

I had also found out that my birth great-great-grandmother, Verena Wanner, was from Schleitheim in Canton Schaffhausen, Switzerland. They originally met onboard the ship during the Atlantic crossing. I still have no records of where they entered the United States. Still, I did learn that Wilhelm ended up on the Illinois river south of Chicago and Verena became an indentured servant in La Crosse, Wisconsin. Their paths crossed again when, during the Civil War, soldier Wilhelm was a patient at a military hospital in Iowa and Verena was his nurse. They married, moved to Lake City, Minnesota, had four children – one who migrated to Rapid City, South Dakota, and became my maternal grandfather.

Traudl's Long Goodbye

In 1999, things began to change, as Traudl started complaining about pains in her back. We soon learned that she had serious cancer that would require surgery and chemotherapy. That battle lasted two years and involved specialists and 260 days of hospitalization including The University of Ulm Surgery Clinic in Ulm, on the Baden-Württemberg/Bavarian border; Kurklinik Eggensberger in Hopfen near Neuschwanstein Castle; St. Johannis Krankenhaus in Landstuhl; and the University Clinic of the Saarland in Homberg.

Thus began a spiral of hope and fear as she went through treatment after treatment. The cancer metastasized, and by mid-2000, we both knew there was no hope for her recovery. Traudl's final months were spent at home in Weilerbach. She had full-time nursing care. We changed the living room into her room that gave her a picture window view of our patio and the greenery of our back yard. Her final days were spent at the St. Johannis Krankenhaus in Landstuhl, Germany. She was provided with a private room that allowed me to remain with her. I was able to hold her hand in her final hours through her last breath in the early morning hours of September 3, 2000.

Funeral services were held in Kaiserslautern with burial next to her first husband, Franzl Karolyi, in the family plot. German cemeteries are parks with well-maintained paths through majestic trees and always-beautiful flowers. It is a magnet for people who enjoy the outdoors to wander and feed the numerous squirrels and birds.

I continued to reside in Weilerbach to take care of Frau Fritch and arrangements following the funeral. In December of 2000, I began the daunting task of determining what to do with Traudl's possessions. I did that in concert with Frau Fritsch, Dr. Barbel Rygula (Traudl's goddaughter) living nearby in Kaiserslautern, and my granddaughter, April. She had become very close to Traudl while we lived in Vienna, Virginia, and her visits to Germany.

April came to Weilerbach to assist. During this visit, April accompanied me to the annual TKS Christmas party in Kaiserslautern. As luck would have it, April was the winner of a drawing for the Tour de France racing bicycle used by Deutsche Telekom's Jan Ulrich. He was the winner of that race that summer.

Deutche Telekom's Jan Ulrich Tour de France winner

Now April was faced with returning to Kentucky and having a valuable bicycle in Germany. Through my contacts with my old office at Ramstein, I found a military family who was being reassigned to Ft. Campbell, Kentucky, about 30 miles from where April was living. They agreed to add the bike to their household goods shipment, and April could pick up the bike. Today, the bike is still in the family and used frequently by my great-granddaughter, Brylee Sanford.

In the summer of 2001, Traudl's cousin Gitta arranged for Frau Fritch to be moved to a senior care center in Koblenz, Germany, near where Gitta and her husband Seppl resided.

In the winter of 2003, Frau Fritsch died, with services and burial, in the family plot in Kaiserslautern in May 2004.

Frau Fritch's move to Koblenz allowed me to focus on selling our house in Weilerbach and move back to the United States. Traudl and I particularly liked the Sarasota area, where we had vacationed many times in the 1980s. My long-time Air Force friend, Jack Olsen, gave me a lead on a real estate agent, and my search for a new home and a new life began. I was extremely lucky in selling my house in Weilerbach. Issue No. 1 solved. Now I had to plan on what to ship back with me. I had arrived in Germany with more than 15,000 pounds of household goods. That move was at government expense. I no longer had the benefit of shipping anything back to the U.S. Shipping costs were about $1 per pound. That meant getting rid of lots of stuff. In the end, I shipped back about 2,000 pounds of things I considered personally important or of high value. That turned out to be books, paintings, and oriental rugs. Everything else I would buy new.

In 2002, real estate offered on the Internet began including videos of the properties. I began checking many of those each week. I could tell my agent that I visited about 50 homes this week on my computer, and of those, about five appealed to me. I could also tell her why I liked them. I knew none of the homes would be available when I got to Sarasota about 60 days later. But, I reasoned, she would have a pretty good idea of what I liked and why. I finally got everything in order, shipped and arranged my flights to Florida, departing Frankfurt International Airport in late January 2002.

Sarasota Citizen with Partner Gayle Maxey 2002 to Present

My long-time fraternity brother and Drake journalism friend Rod Bricker and his wife, Nona, met me with welcome signs at Tampa International Airport. We had dinner, reminisced, and discussed living on the Gulf Coast. He lived in Clearwater. I got a rental car the next morning and headed south to meet my real estate agent for the first time. I selected a restaurant on St. Armand's Circle I knew from vacations in Sarasota and picked her out instantly. She was with her assistant.

As we began lunch, my agent told me she had both good and bad news. I asked for the good news first. She said today was her birthday. I congratulated her and she went on to explain her husband had given her a surprise gift of a trip to Cancun, Mexico – and that she would be leaving the next day. However, her assistant knew everything I had sent back about my virtual home visits on the web.

Her assistant told me she knew the house I wanted, but we couldn't see it until Tuesday. This was Saturday. So began a tour of homes from Lakewood Ranch in Northeast Sarasota to Venice to the south. I did see some homes of interest, but was intrigued about her positive view of the house we would see on Tuesday. Turns out she was dead right. The home at 133 Inlets Boulevard in Nokomis was perfect.

It had a big modern kitchen with new appliances, s separate laundry room with entry to a 2-car garage, dining room with sliding glass doors opening to a large lanai and swimming pool. The view expanded over the canal below with a dock and boat lift plus a lake across the way – meaning the lanai and pool were totally private, and the nearest neighbors were about a mile away across the lake. Two large bedrooms and walk-in closets, an office on the second floor, three bathrooms, and a Florida basement. (*A Florida basement is the space on the ground floor under a flight of stairs you can use for storage.*)

As part of the lanai decoration I added a large lifesaver ring labeled *Kurpark Halbert*. Kurparks are major health spas in the German-speaking world located in more than 160 communities that have 'Bad' in the name. The word *Bad* is used as a prefix (*Bad Vilbel*) or a suffix (*Marienbad, Wiesbaden*) to denote the town as a spa city. In any case, Bad as a prefix is an official designation and requires governmental authorization.

I had leverage from the sale of my house in Weilerbach. I negotiated a cash price well under the listing price, and also that I could take occupancy of the house on March 1, 2002. It worked. We closed and I moved in as planned, including having delivery of my basic just-purchased furniture.

New Home, New Life – 133 Inlets Blvd.
A House with History

Before I moved in, the occupants of the house were two young men and a large dog. The one that I met during visits to the house was a 'car salesman' at nearby Matthews Currie Ford in Nokomis. He was from Oklahoma, and his brother was Secretary of the Army in Washington, D.C., who I had met in my Pentagon years. That puzzled me. The puzzle continued when I would take his mail sent to 133 Inlets Boulevard to his office at Matthews Currie Ford. Supposedly he was a new car salesman. His office space was not with the other car salesmen. In fact, it was an isolated office at the back of the dealership.

The next oddity was when I found a .38 caliber pistol on the top of a guest bedroom cabinet. Two days later, I found a Secret Service badge at the back of another cabinet. He was not at the dealership when I returned these items. I never saw him again at the dealership or in the Venice area.

During the closing, I found out the house was previously owned by Serguei Lepekha, a Ukrainian who was not present but represented by a lawyer. On getting to know my immediate neighbors I learned that Lepekha was noted for all kinds of odd behavior. This involved speeding panel trucks that pulled into the garage and never unloaded when the garage door was open. My neighbors told me that he departed the Inlets in the middle of the night right after 9/11. The next morning, the entire street was loaded with marked and unmarked police cars. As each neighbor, awoke the police would conduct interviews focused on the Ukrainian owner. Shortly after, the 'car salesmen and his companion' moved into the home.

The same morning, neighbors of the home that Mohamed Atta and others had rented three blocks away on Laurel Road were interviewed. It was the same situation. Laurel Road was blocked by marked and unmarked police cars as interviews of neighbors were conducted. These Saudi pilots involved in 9/11 got their flight training at Venice Municipal Airport.

Other oddities included that the garage was air-conditioned. Both sidewalls had built-in storage cabinets, and each shelf was filled with empty plastic 'inboxes'. The entry hall, the guest bedroom, the master bedroom, and closet had elaborate electrical boxes installed that appeared to be associated with communications technology. Entry to the master bedroom was hidden behind a bookshelf door.

My journalism curiosity led me to ensuring that no other hidden surprises might surface. I had a complete wall to wall, attic to floor inspection conducted – and nothing new was found. However, finding a pistol and secret service identification badge in the house led me to believe that the 'car salesman' and his companion officially occupied the house to ensure they could learn any useful information in the aftermath of 9/11, including mail and telecommunication reception. I am convinced that the secret service surveillance must have ended by February 2002, and that is why the house was finally listed for sale shortly after I arrived in Sarasota.

Inlets Welcome Wagon

Getting settled became a full-time occupation. My main focus was shopping for furniture, kitchen and dining area needs, picking up packages I had mailed from Germany to my real estate gal, and buying a new car.

And then came a knock at the door. Gayle Maxey, who lived just up the street at 125 Inlets Boulevard, was the official greeter for informing new residents about the Inlets community and the Sun Coast of Florida. She provided a package detailing benefits of Inlets residents, including Club House events and excursions, tennis, swimming pool, boating and biking opportunities, lots of restaurants, and local events.

She showed up on her bicycle wearing a pair of white shorts.

That led to our meeting at clubhouse events and eventually to dinners together. We had both lost our spouses on the same September day in 2000. Our first date was in June 2002 at the Summer House restaurant, a 2-story glass building hidden in tropical lushness on Siesta Key. Five months later, we had become an 'item' being together at Inlet's clubhouse events, beach parties, and theater and restaurant excursions.

At this time, Gayle invited me to dinner at her home eight houses away. When I walked in, I was impressed with the Florida-style home décor and then noticed a painting on the wall. It was an Air Force Art Program painting by Betty Maxey, one of several

Tom and Gayle

that Betty donated to the Air Force when I was in the Pentagon. I asked, "Where did you get this painting?" Gayle explained that it was a copy of a painting Betty did for the Air Force. I responded, "I know your sister-in-law, in fact, long before I met you."

By now my household goods the Air Force shipped from Germany had arrived. One major problem was where to put all of the paintings that we collected in Germany, many done by well-known European artists and several by Traudl. So I enlisted Gayle and two of her female friends to give

349

me decoration ideas and suggest painting placements. That worked out well with the aid of several bottles of wine. The paintings have remained in place ever since.

The 'I Love Me' Room

Another part of the decoration 'aid' in creating my upstairs office, which became my designated 'I love me' room where my Volksmarch medals, mementos, awards and certificates are all displayed. Some of those included:

Deutsche Telekom
"Simply the Best" Award 1989–2002

John Halbert

U.S. European Command Plaque – 1987–97
Cable and Satellite Management

U.S. Army Europe
Certificate of Service 1987–1997

The Inlets Airshow

Our daily ritual at Kurpark Halbert centered around the Inlets Airshow. Each morning we would begin our day with a glass of tea in the Kurpark Halbert lanai pool. Greeting the sunrise to the sounds of ospreys, gulls, cardinals, whistler ducks, and witnessing countless other birds, flybys of flocks and individual birds plus squirrels jumping from our lanai cage to trees, and fish jumping in the canal. We would often enjoy sunsets from the pool with the same nature bonuses abounding. We came to call it the Inlets Airshow.

We divided the Air Shows into two parts: before Hurricane Charley and after Hurricane Charley. Before that hurricane, birds of all types were in and above the Inlets. Not so after Charley. Before, we had large and small cranes, egrets, whistler ducks, gulls, and sandhill cranes in large numbers on our lawns – today seldom. The same on our beaches.

While we still see flocks flying, their numbers are dramatically reduced. We believe that Hurricane Charley destroyed nearly all of the coastal rookeries resulting in a huge bird population reduction. In early 2000, it was common to see the big birds patiently standing at front doors to get handouts, usually hot dogs, from residents. Birds were all over the Inlets searching for geckos in the shrubbery then. This is rare today.

Sarasota Sister Cities Involvement

We became members of Sarasota Sister Cities through 'gentle persuasion' by Bill and Jean Wallace, who I introduced

Gayle to early on. Bill, Jean, and I go back to being freshmen together at Drake University in Des Moines in the fall of 1950. Bill and I were journalism graduates at Drake in 1954. He went on to join Hallmark Cards in Kansas City, and I entered the Air Force. Bill and Jean eventually moved to Sarasota, where he became a financial advisor.

Bill was city director for SSCA (Sarasota Sister Cities Association) and was deeply involved in 2002 with the establishment of Dunfermline, Scotland, as a Sarasota Sister City. Dunfermline is the birthplace of Andrew Carnegie, the industrialist and philanthropist. He led the expansion of the American steel industry in the late 19th century, becoming one of the richest Americans in history.

The signing ceremony was a major weeklong event. Bill recruited me to head public relations outreach for this event. Since then, Gayle and I have been deeply involved with the international outreach program. It was started by President Eisenhower after World War II, based on the premise that if people in other countries got to know each other, there might be fewer wars. President Eisenhower was responsible for the term 'Sister Cities,' a program that is termed 'Twinned Cities' throughout the rest of the world.

We both became SSCA members in 2002, both of us serving many of those years as board members, and are still members today. The Sarasota outreach grew to including Hamilton, Ontario, Canada; Dunfermline, Scotland; Perpignan, France; Treviso Province in Veneto, Italy; Tel Mond, Israel; Vladimir, Russia; Xiamen, China; Mérida, Mexico; and Rapperswil-Jona, Switzerland.

Gayle Maxey

I began on the board as Vice President for Public Relations and later served as President. Gayle created the organization's first 'Meet and Greet' happy hour outreach program. Her first monthly event was at a downtown Sarasota restaurant and drew eight people. That quickly expanded to a monthly event that consistently drew more than 50–70 members and potential members. She made sure the venues changed monthly to get members to experience new restaurants and the business owners getting to know the impact of SSCA on the community.

Serendipity

One of the many benefits of living in The Inlets is that a third of the homes are situated along canals. These lead to the Intracoastal Waterway with access to the Gulf of Mexico. My home was one of those. The home came with a long dock and boat lift. Boat size in the Inlets is limited because of two bridges over the canal between my home and Lyons Bay to reach the Intracoastal and the Venice Jetties. But it was not a problem for our 24-foot Grady White, Cuddy Cabin, and Bimini roof boat powered by a 65-horsepower Yamaha engine. Our only adjustment was during the high tides of winter months when we would have to lower the Bimini to get under the bridges when traveling between our dock and Lyons Bay.

Gayle and I had been to boat shows in Sarasota and Ft. Myers to learn about various options that would be best for our needs. The one we selected was the Grady. The dealership was owned by the chairman of the board of Pfizer Corporation, best known for Viagra. The dealership delivered the boat by truck to the launch area in Venice on the waterway. Our first excursion was to cruise the waterway to our canal and our dock.

We named our boat *Serendipity* – reflecting on the relationship Gayle and I formed tracing back to our chance meeting Salzburg, Austria, in 1987, my having known her sister-in-law Betty Maxey as an Air Force Art Program artist during my Pentagon years, and her welcome wagon introduction to the Inlets.

In the early years in the Inlets, we were active in Inlets flotillas. This is a boating community. Our boats flew the Inlets burgee (a pennant originally designed by Gayle and her husband David) on monthly outings to restaurants along the Intracoastal Waterway. The flotillas, originated by David in the late 1990s, drew about 30 boats filled with owners and their guests. Outings extended north to Marina Jacks in Sarasota, south to the Fishery by Boca Grande, and lots of locations in between.

The flotilla era began to decline around 2010 as gas prices kept climbing. Also, a huge number of restaurants were sold to developers to build high-rise condos. By the time we sold the *Serendipity* in 2015, flotillas had ceased to exist. Today boaters in the Inlets are mostly offshore fishermen or kayakers.

Family Visits to Lombard, Oak Park and Westmont, Illinois

I became a member of the road team with Gayle for her annual pilgrimage to the Chicago area to see family and friends. Eldest son Steve resided in the Oak Park suburbs. Her youngest son, Craig, lived with his wife Barbara and two daughters (Jessica Lynn and Laura Ann) in a second-story apartment in Westmont.

Barbara's health was declining, and Gayle began a serious hunt for a one-story house to purchase in the suburbs for Craig's family to move to. One day while we were driving in Lombard, I got a glimpse of a for-sale sign on a side street. We stopped; it looked like a possibility. Gayle called the realtor listed on the sign. Shortly after, she could gain access to see the three-bedroom home, with a two-car garage that included a large workshop area, and a large, landscaped fenced-in backyard. The next day she arranged for Craig, Barbara and the girls to view the house. All agreed it met their requirements, including being within four blocks of an elementary school and one block away from a huge city park with playgrounds.

Gayle became the owner of 927 South Grace in Lombard, and Craig and family became her tenants. The family was now in the home they would reside in until 2015.

Barbara's health continued to decline, and unfortunately, she died three years later. It was a major blow to Craig and the girls, as he continued to be the breadwinner and father. But Gayle's decision to purchase the home provided the anchor that allowed the girls to have community continuity throughout high school. Both girls went to college – Jessie to Northern Illinois University in nearby DeKalb and Laura to the College of DuPage in Glen Ellyn.

New Orleans, Lake of the Ozarks, Omaha, Red Oak, Des Moines, Chicago, Bloomington, Indiana, and Nashville Marathon

Our first major trip together was a 30-day nostalgia excursion where we were together in a car for long hours at a time. We survived and even solidified our relationship!

Our first stop was New Orleans, where Gayle was born and spent her early childhood. It was a chance for Gayle to show me her New Orleans. I saw the historical homes of the Boday and Carroll families that provided her parentage, her grade school, the former drug store her father managed, and where the family lived in an apartment above the store. We met many of Gayle's cousins and aunts, and that sparked an interest in Gayle to explore her family genealogy.

From New Orleans, we had a long drive to the Lake of the Ozarks in southwest Missouri. My two Pilkington cousins (Jim and Ross) had retired on the lake following their careers as college professors. We spent several days there, and I gave a genealogy presentation on the Pilkington family at a Pilkington reunion and enjoyed boating on the Lake of the Ozarks. As always, there was one annoying member of the 'family' in attendance. It was a male peacock who had chosen Jim's home as his. The peacock screeching celebration at sunrise each morning was unforgettable.

We then made our way north to Omaha, where I had lived in fifth grade and later when I was assigned to SAC Headquarters at Offutt AFB. Our first stop was Arbor Lodge in Nebraska City, just south of Omaha. That stop was for two reasons. First, I wanted Gayle to see the historical Morton mansion, my mother's most favorite spot in the world. Second, to see where the pioneer family lived before they migrated and created the Morton Arboretum in Glen Ellyn – Gayle's favorite park in Chicagoland.

In Omaha I showed Gayle my highlights. That included the home where I lived during the early WWII years, Field Club School where I attend fifth grade, Hanscom Park, Offutt AFB, and Carter Lake. I also showed her the warehouse district where I was a teenage employee of Red Oak Wholesale Fruit grocery and helped fill our truck with produce.

From there, it was on to Red Oak and Montgomery County where I spent my youth and formative years. Gayle got to see the huge Swedish Coffee Pot and Swedish Coffee

Cup water towers in Stanton. She bought groceries in a store that was at a location where I used to swim when the site was a bayou, have dinner at the Red Oak Country Club, and see the historical family homes that were part of my heritage. The visit was timed to coincide with my high school reunion where Gayle knew no one, and I couldn't recall half of those attending.

The next stop was Des Moines. It was my chance to show Gayle the last home my family used to live in. But it was no longer there – it was now just empty airspace. The entire hill was destroyed for the construction of Interstate 80. A second home we lived in earlier was demolished, and that location is now the Drake University Field House. Urban renewal in downtown Des Moines had destroyed my second-floor United Press office. Now, it is the lobby of a Marriott Hotel. I was able to show Drake University and the library where my mother had worked to allow me to gain a college education. The high school I had attended was now a senior citizen home. Nostalgia is not what it used to be!

Onward to Lombard, Illinois, and the Hyatt Hotel we used as our headquarters during Gayle's annual family week each summer. The hotel had an indoor pool providing a great vacation stay for us and Gayle's young granddaughters, Jessi and Laura. We had easy access to the Greek Isles restaurant, the Yorktown and Oakbrook Shopping Centers, Brookfield Zoo, and the homes of Gayle's sons.

We made a special stop in Bloomington, Indiana. Then, we began our trip south to visit Betty Maxey, Gayle's artistic sister-in-law. Betty was well known to me as one of the famous artists who participated in the Air Force Art program when she was a member of the New York Society of Illustrators. While I was in the Pentagon, Betty had donated more than 20 oil paintings to the program. Betty was retired and lived near Indiana University, where many of her paintings are on display. After a very enjoyable dinner with Betty, we took off early the next morning for Tennessee.

Our stop in the Nashville area was to introduce Gayle to my granddaughter April Dawn and her husband, Brad Sanford. Their marriage was April's first and Brad's second. Brad was raising his daughter Brooke who was eight years old. Brooke became my first great-granddaughter. April was born in Nashville and had lived in nearby Adairville, Kentucky, when her mother, Debra Elaine, had married Grady Peay. It provided me a chance to introduce Gayle to the wonders of Nashville including the Grand Ole Opry, Opryland, my former home at 2740 Mossdale Drive, Percy Priest Lake, favorite restaurants, and the Civil War grave of Gayle's maternal great-great-grandfather, Adam Boday.

Heading home we made an overnight stop in Valdosta. My two sons, Mike and Curtis, who were living in the Thomasville, Georgia, area, joined us for dinner. The next morning, we left for the last leg of our Journey for Nokomis, Florida. Exhausted, but still talking to each other and now joined by learning more about our families and their histories.

Marriage Decision

We had been considering marriage for quite some time. Even before Jessi, then a second-grader asked us, "When are you two going to get married?" With a follow-up statement that if we did get married she would not stand up at our wedding. When we asked her why, she said she had "Just stood at my dad's friend's marriage, and had to wear long white panty hose – and that it itched terribly – and I would never do that again." I told her if we got married it would be on the beach, and everyone would be barefoot. She said she could accept that option.

As we mulled marriage, we found out there was a major showstopper. Florida laws forced us to not marry. Florida is a common property state, meaning that our desires to have what we have acquired in our life go to our families would be lost. Gayle's assets would no longer go to her sons and granddaughters; my assets would no longer go to my kids. The only thing economically positive in our getting married would be Gayle would qualify for military retiree Tricare for Life health insurance. We elected not to combine our assets because of Florida laws. Our commitment has now reached 19 years of wonderful, loving experiences that have only grown stronger.

Gayle and Tom

Trier, Kaiserslautern, Bavaria, Südtirol and Koblenz

In May 2004, I had to return to Kaiserslautern for the burial of my mother-in-law, Frau Maria Fritch. I asked Gayle to accompany me. We flew from Ft. Myers, Florida, to Düsseldorf, Germany, arriving early in the morning. We got a rental car and headed first to Trier to spend a couple of days along the vineyards of the Mosel River with Eckhard Dohm. He is the Deutsche Telekom executive that created the avenue for providing Armed Forces Television to U.S. military communities by cable.

Eckhard met us at an Autobahn rest stop near his home to ensure we could get to his wine village without getting lost. We greeted each other, and he opened the trunk of his car, passing out glasses, popping a champagne bottle cork, and greeting us with a toast. He led us to a charming wine country hotel. Here, we recovered from the all-night flight, allowing us to enjoy their hospitality and guided tours of Trier and the Mosel Valley.

We then drove to Weilerbach, Germany, for visits to Ramstein AB and Kaiserslautern, meeting with Air Force Public Affairs friends on the base and members of the German-American Press Club and German-American Club Weilerbach. Gayle got personal tours of the area, while I was with Traudl's cousin completing burial arrangements at the Kaiserslautern Friedhof (cemetery). Frau Fritch was buried in the family plot with Traudl.

Following the burial, we departed for several days of enjoying my favorite locations in Munich and Bavaria. Eventually, we ended up in Südtirol (the historical Austrian area of what is now the Dolomites area of the Italian Alps). The resort hotel was spectacular, offering gourmet meals, a FKK sauna, a massage center, a heated pool, and *National Geographic* views of the Alps. Gayle loved the massages and finally learned what FKK is in German-speaking Europe.

FKK is 'Frei Körper Kulture' (or nudity) in the coed sauna. After a sauna, guests would recover in lounge chairs in a room with windows facing the scenic Alps. Following her first massage, she came back to the room to tell me a guy was completely naked in the sauna's lounge area. I had to explain what an FKK sign means. FKK areas are frequent in Europe, including beaches and public parks such as the English Gardens in the center of Munich. At dinner, as each male guest arrived, I would ask her, "Was he the one?"

On that way back to Dusseldorf for our return flight to Ft. Myers, we spent a couple of days with Traudl's cousin Gitta, and husband Seppl, in their home high above the Rhein and Koblenz. Later Gitta and Seppl would come to visit us on vacation in Nokomis.

Drake 50th Reunion

In May 2004, Gayle accompanied me on a trip back to Des Moines for my 50th Class Reunion at Drake University. It was a three-day event packed with activities, culminating with the class of 1954 decked out in golden robes and mortarboard headgear leading the procession for the 2004 graduation exercise.

It was a bit easier for Gayle as both Bill and Jean Wallace were both class of 1954 grads. It was a time for telling tales, some of them true, at the journalism grad reception at the home of the college dean. It was also another chance to show Gayle the highlights of Des Moines, including the State Capitol complex where I used to work when I was a reporter with United Press.

Hurricane Evacuations

Because of my experiences with category 5 Hurricane Camille at Gulfport, Mississippi, I am cocked to leave the area any time a hurricane is projected to be a category 2 or higher. So many summers, we would drive or fly to Chicago (Lombard), Nashville, Tallahassee, and Valdosta, Georgia. These trips gave us additional family time.

For Hurricane Charley in August 2004, I made our only wrong decision. Charley was projected to move rapidly up the Gulf of Mexico over water to North Florida. Our only option was to head east, and I chose Orlando. Jack and Shirley Olsen joined us as the potential for damage at Venice was looking highly likely. But as it approached, it suddenly made a 90-degree turn into Charlotte Harbor about 40-minutes south.

Charley then continued to produce severe damage as it made landfall on the peninsula in Punta Gorda. It continued to the north-northeast along the Peace River corridor, devastating Punta Gorda, Port Charlotte, Arcadia, Zolfo Springs, Sebring, and Wauchula. Zolfo Springs was isolated for nearly two days as masses of large trees, power poles, power lines, transformers, and debris filled the streets. Wauchula sustained gusts to 147 mph; buildings in the downtown areas caved onto Main Street. Ultimately, the storm passed through the central and eastern parts of the Orlando metropolitan area, still carrying winds gusting up to 106 mph.

We had hunkered down in a Marriott Courtyard in the Disney area of Orlando. As the storm approached, we were told to leave our rooms and shelter in the main dining area. When the storm first hit, we could tell that it was really rough outside. Tiles from the roof were flying everywhere, and an old, large oak tree had toppled, blocking the motel's front door. When the eye of the storm came by, we could see lots of fallen trees, downed power utility poles and lines, damaged cars, and missing roofs.

After the eye passed, the storm resumed with trees now bending the opposite direction. The storm slowly exited the state over Ormond Beach just north of Daytona Beach. We remained at the motel for two days after the storm passed to stay off the roads and not impede the emergency response teams and vehicles. When we did leave, we elected to avoid Interstate 4 to Tampa and Interstate 75 home for the same reason. We drove back roads on the return that took most of a day, passing by mile after mile of destruction from Orlando to Arcadia. This trip would normally take two hours.

When we got home, we found Venice had (again) missed the wrath of the storm. The meteorological guess is Venice misses the hurricanes as it lies between huge Charlotte Bay and Tampa Bay. The bays seem to be an attraction for major storms, and Venice has historically avoided any major impact from hurricanes since records have been kept.

Visits to San Francisco, Sacramento – Gold Rush Country

Over the years, we made several trips to visit Gayle's sister, Dorothy Kilgas. She lived in Orangevale, California, a suburb of Sacramento. The primary purpose was for Gayle to have 'Dottie time.' Dorothy had been widowed for several years and taught piano at her home to a large group of students. It also allowed me to explore the Sierra Nevada foothills, including gold rush communities. My birth mother lived there after leaving Death Valley, where her husband was an engineer for borax mining.

My birth mother had died in Grass Valley, California, about a year before we began our trips to visit Dottie. Her husband had died several years before. But I met several of her friends during two of my genealogy visits. They provided me several mementos, photos with her, and tales of her active community role in Democratic politics.

The Musical Danube Cruise

Our grandest trip was from May 29 to June 18, 2015. We enjoyed a Tauck cruise on the Danube from Budapest,

Hungary, to Prague in the Czech Republic aboard the *Swiss Jewel*. This was a musical cruise that only happens twice a year. Gayle's background as a symphony coronet musician in Chicago, the University of Illinois, and the University of Wisconsin was one of the drivers of joining this cruise. The other is my love for Vienna, Austria – the music mecca since the 1800s.

Because of Gayle's musical background we extended the trip. We started with a week in Vienna, where we flew direct from Chicago on Austrian Air prior to joining the cruise in Budapest. In Vienna, we stayed in the K&K Maria Theresia Hotel within walking distance of downtown Vienna, The Hofburg (the home of the Habsburg dynasty), Café Demel, the Lipizzaner Horses, the Vienna Boys' Choir, St. Stephan's Dom, the Capuchin Crypt, the Vienna Opera House, and the Musikverein (home of the famous New Year's Concert). We also attended concerts and musical events every day, none of which were on the cruise itinerary for the scheduled two-day stop in Vienna.

Two impromptu events added to our extraordinary visit. One was when we hopped on a horse-drawn carriage outside The Hofburg for a historical tour of Vienna narrated by the female driver. The second was a specialized tour by Margaret and Walter Gerhold. They were both born in Vienna and are now friends and residents in a community just minutes from our home in Nokomis. Margaret is a concert pianist educated in Vienna. Walter is a medical doctor trained in Vienna, but who practiced in Chicago many years before they retired nearby.

We met early on a Sunday morning when they took us to a midday concert in a music hall where Margaret had gained her piano virtuosity. Margaret was joined at the concert by a conservatory classmate who was the daughter of Johannes Heesters. Heesters was a famous Dutch actor, singer, and entertainer who specialized in Viennese operetta. To Americans, Heesters would probably equate to a Bing Crosby of Europe. Heesters made his Viennese stage debut in 1934. His career continued until his first 'final' concert on December 5, 2006, on his 103rd birthday at the Wiener Konzerthaus. His actual final concert was on December 5, 2007, as he celebrated his 104th birthday with a concert at the Admiralspalast, Berlin.

What made this unique on this Sunday was that Heesters' daughter broke her glasses during an intermission refreshment break. Gayle came to the rescue by reaching into her purse to retrieve a jeweler's screwdriver to repair them on the spot.

Following the concert the Gerholds gave us a tour of their Vienna, where they had grown up. They showed us their favorite restaurant in the Vienna Woods, a fantastic hilltop park with a spectacular view of Vienna and the Danube below, and a Heuriger winery for folk music and dinner in the evening.

Onward to Budapest

We took the train from Vienna to Budapest on June 3, amazed at the number of fields (usually in marshy areas) filled with wind power generators and solar power panels producing 'green power' to electricity grids. We grabbed a taxi at the Budapest train station and checked into the 5-star Kempinski Corvinus Hotel for a three-day stay and guided explorations.

We had two days on our own to explore the historic city on foot. The Tauck portion of the visit began on June 4, with a grand reception at the Hungarian Academy of Science. The next day we had a bus tour of both Buda and Pest, located on the west and east side of the Danube. The tour included concerts at the Opera House in Buda, a piano concert in Pest, stops at the famous market, spas, World War II and Russian occupation sites, castles, and the Hungarian Parliament. On Saturday, June 6, we embarked at 4 p.m. aboard the *Swiss Jewel*. We enjoyed the Captain's welcome dinner and initial onboard concert in the Panorama Lounge as we headed upriver to begin our excursion.

Bratislava and a Slovakian Wedding

The next day we departed at our first stop in Bratislava, Slovakia. Following breakfast, we had the first of daily lectures by professional music conductors on what we would see and hear each day. On reaching Bratislava, we enjoyed a walking tour of the city and a visit to the Opera House, where we were greeted by arias sung by resident vocal artists.

In town, the numerous whimsical bronze statues were of special interest. One statue depicted a bronze guy in a hard hat manhole cover looking up girls skirts as they walked by. Another sculpture was of a guy looking over your shoulder as you sat on a park bench, while one was of a guy looking around a building at an intersection – plus tons of others.

In the evening, we were bused to a large rural restaurant. The group participated in a Slovakian wedding and celebration dinner before resuming our cruise toward Vienna at 9 p.m. Gayle joined the wedding party as a participant in the famous 'Hat Dance.'

Return to Vienna

We returned to our ship and slept en route to Vienna, awaking in port the next morning. Following breakfast on board this Monday morning, we were bused to the city, passing the famous Riesenrad (Ferris wheel) of *The Fifth Man*" movie fame. We were on our way to Schoenbrunn, the main summer residence of the Habsburg rulers. The 1,441-room Rococo palace is one of the country's most important architectural, cultural and historic monuments. Schoenbrunn is Vienna's most popular tourist destination, attended by 3.8 million visitors annually. The Schoenbrunn Palace Strauss Concerts account for more than five million visitors. We returned to the ship for dinner before departing for an evening Mozart concert in the Karlskirche in downtown Vienna.

Our second day in Vienna took us to a two-hour Auersperg Palace concert rehearsal and afternoon free time for a more detailed tour of The Hofburg, and the royal rooms of the

Habsburgs, particularly Franz Joseph and Sissi. And, importantly, to relax at Café Demel and watch the world parade by. That evening we were treated to an imperial dinner and Strauss concert in a former Habsburg residence before our cruise departed when we arrived back on board.

Cruising the Danube

On Wednesday, June 10, our next leg took us into the Wachau Valley to Dürnstein, Melk, and Linz. As we cruised upriver from Vienna, we entered this beautiful valley and it famous vineyards. We eased past Dürnstein with its historical, renowned white and blue church and ruins of the castle where Richard the Lionheart was held for ransom following his return from the Crusades. We made a stop at Melk for a visit to the beautiful monastery before proceeding to Linz while enjoying a dinner concert aboard. Linz is the second-largest city in Austria and became a stop for our next morning's day-trip to Salzburg and back by bus.

Salzburg and *The Sound of Music*

Shortly before reaching Salzburg on the morning of June 11, we pulled into an Autobahn rest area, at a rustic restaurant overlooking multiple lakes, for a coffee break. The next stop was Salzburg, where we got off the bus and we walked across a bridge on the Salzach River into the formal gardens. The bridge handrails were covered with love locks (padlocks) holding messages of love – a kind of colorful graffiti with messages from the heart.

'Love locks' of Salzburg

Cruise End at Passau and Regensburg

The morning highlight was the walking tour of Passau and the famous St. Stephen's Cathedral, home of the largest church pipe organ in the world. Gayle sat next to the organist in the loft as he conducted a mini-concert.

Back aboard the ship, we enjoyed the Captain's final reception and dinner. Bavarian musicians and dancers provided the entertainment as the ship proceeded for our last port of call in Regensburg, Germany. I was in my element, singing along to the German beer-drinking songs aided by half-liter mugs of Bavarian beer. We had a walking tour of historical Regensburg before boarding buses and the beautiful drive to Prague for the final two days of the cruise.

Tour Extension to Prague

I had never been to Prague, but I knew its history well, as it was a city so important to Traudl and her Egerland heritage. I knew that Prague was the home of the oldest German-speaking university. Also, Prague was a city that had not been destroyed in World War II. Our five-star hotel was the Intercontinental along the Moldau River within walking distance to the city center. Here we visited the Opera house where musical vocalists performed as we luxuriated in box seats. We had lunch in a nearby Café to enjoy the Prague Astronomical Clock, which for 600 years has been one of the greatest treasures of the city. It still amazes people with its procession of Apostles, moving statues and visualization of time like no other instrument in the world.

Prague Astronomical Clock

In the evening, we were guests for dinner at Lobkowicz Palace in a beautifully decorated concert hall with impressive 17th-century painted rococo ceilings. Professional musicians, including members of the Czech Philharmonic Orchestra, played for our pleasure following our castle art collection tour.

The next morning we were bused to the Prague train station for our tour extension visit to Munich where we stayed at the Eden Wolff hotel across the street from the Munich Hauptbahnhof.

Final Days in Munich

We had two full days in Munich. These centered on relaxing, shopping, and enjoying a narrated city bus tour. We also viewed the glockenspiel clock at City Hall and lunched al fresco at the Nurnberger Bratwurst Glockl am Dom. On both days, we visited the Hofbräuhaus for classic Bavarian food and music. We departed Munich by an ICE bullet train for the 3 hour and 15 minute trip to Frankfurt to make our connecting flight from Frankfurt to Toronto, Canada. We elected to fly to Toronto as it provided a direct flight connection to Sarasota.

We stayed overnight in the Steigenberger Airport Hotel and had an enjoyable layover with Sarasota Sister Cities friends Bettina and Barry Miller. They now had a real estate business in Frankfurt.

Becoming Embroiled in Embezzlement Using Investigative Reporter Skills

My first initiative at becoming involved in my new community was when Bill and Jean Wallace 'nudged' me to assist in the establishment and signing ceremonies of Dunfermline, Scotland, to become an official Sister City with Sarasota in 2002. That led to Gayle and I becoming members of the board of directors and greatly expanding our friendship base, our knowledge of the communities, and civic leadership of Florida's Culture Coast. That culminated in my becoming President of Sarasota Sister Cities in 2011 and walking blindly into a disaster.

Following my election in May, the organization entered a pause time in what has become for Sarasota two seasons. One season when the snowbirds are here and one season when they are not. We held board meetings during the summer months, but not major community events. It gave me time to learn the role of president. Being a reporter deep in my being, I knew my first job was getting to know our finances. Our treasurer gladly shared his monthly finance reports. However, I had no verification of what was in the reports, which bothered me. Two months later, I got access to our banking account. But I could not get the records in our savings account held by a non-bank institution.

By digging into the records I had, I learned our bank balance was $111, not the $24,000 that was reflected in our monthly treasurer's reports. I had nothing to back up whether we had any funds in our savings account. The treasurer's report indicated we had about $20,000 in that account. My first initiative was to inform the senior official in the City of Sarasota of my initial concerns. I formed an advisory committee that included Bill Wallace, a Sister Cities past president, and two members who were retired bank presidents. That was a lucky choice as Bill Wallace still had access to our savings account, allowing us to determine that it was apparently still secure. Further journalistic digging unearthed the fact that our treasurer had several civil legal cases pending for fraud and misappropriation of funds filed by three separate widows in Tampa. I also learned he was not a U.S. citizen but an Italian from Sicily. My advisory panel and the city leader I was working with concurred that I should initiate a criminal case against our treasurer. I turned over the evidence to a city police force detective and the state's attorney in Sarasota.

A year later, the District Court of Florida in Sarasota found him guilty, with a sentence that he would be deported to Italy plus a courtroom surprise. He had made an agreement to make a restitution of $24,885.75. The funds came from an unnamed individual in Guam. The amount was equal to our known banking account losses that covered only two years of the four years he had been treasurer. We could not get past banking records beyond the two-year look back to determine our real losses.

State of Sarasota Sister Cities Speech
April 5, 2013

On April 5, 2013, I gave my State of SCAS report at the annual general meeting held at Sara Bay Golf and Country Club. My report shows the detailed initiatives despite the criminal fraud we lived through. The 2013 State of SCAS follows:

Undoubtedly the most important fact I can provide you in this report is that, based on initiatives in October 2011, as I began my first term as president, we are solidly based today. In October 2001, I discovered we had just $111 in our banking accounts. Today, we are solvent, having created steps to ensure we have full and transparent financial records. This morning, the gross balance in our accounts is $46,335.06 to continue our citizen diplomacy programs. Our membership has increased to 230, including 45 new members in the past 12 months. And all the credit goes to you, our board and members.

This is the time for me to take a moment to say thank you. Because really and truly, as President of Sarasota Sister Cities I am grateful. Grateful to each and every person who has dedicated his or her time, energy, money, and passion to making our Sister Cities Association of Sarasota so special. Grateful because the collective action of the passionate, active membership has supported our mission of making the world a better place. Grateful for the words of kindness and encouragement that have motivated all of us to do our volunteer jobs well every day.

We are excited about the new membership that has joined us in the past year. We hope to connect you with our Sister Cities exchanges in the remainder of 2013 and beyond. We are excited about the initial special events that kicked off our 50th anniversary year, including the Thistle Ball in February and the One World Gala in March. In nine days, the La Musica Celebration concert at the Sarasota Opera will honor Sarasota Sister Cities. We hosted the Florida Sister Cities State Convention in May followed by involvement with the Sister Cities International annual convention on the River Walk in San Antonio, Texas, on July 12–13.

More anniversary events are in the works. The monthly Chinese Film program in conjunction with Alliance member Ringling College of Art and Design continues. We are excited about the timely blog and social media innovations we have initiated. We are also excited about the travel opportunities available to Russia and Italy in 2013 and Israel in 2014.

Two other special events are already ongoing. The 10th annual Embracing Our Differences outdoor art exhibit is on display until June 2 at Sarasota's Bayfront Park, plus now until April 29 at Rossi Waterfront Park in Bradenton. It will be on display from May 1 to June 2 at North Port High School. The annual exhibit attracted more than 2,400 entries submitted by individuals from 44 countries and 32 states. Sister Cities Association of Sarasota has partnered with Embracing Our Differences through our Alliance member of the Sarasota Manatee Jewish Federation since the initiative began.

The second is the Sarasota Film Festival which is also ongoing. This event traces back to the 1994 Sarasota twinning with Perpignan. That tie was initiated by Alain Taulere, who had homes in Perpignan, France, and Sarasota. He owned the Cafe of the Arts in Sarasota. He was very prominent in organizing the French Film Festival in Sarasota, which evolved into the now prestigious Sarasota Film Festival.

Our successes certainly began with Sarasota itself. Sarasota, on Florida's Cultural Coast is home to the greatest concentration of natural beauty, art museums and galleries; an abundance of theaters; performing halls featuring orchestra, opera, choirs; film production, and educational centers that make this remarkable city an important venue of creativity. The wealth of cultural resources and creativity in Sarasota match well with the diversity of our sister cities relationships that began in 1963 in response to President Eisenhower's vision to enhance worldwide understanding one handshake at a time.

During the past year, we have been busy with events, visits, and looking forward. For example, Tel Mond came to Sarasota in a big way in December with the NOOA dancers, 27 young women who danced and participated in discussions with students at Sarasota Military Academy, Booker and Riverview High Schools as well as the Sailor Circus. They visited a Sarasota Ballet workshop and danced at the 12th Annual Holocaust Luncheon sponsored by our alliance member, the Jewish Federation of Sarasota-Manatee. Particularly spectacular was the closing show that was co-sponsored by the Federation and ourselves. The dancers received Honorary Citizenship

Certificates from Sarasota Mayor Suzanne Attwell, toured Mote Marine, and the John and Mable Ringling Museum. All of this in five days!

One very active city has been Xiamen, China, led by City Director Dr. Carolyn Bloomer. In June, we learned the results of a University of South Florida business opportunity research project conducted on behalf of SSCA. The research was by 11 MBA students who were divided into three teams to identify export opportunities from Sarasota to Xiamen. The students created three business models that could be adopted for expansion to our seven other twinned cities. One plan has led to further exploration with meetings in Xiamen this fall.

In late October 2012, our alliance member State College of Florida hosted the 2012 Sarasota-Manatee China Town Hall at their Lakewood Ranch campus. Presentation speakers included Dr. Charles Steilen, our VP for Business and Economic Development; The Honorable Gary Locke, U.S. Ambassador to the People's Republic of China, participated by webcast. Locke's remarks placed great importance on citizen diplomacy initiatives. Locke said, "We need more people from America to come to China to understand China's history, culture, language and values to gain greater cooperation." These contacts provide exposure to citizens of both nations with a positive impact of calming fears and tempers.

Another success story happened this fall. Sister City member Dr. Edward Lin, who is founder and CEO of HealO-Medical, won a $1 million technology innovation contract in an international competition sponsored by Sarasota's Chinese sister city of Xiamen.

A *Beijing Review* magazine writer/photographer team from New York City visited Sarasota January 9 to research the Sarasota Sister City innovations involving Xiamen. They interviewed our SCAS team, leaders of our alliance organizations, and Mayor Suzanne Atwell.

As a follow-up to the University of South Florida Sarasota Manatee MBA graduate student study, we held an initial meeting on July 23 with Tidwell. It concerned the concept of acquainting Xiamen contacts with Hospice care concepts in an era of aging populations. The initial meeting expanded to bringing Tidewell officials together with medical contacts in Xiamen this fall.

Vladimir, Russia, also had several activities during the past 12 months, beginning with an international photo contest titled *A Day Together* on July 13, 2012. Sarasota is one of 20 sister cities in 12 countries twinned with Vladimir. Our mutual cooperation is about being real friends, so let us start small and tell each other about our organization using photographs.

We learned about the death of Yuri Federov, our primary point of contact in Vladimir since our establishing the twinning with Vladimir. Yuri enriched Sarasota's Sister Cities program with Vladimir through innovative ideas that served to bring people closer together. Mayor Suzanne Atwell proclaimed June 20 as Yuri Federov Day in Sarasota.

Vladimir Chief of Police Alexander Rasov visited Sarasota October 17 to reactivate the relationship that had been dormant for several years. Rasov met with Sarasota Mayor Suzanne Atwell, City Manager Thomas Barwin, police counterparts, and Kate Alexander of Florida Studio Theater. Kate had been the houseguest with the Rasov family when she was in Vladimir with the Florida Studio Theater Young Playwrights program. As a result of this visit, SCAS gained Yulia Gauckhmann as our city director for Vladimir. Yulia is leading the Golden Ring tour of Russia to St. Petersburg, Moscow, and Vladimir.

City Director Pauline Mitchell skillfully handled the visits of the Florida Studio Theater Young Playwrights winners from Dunfermline, Scotland, in May. Plans were also made to host winners from Vladimir and Tel Mond, but conflicts prevented their travel to Sarasota. But for Kelly Fairbairn, Matthew Walton, and Teacher Elspeth McDonald, it was an eventful five days in Sarasota. It included viewing their play, *Hagis Hunt*, presented by FST actors on the FST stage. The Poet Laureate of the United States presented their awards at Holly Hall.

The 10th anniversary of our twinning with Dunfermline was celebrated as our first SCAS 50th anniversary event in February 2013. Dunfermline city director for the twinning, Ben Conway, was on hand with a delegation from the Kingdom of Fife community. The event, complete with pipers and tartans, packed the Bird Bay Yacht Club banquet room. SCAS continued to play the host. Our Sarasota Sister Cities golfers won the Competition Cup for the fourth straight time. The tournament is held biennially with revenge on Dunfermline's mind for 2015.

Our final luncheon at the Sarasota Yacht Club was in November 2012. We were notified that the yacht club had to restrict business events due to concerns about maintaining IRS tax-exempt status. A review of options included Bird Bay Yacht Club, Marina Jack's, Michael's on East, and the Sara Bay Golf Club. Sara Bay Golf Club was selected as the best option considering price, availability, technical support, and quality of meals.

Our luncheon season began in October 2012 by honoring Dr. Mary Elemendorf. She has been an active member for more than 41 years and released an interesting new book just days before her 95th birthday. *From Southern Belle to Global Rebel, memoirs of anthropologist and activist Mary Lindsay Elemendorf* has several references to the history of Sarasota Sister Cities.

Our November luncheon featured guest speaker Hadda LaMotte, a teacher at the Pablo Picasso Lycée in Perpignan, France. She reported on her students' preparation for the SCAS sponsored Sustainability, Renewable Energy Conference to be held in Sarasota in November 2013. Hadda had just hosted SCAS Board members Beth Ruyle Hullinger and Craig Hullinger in Perpignan in September 2012. It was their first visit to a Sarasota Sister City, but they are veterans of other visits to sister cities in Europe and Asia while in key city positions in Illinois.

Our first luncheon at Sara Bay Country Club featured Fran Harris. She presented a special program about her late husband's passion for the architecture of Venice, Italy – the capitol city of Veneto where our Sister City of Treviso Province is located.

The hit of the year has been our meet and greets arranged by Gayle Maxey. This event has provided double benefits – bringing customers to Sarasota businesses and enhancing our membership roll. What began with a modest attendance made up of mostly board members has now mushroomed to where 40 is a small number of attendees – and many of them first-time visitors to a SCAS event. Our last event at Blue Rooster drew 66 attendees. Our membership has grown to 230 members on the roll – including 12 we can only reach by snail mail. Thank you all for being involved in the use of this event to provide new members who see value in the Sister Cities Citizen Diplomacy concept!

And speaking of technology, we all owe a major vote of thanks to Craig Hullinger. As VP for Communications, he has brought us into today's digital world through our complete social media presence. Besides our new website being completed, we have an up-to-date blog for learning what is happening– now! It has replaced our newsletter, which could not compete with the speed of our blog in getting you information. He has us connected to Facebook and Twitter also.

But my favorite site is Pinterest. No longer are photos of events and our history just collections in our office. Pinterest is where we now have an unlimited collection of current and historical digital images. Anyone in the world can learn who we are, what we do, and the community impacts we have made. Consider it a pinboard or even a refrigerator door where you have your favorite photos to informally share with friends.

What's in it? It is divided into sections, including a section for each sister city, great photos of Sarasota, Meet and Greets, Current Events, and Historical Collections. More than 1,000 photos in all and more to come.

What can you do with it? Pinterest is not just to look at. It is to share. It is our best opportunity to expand community knowledge about SCAS – bypassing the established news media. It allows anyone in our twinned communities to learn more about their Sister City and the cities we are twinned with.

Who views our Pinterest site? As of this morning, in the short time we have had our Pinterest site active, we have followers from Australia, Canada, Italy, New York City, Chicago, San Francisco, Nevada, Massachusetts, California, Virginia, seven media outlets, Tervis, Sarasota Memorial Hospital, Florida House, Homosassa Springs, Bradenton, Lakewood Ranch, and Sarasota, plus seven SCAS board members.

And with this report I pass on the Presidency to Beth Hullinger – knowing that the Sister Cities Association is in good hands and knowing that the framework for our organizational future is solid.

Despite the extraordinary challenges I faced, my best memories remain at the forefront. Those are being involved with an outstanding group of people, finding close friendships with people globally that I would have never met otherwise, and being so deeply involved in an organization that has such a great mission. Again, thank you – thank all of you!"

Media Roundtable, Broadcasters Club, Air Force Public Affairs Alumni Activities

Impact of Len Gumley

Len Gumley opened doors for me in several Sarasota media organizations. He is the New York City journalist I first met during Air Force public affairs workshops in Manhattan, later as a reserve officer at Wright-Patterson AFB in Ohio, and the Air Force Lookout Mountain Studios in Hollywood. I had met Len when he was an active member of Sarasota Sister Cities, where we traded Air Force Public Affairs memories. These organizations included Broadcast Pioneers of Florida (later the Broadcasters Club of Florida), the George Allen Media Roundtable, Veterans for Common Sense, and Fly Boys.

George Allen All Media Roundtable

The George Allen Media Roundtable was started in New York City in 1950 by Media Executive George H. Allen. George and The Roundtable moved to Sarasota, Florida, in 1991, where 35 or so active and semi-active media executives continued to meet 12 to 15 times a year at a restaurant on St. Armand's Circle.

With additional seating capacity at The Field, club attendance averaged 43 participants at each meeting. When Len introduced me to become a member, the Roundtable was moderated by Irwin Starr, former Vice President and General Manager of KGW-TV, Portland, Oregon; KREM-TV, Spokane, Washington; KGGM, Albuquerque, New Mexico; WDJT, Milwaukee-Racine, Wisconsin; Alaska Broadcast Network, Anchorage; and Program Manager of WJLA-TV, Washington, D.C.; and WJXT-TV, Jacksonville, Florida.

The Media Roundtable was unique in Florida, in the U.S., Canada, and the world, in the field of communications All members had been on-payroll or on-camera, or the equivalent, in any communication industry: radio AM, FM; TV; Cable; newspapers; magazines (national or local); book publishing; the theatre arts; trade papers; direct mail; outdoor advertising; movies; music; Internet editorial content or business; male or female; now or past.

Each medium of communication has its own industry association and multiple meetings. The Roundtable competed with none, and involved any or all media as an entirely 'voluntary' conversation group; no dues; no officers, no budgets, no bylaws, no standup speakers, no social or hidden purpose or agenda . . . just an informal interchange of opinions, news, and developments among interesting, and occasionally, even well known, personalities under informal circumstances involving any or all media of communication…current or in the future.

Discussion emphasis was on current developments and experiences – not the past. The Roundtable was not a retirement group. Politics and religion were considered 'out-of-order' unless discussing media coverage of the topics. All comments are always 'off-the-record.'

Each Roundtable meeting was unique in subject matter, the profile of attendees, and the industries represented. Discussions were held along two long, facing tables, people spoke while seated. Each meeting usually had four to five speakers and an introduction of new participants. Only 40–43 of the 300+ active members could get reservations for any one meeting. There is usually a waiting list, assuring few empty chairs, if any. A Social Hour was from 11:30 a.m. to noon. The program began at noon and ended promptly at 2 p.m.

Both Gayle and I became members of the Roundtable. Gayle qualified with her background as a columnist for the *Wheaton Leader* and the *Glen Ellyn News*, and author of a how-to book for real estate agents. I qualified through my newspaper and broadcast experiences. Each first-time member was introduced by his or her sponsor, and had 8–10 minutes to make comments (seated or standing) and respond to questions. The only obligations of membership were:

1. Pay for your own luncheon;
2. Create a 150-character bio for the back of the program that provided background on attendees for the luncheon.

Broadcast Pioneers of Florida

Broadcast Pioneers of Florida was "a society of broadcast professionals contributing to the past, present, and future of broadcasting." The group was founded by broadcast pioneers Dallas Townsend and Wallace Dunlap in Bradenton. The original and long-time President was William F. 'Rusty' Russell, a broadcast pioneer in Kentucky, and the original meeting location was the Quay on the downtown Sarasota bayfront.

Beginning in 1995, the club partnered with the Foundation of the State College of Florida to create the Broadcasters Club of Florida Scholarship honoring broadcast pioneers Dallas Townsend and Wallace Dunlap to encourage students to pursue broadcasting and electronic media as a career. The $1,500 scholarship was provided annually to a student for as long as the student maintained a 3.0 grade point average and continued to work toward a baccalaureate degree in the broadcasting, electronic media, and mass communications fields.

The name was changed to the Broadcasters Club of Florida several years after Len Gumley introduced me as a speaker to the group. It was becoming harder and harder to find broadcast pioneers. The group met on the second Friday of each month from October to April at the Sara Bay Golf and Country Club. The Quay complex had been leveled as it had fallen into disrepair. The meeting format remained unchanged, featuring luncheon speakers and panel discussions on broadcast issues and history.

The new Broadcasters club was composed of anyone who has been involved broadcasting (past and present). The club had nearly 180 members who resided in 44 communities in Florida when I became the club's third President in 2015.

Fly Boys (The Flying Liars)

Len Gumley had been an Air Force glider pilot in World War II. He created the Fly Boys group at The Landings, a gated community in south Sarasota among residents of the housing complex. It was an informal group and met monthly in The Landings' clubhouse for brown bag do-it-yourself lunches and storytelling. The popularity expanded, as did the membership that extended to former pilots (U.S. and foreign, male and female) throughout Central Florida.

National President Air Force Public Affairs Alumni Association

The Air Force Public Affairs Alumni Association (AFPAAA) is a non-profit, veterans' organization of past and present U.S. Air Force Public Affairs, Band, Combat Camera, and Broadcast professionals. It was founded in 1993 from the informal public affairs alumni group I created in the 1980s at the request of Brig. General Jerry Dalton. AFPAAA has been committed to preserving the heritage and profession-alism of the Public Affairs community, helping members transition into new jobs, and maintaining contact with friends and co-workers. It is more a fraternity than an as-sociation - a fraternity of over 500 men and women whose generations were defined by the conflicts they were involved in and the deployments they were sent on. These include World War II, Korea, the Cold War, Vietnam, Bosnia, Iraq, Afghanistan, and many other places around the globe, all sharing a singular common experience.

In 2004, I was elected to the board of AFPAAA, serving as secretary. Board positions are elevated annually, and I became Vice President in 2005, President in 2006, and Chairman of the Board in 2007. In 2008, Gayle and I were in charge of arranging hotels, entertainment and program for the reunion held in Orlando.

Beginning in 1994, AFPAAA has held an Annual Reunion and Membership Meeting. This allowed members to be 're-blued' as we tour active-duty installations amid ample opportunity to see old friends and make new ones. The first reunion as AFPAAA was held in San Antonio, Texas. During the informal years, annual reunions were held at the Sheraton Park Hotel in Washington, D.C., during the annual Air Force Association convention.

Since 1994 reunions have been held in Colorado Springs, Colorado (1995); Hampton, Virginia (1996); Las Vegas, Nevada (1997); Dayton, Ohio (1998); Satellite Beach, Florida (1999); Long Beach, California (2000); Alexandria, Virginia (2001); San Antonio, Texas (2002); Dayton, Ohio (2003); Destin, Florida (2004); Tacoma, Washington (2005); Baltimore, Maryland (2006); Colorado Springs, Colorado (2007); San Antonio, Texas (2008); Dayton, Ohio (2009); Orlando, Florida (2010); Fairfield, California (2011); Saint Louis, Missouri (2012); Las Vegas, Nevada (2013); San Antonio, Texas (2014); Washington, DC (2015); Colorado Springs, Colorado (2016); Destin, Florida (2017); San Diego, California (2018); and Charleston, South Carolina (2019).

German-American Club Sarasota

For fun and friendship, we became active members of the German-American Club that met monthly in Sarasota for a German dinner and dancing. As in each case, we expanded our friendship circle, with the bonus of retaining my German language skills. A most memorable character was a young 90-year-old named Frieda May. When we first met her, she had a man in tow for dancing and later explained that she was leaving with another man for Hawaii the next day. She delighted in her introduction that went, "My name is Frieda May, as in Frieda may, or Frieda may not."

Cheers for Venice – where everybody knows your name while enjoying music, wine, and friendship. This specialty wine and piano bar is a Venice jewel. Nestled along Miami Avenue, owner Arieh (Ari) Aizenberg has wines and beers from all over the world. He offers tapas, paninis, desserts, and some dinner cooking. Food is available after 7 p.m., and the pianists begin playing at 7:30 p.m. This French-style setting featuring inside and outside seating has an atmosphere that provides a special escape from life's everyday hustle and bustle. The Zebra has become our favorite place in Venice since 2018. A place we always take visitors to and encourage new acquaintances to join us. The outstanding piano players and volunteer vocalists make every evening a special showcase of talent.

The Zebra was our entertainment 'go-to' establishment. We enjoyed the talents of piano entertainer Ray Goines of Minnesota on Tuesday and Friday, concert pianist Lana Reign of Albania on Wednesday, George De Jong of Herman's Hermits fame, on Thursday, and New Yorker Dave Sayer of *Publishers Clearing House* TV fame on Saturday.

Commemorative bottles of Ray Goines label wines

Ray Goines was an entertainer – a pro. He had many costume gimmicks to match nearly every song. Whenever we arrived, he would loudly announce, "Gayle's here!" Unfortunately, we lost Ray to a heart attack in early March 2020 – just before the Coronavirus pandemic closed all 'non-essential' business establishments. Memorabilia from Ray's tenure, including hats, boas, glasses, and wigs, are now part of the Zebra decor. One of his featured singers was Johnny K noted for his duets of "Jeremiah was a Bullfrog" with Ray who wore a stuffed green bullfrog on his head.

We extended our friendship circle greatly at the Zebra to include talented singers like our best friends Dawn and Eric Spitz, Greg Wollaston, Marty Hoffman, Ray Rees, Sylvia Hollister, Marcia Mackey, Amy Peck, and Eileen Campo Gerle.

Eric & Dawn Spitz with Pianist Dave Sayer

We also created many new friends, who like me, majored in 'audience,' and just enjoyed the ambience. This includes Poppi Rossano, a bubbly, cute, petite gal you remember from your high school days who was the most popular cheerleader and homecoming queen. Poppi came from New York City, where she was one of the originators of the Barbie Doll.

Others included Shirley Remondi, who is caretaker for Jim Gray, a handicapped Viet Nam vet; Former Bitburg AB, Germany Flight Surgeon Dr. Tom and Patty Shreeve; Doreen Schreiber, who was born and raised in Corner Brook, Newfoundland, where I had golfed and was on a curling team in the 1960s; and two beautiful sisters, Joanie Evans and Ellen Ryan; plus Barbara Isaacson, a former Playboy Club Playmate.

During the Coronavirus pandemic, many businesses shut down. Several entertainers, including Gregory Wollaston, Amy Peck, Marty Hoffman, and Ray Rees, created virtual concerts from the closed, empty Zebra bar that were streamed live and are still retrievable on computer devices and home television sets using Facebook and YouTube access.

Following the opening of some businesses in Florida in the summer of 2020, Ari was able to open as he already had a restaurant license. However, while the ambiance was the same, spacing limitations dramatically reduced the numbers of guests allowed inside. He did, however, expand his outside seating with wide separation between tables.

As the impact of COVID diminished new "stars' brightened the Zebra featuring young Tom Cahalan who quickly became popular bringing in new generations for music lovers,

Gayle matching colors with an artistic sea horse in Venice, like the one at the Zebra which was destroyed by Hurricane Ian.

Others who joined as entertainers included Michael "Sparky" Edelstein featuring "Broadway on Miami Avenue" plus the talents of Jimmy Gillis, Vince Addesa, and Nick Sperry.

Death of Sons John Michael Halbert; Curtis Charles Halbert; and Grandson Billy Jack Hanson

The period beginning in April 2021 and ending in November 2022, was a series of tragedies even Russian author like Dostoyevsky could not have imagined. First, my oldest son Mike died at home on Lake Iamonia just north of Tallahassee on Saturday, April 24, 2021. Graveside services were held at Murphy Cemetery, Moultrie, Georgia on Wednesday, April 28, with Rev. Kerry Walsh officiating. Mike had worked most of his adult life as a machinist at C&S Machine in Thomasville, Georgia. His sister Tomajean, and her son, Willie Hanson, represented our family at the services. Mike had suffered a serious industrial accident at his workplace when he was nearly crushed when a heavy machine was being removed and fell on him. He was nursed back to health by his mother who was a nurse. At that time, his mother told him that I was not his biological father. That resulted in his request for me to never contact him again. While I have honored his request, I have never wavered from being his father.

It began, of course, on a dark and stormy night - in a small settlement on the Georgia/Florida border on November 3, 2022, just as Hurricane Ian reached Georgia. My youngest son had just been hospitalized in Thomasville, GA. He lived alone and was never married. For unknown reason he was able to leave the hospital with his IV still in his arm. His body was found 6-days later in his home - in a a situation the coroner said was the worst he had ever seen. His body was decomposed requiring the home to be sealed and condemned.

My daughter in Tennessee was notified, as she was the only family member residents could recall. Tomajean and Curtis have always had close bond. Tomi, and resides near her four sons and family members. She, one son and two daughters-in-law drove to Georgia to assist. My former wife and Curt's mother lives in Thomasville, unfortunately in lates stages of Alzheimer's. Tomi spent five days handling Curtis's burial services and to begin probate for his estate.

She checked out of the motel and was heading out of town when she was involved in an intersection collision. She was severely injured from air bag deployment (pelvic fractures, loss of teeth) . She was hospitalized three days. Her car was totaled and drove back to Tennessee in a rental car arriving on Sunday, November 11.

Then November 12 her youngest son Billy Jack Hanson, died at age 41, adding grieving on top of grieving, with family support, all while needing to begin medical rehab and finding a replacement car. Her injuries were still serious and restricted her mobility and ability to work. Following Billy's funeral, Tomi moved to her son Will Hanson's home near Chattanooga, TN to begin medical rehabilitation and recover from her injuries.

No parent expects to outlive their children. It is the downside of reaching 90 that no one ever tells you about.

Epilog Reflections

Monetary Reform

My greatest fear in 2021 is that my descendants will be impacted by currency reform someday. I have seen that happen three times, twice in Germany and once in Italy. In those cases, the currency of those nations was changed overnight. In both nations, the change was to declare one currency valueless and create a new one. All the funds you had in banks, billfolds, and hidden under mattresses were worthless. Each individual was issued a starter fund of the new currency. The only thing of value that remained unchanged was homeownership. However, those proceeds were valueless if you sold your property the day before the change. If you bought a home that day, you now owned a home, the seller lost it plus any proceeds from the sale.

I look back on watching a systematic reduction of the dollar's value over the years. As a kid, I could watch double feature films and also get a box of popcorn and a candy bar for 25 cents. Today, it costs more than $20 for a single ticket for a single move, with nothing left over for popcorn. As a college freshman in 1950, I could take my date to a movie and share a pizza afterward for $2.50.

My salary as a GM-15 (the highest 'rank' in Civil Service) in 1985 was $50,000 a year. In 2021, the pay scale for a GS-15 was $150,000 per year.

The first home I purchased was in Omaha. The new two-bedroom home at 4706 South 52nd Street was $10,000 paid by a monthly mortgage. In mid-2021, the value of that house was $156,700 based on Zillow listings. In 1965, I purchased 2740 Mossdale Drive in Nashville for $20,000. In mid-2021, that home was valued at $305,500. My home in Fairfax, Virginia that I purchased for $65,00 in 1980, is now valued at $858,600.

Based on history, I worry that what happened in Germany and Italy could happen here. In both cases, the nations rebounded over time. It is the in-between time that hurts the most to everyone.

Schadenfreude
That Wonderful Feeling You Get from Someone's Misfortune

One thing you learn very early in your flying career is your crew is a team, each equally important in getting the mission accomplished. It didn't matter whether one was an officer or enlisted – you worked together.

On the other hand, fighter pilots are loners. Whenever we could, those of us in multi-engine aircraft would frequently interject that fighter pilots only have two working parts – a mouth and an asshole, and the parts are interchangeable.

So the schadenfreude comes to the forefront when you note that the leading Ace in the Viet Nam war was a navigator, Capt. Charles DeBellevue. He was credited with downing six enemy MIG aircraft with air-to-air missiles. Chuck was an F-4 Phantom GIB (guy-in-the-back) or weapon system officer (WSO). The F-4 was a 2-seat fighter – the pilot in the front seat and the radar navigator in the back seat. De-Bellevue was one of five who achieved flying Ace status in that war.

Politics – An Independent Voting for Best Candidate or Issue

In mid-September 2020, as things were heating up in the Presidential election race, I was stunned by revelations surfacing daily in book after book about President Trump by members of the news media, those who had been in senior White House positions, and family members. But the voice recordings released by *Washington Post* investigative reporter Bob Woodward as his book *Rage* was released and excerpts from a 'tell all' book by Trump fixer Michael Cohen were released publicly.

As a combat veteran of the Korean War, Viet Nam, Dominican Republic Incursion, Cold War and Desert One in Iraq, I was totally appalled by our Commander-in-Chief using derogatory slurs toward those who have served their country. My personal background reached the Quadruple Champion level, being recognized by five slurs. Two for being a military veteran (loser and sucker), and three more for being a Christian by faith (fool, idiot, schmuck) coupled with an opinion that religion is 'bullshit.'

I am still very proud of my 27 years as an Air Force pilot in service to protect our nation and democracy. I am not proud of a Commander-in-Chief voicing slurs in statements demonstrating his true feelings about those who chose to protect our nation from all enemies, foreign and domestic, and those who don't consider Christianity as being a 'bullshit' faith or Republicans in Congress who continue to betray the constitution they swore to defend.

This historical election became the impetus for finally allowing me to live the dream job I had determined while getting my journalism degree at Drake in the 1950s. My dream job was to become cartoon editor for the *Wall St. Journal* that published just one political cartoon a day. Thus during this campaign, I succeeded in meeting this personal goal. I collected and emailed three to nine cartoons daily to friends from the Media Roundtable and Broadcasters' Club. These were cutting rebukes of Donald Trump and his goal of destroying our democracy. It was a mission of passion. And it met a need as the daily cartoon packages were retransmitted to friends, and multiplied further to friends of friends and beyond.

The resounding firing of Donald Trump and the promise of restoring our nation to the leadership of the free world gave me unbridled comfort. I know that our nation can begin the recovery to a leadership role in the free world. My contributions as a citizen, combat veteran, and community leader were a part of this effort.

A dictionary definition of veteran explains my sentiments exactly:
Vet-er-uh-n – Noun: A person who wrote a blank check payable to the United States of America for the amount of and unto and including one's life

Final Thoughts

My summary today is based on the lyrics to the hit song from the 1940s movie *Casablanca*. They seem to be perfect for completing this biography of a long and wonderful life. Especially after expressing our wonderful nostalgic times at the Zebra Piano Bar. *As Time Goes By* was performed for the first time in 1931 in a Broadway musical, *Everybody's Welcome*. It was written and composed by Herman Hupfeld (now there's a trivia question for you). It became popular in 1942 when Humphrey

Bogart told the piano player, "Play it, Sam." And Sam did as he sang:

You must remember this:
A kiss is still a kiss,
A sigh is just a sigh.
The fundamental things apply
As time goes by.

And when two lovers woo
They still say, "I love you"
On that you can rely,
No matter what the future brings.
As time goes by.

Moonlight and love songs; never out of date.
Hearts full of passion, jealousy and hate.
Woman needs man, and man must have his mate.
That no one can deny.

It's still the same old story.
A fight for love and glory.
A case of do-or-die.
The world will always welcome lovers
As time goes by.

-30-

Made in United States
Orlando, FL
26 February 2023

30432498R00232